FUNDAMENTALS OF
LOGIC DESIGN AND SWITCHING THEORY

FUNDAMENTALS OF
LOGIC DESIGN AND SWITCHING THEORY

ARTHUR D. FRIEDMAN
George Washington University

COMPUTER SCIENCE PRESS

Computer Science Press, Inc.
1803 Research Boulevard
Rockville, Maryland 20850

1 2 3 4 5 6   90 89 88 87 86

Library of Congress Cataloging in Publication Data

Friedman, Arthur D.
   Fundamentals of logic design and switching theory.

   Bibliography: p.
   Includes index.
   1. Logic circuits.   2. Logic design.   3. Switching
theory.   I. Title.
TK7868.L6F75   1985   621.3819'5835   84-23315
ISBN 0-88175-098-0

PREFACE

The study of the techniques of digital circuit and system design has been referred to as *logic design* or *switching theory*. Although frequently used interchangeably, these terms may have different connotations. Thus logic design may be used to refer to the development of procedures for the design of digital systems. In practice many design techniques are heuristic in nature and may be based primarily on the experience and knowledge of the circuit designer. Switching theory studies properties of switching circuits and considers the development of design procedures which optimize some parameter of the design. Frequently concepts originally developed as theory become important aspects of practical design. Furthermore adaptation to technological change is simplified for the person with a strong theoretical background. Consequently I have attempted to cover both practical design techniques as well as theoretical problems with emphasis on general concepts and problems of potential relevance to current technologies.

The book is intended for an introductory one-semester undergraduate or basic graduate level computer science or electrical engineering course in switching theory or logical design of digital systems. No specific previous knowledge is required on the part of the student other than some general mathematical ability. The book features many topics relevant to current technologies which are usually not presented in an introductory text. With the advent of integrated circuits and especially large scale integration, the classical switching theoretic design objective of component minimization has been replaced by an interest in system level design or modular design, in which systems are designed as interconnected sets of relatively complex modules. Related topics presented herein include modular design of combinational circuits, system level design using register transfer languages and logic design using MSI and LSI components such as ROM's and PLA's. Beginning with the simplest precepts of gate level logic design, the concepts of combinational circuit design, sequential circuit design, and finally system level design are developed in a systematic and unified manner, culminating in an introduction to the design of digital computer systems, which is presented as a natural extension of circuit design rather than as a totally different subject.

The first two chapters introduce the subject of digital systems, and present basic required mathematical concepts, including Boolean algebra, number systems, arithmetic procedures, and codes. In Chapter 3, procedures for the design of minimal combinational circuits are developed. More advanced topics of combinational circuit design are covered in Chapter 4. Topics include multilevel circuit design by factorization, which is illustrated by the design of decoders;

and modular realizations, illustrated by the design of a comparison circuit and a parallel adder. Finally logic design using MSI and LSI components such as ROM's and PLA's is presented. In Chapters 5 and 6 the subject of sequential circuit design is presented for the synchronous and asynchronous case, respectively. Topics include sequential machines, state tables, and flow tables as models and representations of sequential circuits, the state assignment problem and state minimization including the case of incompletely specified state tables. Chapter 7 develops a register transfer language and demonstrates how it can be used to design complex systems from basic combinational and sequential circuit modules, including the specification of a control unit as a sequential machine. A model of a stored programmed digital computer is presented and the concepts of macro- and microinstructions are introduced.

The basic ideas are presented in an informal manner, and illustrative examples are used to demonstrate these concepts. In addition formal proofs of most theorems and algorithms are presented. Problems at the end of each chapter range from simple exercises to problems of considerable difficulty and some unsolved problems demarcated by a flag (†). (A solution manual is available for course adoptions). Each chapter also contains a guide to the literature for topics covered in that chapter. The complete contents of the book can be covered in a one-semester course.

I wish to thank Dr. J.P. Roth for permission to reprint Figure 3.14 which previously appeared in *Computer Logic, Testing & Verification* as well as Dr. P.R. Menon and Bell Telephone Laboratories for permission to reprint parts of Chapters 5 and 6 which previously appeared in *Theory & Design of Switching Circuits*.

I wish to express my gratitude to Professor S. H. Unger of Columbia University, New York, NY who initially stimulated my interest in this subject. I also wish to thank Lisande Bissonette for her careful editing. Finally I wish to thank my wife Barbara and my sons, Michael and Steven, for their encouragement and assistance.

Arthur D. Friedman

CONTENTS

Chapter 1 **FUNDAMENTAL CONCEPTS: BACKGROUND AND**
PRELIMINARIES **1**

1.1 Introduction 1
1.2 Logic Gates 2
1.3 Boolean Algebra 8
1.4 Design Hierarchy... 14
References 15
Additional Reading 15
Problems... 15

Chapter 2 **BINARY REPRESENTATION AND ARITHMETIC**..... **19**

2.1 Binary Number System Representation..................... 19
2.2 BCD and Hexadecimal Codes............................... 22
2.3 Binary Number System Arithmetic.........................
    2.3.1 Binary Number System Addition.................... 25
    2.3.2 Binary Number System Subtraction 27
    2.3.3 Binary Number System Multiplication 33
    2.3.4 Binary Number System Division 34
2.4 Floating Point Arithmetic 35
2.5 Other Codes.. 36
References 38
Additional Reading 38
Problems... 39

Chapter 3 **FUNDAMENTALS OF COMBINATIONAL**
FUNCTIONS AND CIRCUITS **41**

3.1 Introduction 41
3.2 Combinational Function Minimization 47
    3.2.1 Generation of Prime Implicants—Tabular Method ... 51
    3.2.2 Generation of Prime Implciants—Map Method 53
    3.2.3 Selection of a Minimal Covering Set of Prime
          Implicants 59
    3.2.4 Selection of Minimal Covers from Karnaugh Maps .. 64
    3.2.5 Minimal Product of Sums Realizations.............. 67

            3.2.6   Minimal Two Level *NAND* and *NOR* Realizations ... 69
            3.2.7   Multiple Output Combinational Circuit Minimization   71
      References 75
      Additional Reading 76
      Problems 76

Chapter 4   MULTIPLE LEVEL AND MSI COMBINATIONAL
            CIRCUITS 83

      4.1   Introduction 83
      4.2   Multiple Level Design of Random Logic 85
      4.3   Modular Realizations of Combinational Functions 86
            4.3.1   A Comparison Circuit 87
            4.3.2   Parallel Adder 89
            4.3.3   Speedup Techniques 91
            4.3.4   Decoders 91
            4.3.5   Parity Check Circuit 94
      4.4   MSI Design Concepts 96
            4.4.1   Multiplexers 97
            4.4.2   ROM's and PLA's 98
      References 101
      Additional Reading 102
      Problems 102

Chapter 5   FUNDAMENTALS OF SEQUENTIAL MACHINES
            AND SYNCHRONOUS SEQUENTIAL CIRCUITS 104

      5.1   Introduction 104
      5.2   Memory Elements, Delays, and Clocks 109
      5.3   Sequential Circuit Synthesis 116
            5.3.1   State Table Derivation 116
            5.3.2   Reduction of State Tables 120
            5.3.3   State Minimization in Incompletely Specified
                    Machines 124
                    5.3.3.1 Generation of Compatible Sets of States .. 125
                    5.3.3.2 Selecting a Minimal Set of Compatible Sets. 130
            5.3.4   Sequential Circuit Realization 135
                    5.3.4.1 State Assignment 142
            5.3.5   MSI Sequential Components 144
                    5.3.5.1 Registers 144
                    5.3.5.2 Shift Registers 145
                    5.3.5.3 Counters 146
                    5.3.5.4 Buses 148
      5.4   Limitation of Finite, State Machines 149
      References 150
      Problems 151

Chapter 6 **ASYNCHRONOUS SEQUENTIAL CIRCUITS** **161**

6.1 Introduction 161
6.2 Classification of Asynchronous Flow Tables 164
6.3 Flow Table Specification 167
6.4 Flow Table Reduction 167
6.5 Synthesis of Asynchronous Circuits 171
    6.5.1 State Assignment 174
        6.5.1.1 Connected Row Set Assignments 176
        6.5.1.2 Universal Connected Row Set State
                  Assignments 183
        6.5.1.3 Shared Row Assignments 185
        6.5.1.4 Single Transition Time Assignments 188
    6.5.2 Specification of the Y-Map 194
6.6 Delays and Hazards 198
6.7 Tying It All Together—A Complete Synthesis Example 201
6.8 Analysis of Hazards 203
    6.8.1 Combinational Hazards 203
    6.8.2 Sequential Hazards 208
6.9 Multiple-Input Changes 214
6.10 Other Delay Models 217
References 218
Problems 219

Chapter 7 **FUNDAMENTALS OF SYSTEM LEVEL DESIGN** **227**

7.1 Design Language 227
7.2 Simple Algorithms 232
7.3 Status Dependent Control Units 238
7.4 Instruction Dependent Control Units 246
7.5 Digital Computer Model 248
7.6 Macroinstructions and Microinstructions 252
References 254
Problems 254

Index **259**

Chapter 1

FUNDAMENTAL CONCEPTS: BACKGROUND AND PRELIMINARIES

1.1 INTRODUCTION

Digital switching circuits are characterized by the feature that signals (voltages and currents) in the circuit are normally restricted to two possible values. Such circuits have many important applications. In a telephone system digital circuits are used to connect a call. The inputs to the system are a sequence of dialed digits which specify the desired connection. Thus there are a finite number of inputs and a finite number of possible connections and, hence, the network that creates the connection can be digital. Digital systems are also useful in pattern (character) recognition machines. If a character is written on a fine grid, each section of the grid can be interpreted as being black or white. These grid segments can thus be converted to electrical signals with two possible values. The character can then be decoded by a digital system.

Undoubtedly the most important application of digital circuits is in digital computers. These systems can perform sequences of arithmetic computations at very high speeds under the control of a program stored within the system. In this book we shall be concerned with the analysis and synthesis of such circuits and their interconnection to create digital systems.

Digital circuits are frequently designed from devices that have two stable states. A switch that can be ON or OFF is a common two state device. Consequently these circuits are sometimes referred to as *switching circuits*.

The subject matter contained in this book has been described as both *logic design* and *switching theory*. Logic design emphasizes development of procedures for the design of switching circuits, whereas switching theory studies properties of switching circuits and attempts to discover design procedures which optimize some parameter of the design. Obviously, these disciplines are closely related and frequently concepts originally developed as theory become important aspects of practical design.

Switching theory makes use of mathematical models and techniques to handle problems associated with the design of digital circuits. The problems of relevance are dictated by the current technology. Switching theory is generally considered to have originated in 1938 with the classic paper by Shannon [1]. Since then the prevalent technology has gone through several generations—relay-contacts, diode gates, transistor gates, integrated circuits, etc., and future technologies are already on the horizon.

For the earlier technologies, the relevant problems were primarily concerned with component minimization. With the development of integrated circuit technology and the advent of large scale integration in digital system design the problems concerned with the minimization of components have become less relevant. These types of problems have been replaced by less well defined and much more difficult problems including structural simplicity and uniformity of modules. Many of these problems cannot be solved in a classical sense and must be treated heuristically. This book will consider both the classical design problems as well as those problems of relevance to the newer technologies.

1.2 LOGIC GATES

The basic elements in circuit level design of digital systems are *gates*. The behavior of a gate can be defined by a *(truth) table* which specifies for all possible input combinations the corresponding output value of the gate (where both input and output values are restricted to two possible values, referred to as 0 or 1). The basic gate types, their representations, and their associated tables are shown in Figure 1.1. The 2-input gates can all be generalized to have *n*-inputs. Practical considerations of an electrical nature, such as amplification requirements, limit the number of gate inputs. An inverted gate input is sometimes denoted by a circle.

Gates are designed from connections of basic electrical components such as resistors, diodes, and transistors. Some simple gates designed from diodes and resistors are shown in Figure 1.2.

In the earlier technologies these components were packaged separately. With the development of semiconductor technology, however, came integrated circuits (IC). In IC technology a small silicon chip contains many elements (transistors, diodes, resistors, capacitors, etc.) which are interconnected within the chip to form circuits. The chip is then mounted on a metal or plastic substrate to form the IC.

Initially IC's were limited to a few gates on a chip. However with advances in technology it is now possible to put in excess of 10,000 gates on a chip. To distinguish the different levels of chip complexity, the following general terminology is used:

> *Small scale integration (SSI)* 1–10 gates on a chip
> *Medium scale integration (MSI) 10–100 gates on a chip*
> *Large scale integration (LSI) 100–1000 gates on a chip*
> *Very large scale integration (VLSI) 1000 + gates on a chip*

Today's digital circuits are invariably constructed with integrated circuits due to advantages in size, cost, speed, reliability, and power consumption. Although

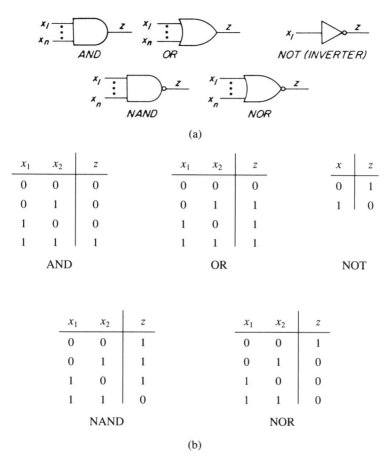

Figure 1.1   (a) Representation of gates (b) Gate truth tables for $n = 2$

in this book we will be dealing with circuits in terms of individual gates and their interconnections, it should be recognized that in practice such circuits would actually be composed of IC's.

In normal switching circuit applications diodes are operated so that the voltage on the cathode side cannot be less than* the voltage on the anode side. Hence, if the input voltage levels e_1 and e_2 in the gate of Figure 1.2(a) are constrained to the two possible values V_+ and V_- where $V_+ > V_-$, then if $V_H > V_+$, the output voltage e_o is approximately equal to the minimum (e_1, e_2) (i.e., the minimum of e_1 and e_2). If $e_o >$ minimum (e_1, e_2), then for one of the diodes the cathode side voltage would be smaller than the anode side voltage, which is not possible.

---

*Actually the cathode side voltage level may exceed the anode side voltage level but only by a very small amount, since the diode forward resistance is very small but non-zero.

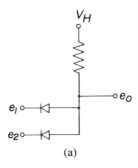

(a)

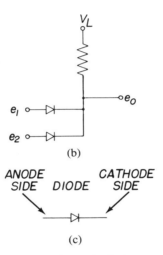

(b)

ANODE   CATHODE
SIDE   DIODE   SIDE

(c)

Figure 1.2 Basic diode-gates

The table in Figure 1.3(a) specifies the output voltage e_o for each of the possible inputs on e_1 and e_2 for the gate of Figure 1.2(a). Thus row 3 of this table is interpreted as follows: If $e_1 = V_+$ and $e_2 = V_-$, then $e_o = V_-$. Instead of using V_+ and V_- to represent the two possible voltage levels it is common to use the symbols 0 and 1. Although $V_+ > V_-$ it is not necessary to associate 0 with V_- and 1 with V_+. There are two possible correspondences ($V_+ \rightarrow 1$, $V_- \rightarrow 0$) or ($V_+ \rightarrow 0$, $V_- \rightarrow 1$). If the first interpretation is used, the resulting circuit is said to have *positive logic* while the second interpretation corresponds to *negative logic*. The tables of Figure 1.3(b) and (c) display the input/output relationship of this gate for positive logic and negative logic assumptions respectively, and correspond to an AND and OR gate respectively. Thus the gate of Figure 1.2(a) behaves as an AND gate assuming positive logic and as an OR gate assuming negative logic.

e_1	e_2	e_o
V_-	V_-	V_-
V_-	V_+	V_-
V_+	V_-	V_-
V_+	V_+	V_+

e_1	e_2	e_o
0	0	0
0	1	0
1	0	0
1	1	1

e_1	e_2	e_o
1	1	1
1	0	1
0	1	1
0	0	0

(a)   (b)   (c)

Figure 1.3   First diode-gate table

The names of the gates derive from descriptions of their behavior. Thus the AND gate output is 1 if and only if for its inputs $x_1 = 1$ *and* $x_2 = 1$, and the OR gate output is 1 if and only if for its input $x_1 = 1$ *or* $x_2 = 1$ (or both). The NOR and NAND names derive from contractions of *Not OR* and *Not AND* since their behavior corresponds to the opposite of an OR gate or an AND gate respectively.

The gate of Figure 1.2(b) can be analyzed in a similar manner. In this case if $V_L < V_-$ the output e_o is equal to the maximum (e_1, e_2), and the gate corresponds to a positive logic OR or a negative logic AND.

The number of inputs on a gate can be increased by connecting additional diodes with the same orientation to the common junction point. In practice the output voltage of a gate may be slightly different from the two possible voltage levels associated with the gate inputs. This signal degradation problem is aggravated when gates are connected to form complex circuits. By using amplification at appropriate points in the circuit, this problem can be eliminated. The transistor circuit shown in Figure 1.4(a) can be used to provide such amplification if the resistor values are properly selected. The input/output voltage level relationships are specified in the table in Figure 1.4(b) and in terms of the symbols 0 and 1, for both positive and negative logic, by the table in Figure 1.4(c). The diode gates and transistor circuit can be combined to form individual gates as shown in Figure 1.5.

Similar gates can be designed from other basic electrical elements. The logic designer usually is not concerned with the precise manner in which a gate is designed or with the choice between positive or negative logic. These decisions may be governed by requirements of compatibility with other subsystems, power supply consideration, or many other factors which are not of interest in the design of circuits on the logic level. In this process, the designer works in terms of the signal value symbols 0 and 1 and gates whose operation is described by tables that specify the input/output relationship in terms of these signal values, rather than by actual voltage levels and actual physical devices which realize gates.

We will be primarily concerned with the logical behavior of circuits. However, we shall briefly consider some of the more important physical characteristics of logic devices which may be of significance in the selection of a specific type of logic:

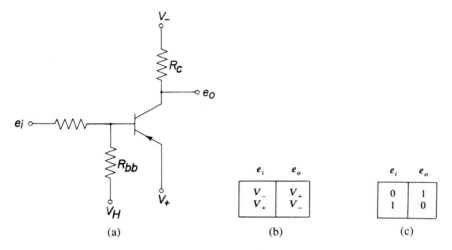

(a)   (b)   (c)

Figure 1.4   A transistor gate

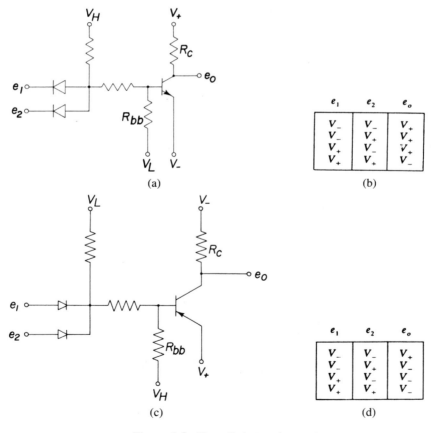

(a)   (b)

(c)   (d)

Figure 1.5   Two diode-transistor gates

Fanout The maximum number of gates that can be connected to (driven from) the output of a gate without improper operation caused by the consumption of power by each gate input.

Fan-in The number of inputs of a gate.

Propagation Delay The amount of time required for input signals of a gate to propagate to (i.e., affect) the output of a gate. The propagation delay of a series of gates is the sum of the delays of the individual gates.

Power Dissipation The power necessary to operate a gate. The power dissipation of a circuit is the sum of the power dissipation of each gate.

Noise Margin The maximum noise voltage which can be added to an input signal without causing erroneous outputs.

Packing Density Measure of the number of gates which can be put on a chip of fixed dimension.

There are two major families of logic, *bipolar logic*, which uses bipolar transistors, and *MOS* (metal oxide semiconductor) logic, which uses field effect transistors (FET). The following table indicates the different families of logic which are used for the different complexity IC chips, and the relative advantages and disadvantages of these families with respect to some of the important properties previously defined.

Logic Family	Advantage/disadvantage	
TTL (Transistor-transistor logic)	Speed and power can be varied over a wide range	Used in SSI and MSI
ECL (Emitter-coupled logic)	Fastest form of logic. Gate provides both OR and NOR outputs, lower fan-in, and fewer gates/package, but higher fanout than TTL	
CMOS (Complementary metal-oxide semiconductor)	Slower than TTL or ECL, very low power dissipation	
I²L (Integrated-injection logic)	Very high packing density	Used in LSI and VLSI
NMOS (n-channel metal-oxide semiconductor)	Slower than TTL or ECL, very low power dissipation, and high packing density	
CMOS (Complementary metal-oxide semiconductor)	Lower power dissipation than NMOS but not as high packing density	

As mentioned previously we will limit our attention to the logical behavior of circuits designed on the gate level and not dwell further on the physical properties of gates and IC's just described.

It is possible, in concept, to analyze the behavior of complex circuits whose elements are gates from knowledge of the behavior of the individual gates. Thus, for the circuit of Figure 1.6, consider the input combination $x_1 = x_2 = x_3 = x_4 = 1$. The outputs of gates G_1 and G_3 are 1 since they are an OR and AND respectively, with both inputs 1. The output of NAND gate G_2 is 0 since both of its inputs are 1. Since G_4 has a 1 input (from G_3) its output is 1. Consequently both inputs to NAND gate G_5 are 1 and the output Z is 0. Similarly if $x_1 = 0$, $x_2 = 1$, $x_3 = 1$, $x_4 = 0$ the output of G_1 is 1 and the output of G_2 and G_3 are 0. Consequently gate G_4 has a 0 output and gate G_5 has a 1 output (since its input from G_4 has a 0 value). This basic approach could be used for all possible input combinations. A more systematic and computationally simpler approach, however, requires the use of discrete algebraic techniques which we shall now consider.

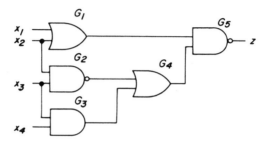

Figure 1.6   A simple circuit

1.3   BOOLEAN ALGEBRA

The basic mathematical tool which is used in the analysis and synthesis of digital switching circuits is *Boolean algebra*, originally developed in the first half of the nineteenth century by George Boole [2]. A binary Boolean algebra is defined in terms of the set $K = \{0,1\}$*, two binary operations, $+$ (sum) and $\cdot$ (product), and a set of basic postulates. The equality sign ($=$) is used to indicate that the functional expressions on both sides are equivalent and parentheses are used for ordering multioperand operations in terms of sequences of two-operand operations. The usual convention is that operations within parentheses are performed first.

The following are a set of basic postulates, which were first proposed by Huntington [3].

---

*A general Boolean algebra can be defined on a finite set K with more than two elements (two of which must be 0 and 1). However, the binary algebra is sufficient for the application to digital circuits.

Huntington's Postulates

1. *Closure*   For all $x,y \in K$ (i.e., x,y are elements in the set K)
   (a) $x + y \in K$
   (b) $x \cdot y \in K$
2. *Existence of Additive and Multiplicative Identity Elements*
   (a) For the element $0 \in K$, $x + 0 = x$, for all $x \in K$
   (b) For the element $1 \in K$, $x \cdot 1 = x$, for all $x \in K$.
3. *Commutativity*   For all $x,y \in K$
   (a) $x + y = y + x$
   (b) $x \cdot y = y \cdot x$
4. *Distributivity*   For all $x,y,z \in K$
   (a) $x + (y \cdot z) = (x + y) \cdot (x + z)$
   (b) $x \cdot (y + z) = (x \cdot y) + (x \cdot z)$
5. *Complementation*   For every $x \in K$, there exists an element $\bar{x} \in K$ (called the *complement* of x) such that
   (a) $x + \bar{x} = 1$
   (b) $x \cdot \bar{x} = 0$

With the appropriate correspondences between the Boolean operators + and and the Boolean complement, with the basic logic gates AND, OR, and NOT, it is relatively simple to determine the validity of Huntington's postulates for logic circuits. The appropriate correspondences are shown in Figure 1.7. The signal value associated with any lead in the circuit can be represented by a Boolean variable which may assume the value of 0 or 1. The behavior of the different types of gates shown in Figure 1.1 can be described by Boolean expressions. Since digital circuits are formed by interconnecting such gates, the binary Boolean algebra may be used in analyzing their behavior.

Boolean entity	Corresponding logic circuit device or property
+	OR gate
·	AND gate
Complement	NOT gate
$K = \{0,1\}$	Set of possible signal values
$\bar{0}$	1
$\bar{1}$	0

Figure 1.7   Boolean algebra entities and corresponding logic circuit entities

If we use the Boolean variables x_1 and x_2 to represent the values of the inputs to the two-input AND gate of Figure 1.1 and z to represent the value of its output, then the output of the gate may be written as $z = x_1 \cdot x_2$.

The validity of this is easily verified. From Postulate 2(b) $1 \cdot 1 = 1$ and $0 \cdot 1 = 0$, and from Postulate 3(b) $1 \cdot 0 = 0 \cdot 1 = 0$. Similarly from rule 5 of Figure 1.8,

$0 \cdot 0 = 0$. This leads to the table in Figure 1.8 which is identical to the logical AND gate defined in Figure 1.1.

Similarly the Boolean sum is defined by $0 + 0 = 0, 0 + 1 = 1 + 0 = 1 + 1 = 1$, which corresponds to the logical OR function. Thus the output of a 2-input OR gate whose inputs are represented by Boolean variables x_1 and x_2, may be represented as $x_1 + x_2$. Similarly, the output of a NOT gate with input x is $\bar{x}$. The NAND and NOR gate outputs are represented by $\overline{x_1 \cdot x_2} = \bar{x}_1 + \bar{x}_2$ and $\overline{x_1 + x_2} = \bar{x}_1 \cdot \bar{x}_2$ respectively.

Using the above correspondence the validity of most of the postulates is obvious. Thus, for example, the closure postulate translates into the statement(s) that if the inputs to a 2-input OR (AND) gate have the values 0 or 1, the output of the gate will also have the value 0 or 1. The commutativity postulates indicate that interchanging the inputs to an OR gate or an AND gate will not change the value of the gate output. These postulates can be used to prove other laws of Boolean algebra. The most important laws of Boolean algebra are summarized in Figure 1.9. For the sake of expositional simplicity we will briefly defer a discussion of these laws and of the methods of their proof.

Many of these laws, including DeMorgan's Law, can be generalized for any number of variables. In its generalized form DeMorgan's Law produces an expression for a complementing by changing all $+$'s to $\cdot$'s, all $\cdot$'s to $+$'s and complementing each variable.

In handling expressions with more than two variables, parentheses are used to define precedence. Due to the law of associativity, it is possible to eliminate parentheses in expressions having only $+$ operations or only $\cdot$ operations without introducing ambiguity. For such expressions DeMorgan's law generalizes to

$$\overline{x_1 + x_2 + \ldots + x_n} = \bar{x}_1 \cdot \bar{x}_2 \cdot \ldots \cdot \bar{x}_n$$
$$\overline{x_1 \cdot x_2 \cdot \ldots \cdot x_n} = \bar{x}_1 + \bar{x}_2 + \ldots + \bar{x}_n.$$

For expressions with both $+$ and $\cdot$ operations, the usual convention is that $\cdot$ takes precedence over $+$, unless parentheses are used. (Parenthetical expressions take precedence over the multiplier operation.) With this convention parentheses can frequently be eliminated. Thus,

$$x_1 + (x_2 \cdot x_3) = x_1 + x_2 \cdot x_3.$$

However, parentheses must be retained in expressions such as $(x_1 + x_2) \cdot (x_3 + x_4)$. It is also possible to eliminate the $\cdot$ in simple products such as $x_1 x_2 x_3$.

DeMorgan's law can also be generalized to apply to complex expressions containing both product and sum operators. Thus,

$$\overline{(x_1 + x_2 \cdot x_3) \cdot x_4 \cdot (\bar{x}_3 + \bar{x}_5)} = \overline{x_1 + (x_2 \cdot x_3)} + \bar{x}_4 + \overline{(\bar{x}_3 + \bar{x}_5)}$$
$$= \bar{x}_1 \cdot \overline{(x_2 \cdot x_3)} + \bar{x}_4 + (\bar{\bar{x}}_3 \cdot \bar{\bar{x}}_5)$$
$$= \bar{x}_1 \cdot (\bar{x}_2 + \bar{x}_3) + \bar{x}_4 + (x_3 \cdot x_5).$$

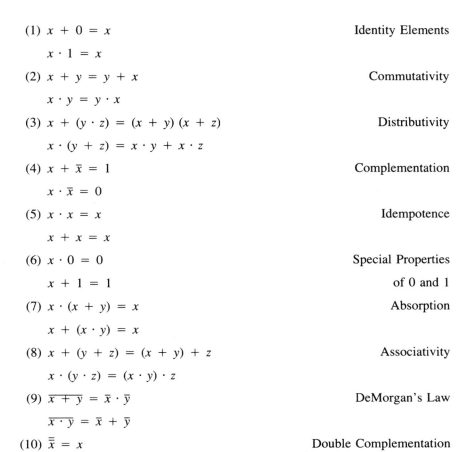

x_1	x_2	$Z = x_1 \cdot x_2$
0	0	0
0	1	0
1	0	0
1	1	1

Figure 1.8   Truth table of Boolean function $Z = x_1 \cdot x_2$

(1) $x + 0 = x$ Identity Elements

   $x \cdot 1 = x$

(2) $x + y = y + x$ Commutativity

   $x \cdot y = y \cdot x$

(3) $x + (y \cdot z) = (x + y)(x + z)$ Distributivity

   $x \cdot (y + z) = x \cdot y + x \cdot z$

(4) $x + \bar{x} = 1$ Complementation

   $x \cdot \bar{x} = 0$

(5) $x \cdot x = x$ Idempotence

   $x + x = x$

(6) $x \cdot 0 = 0$ Special Properties

   $x + 1 = 1$ of 0 and 1

(7) $x \cdot (x + y) = x$ Absorption

   $x + (x \cdot y) = x$

(8) $x + (y + z) = (x + y) + z$ Associativity

   $x \cdot (y \cdot z) = (x \cdot y) \cdot z$

(9) $\overline{x + y} = \bar{x} \cdot \bar{y}$ DeMorgan's Law

   $\overline{x \cdot y} = \bar{x} + \bar{y}$

(10) $\bar{\bar{x}} = x$ Double Complementation

Figure 1.9   Laws of Boolean algebra

Note that the basic postulates are grouped in pairs and that one postulate of each pair can be obtained from the other simply by interchanging all $+$'s and $\cdot$'s, and 0's and 1's. This property is called *duality*. Mathematically, for a given function $f(x_1, x_2, \ldots, x_n)$, the dual function f_d is defined as $f_d(x_1, x_2, \ldots, x_n)$ = $\overline{f(\overline{x}_1, \overline{x}_2, \ldots, \overline{x}_n)}$. Thus for a given Boolean expression, the dual can be derived by the following sequence:

(1) complement all variables
(2) complement the resulting expression

From a generalized form of DeMorgan's Law, step (2) above can be replaced by

(2′) complement all variables
(2″) replace + by · and · by +

Since $\overline{\overline{x}} = x$ steps (1) and (2′) can be deleted thus demonstrating the relationship between the mathematical definition of dual functions and the rule of replacement $+ \rightarrow \cdot, \cdot \rightarrow +$.

Since all the above theorems and lemmas relate to elements of a finite set K, it is possible to prove them *for any particular set K* by enumerating all possible values of each variable. For example, if $K = \{0,1\}$, the table in Figure 1.10 can be used to prove that $\overline{x \cdot y} = \overline{x} + \overline{y}$ for any values of $x, y \in K = \{0,1\}$ since the two columns corresponding to the two sides of the equation (columns 4 and 7) are identical.

x	y	$x \cdot y$	$\overline{x \cdot y}$	$\overline{x}$	$\overline{y}$	$\overline{x} + \overline{y}$
0	0	0	1	1	1	1
0	1	0	1	1	0	1
1	0	0	1	0	1	1
1	1	1	0	0	0	0

Figure 1.10   Tabular proof of DeMorgan's Law

Many results of Boolean algebra can be obtained directly from the basic set of postulates without enumeration. The proofs of these results make use of the *principle of substitution*, if two expressions are equivalent, one may be substituted for the other. The *principle of duality* applies to these results also since if two expressions are proven equivalent by using a sequence of postulates, then the duals of these expressions can be proven equivalent by using the same sequence of dual postulates. We shall illustrate such a mathematical proof for Law 5 of Figure 1.9.

Lemma 1.1 (Idempotence) For all $x \in K$, (a) $x \cdot x = x$, (b) $x + x = x$.

Proof

a)
$$\begin{aligned} x \cdot x &= (x \cdot x) + 0 && \text{Postulate 2(a)} \\ &= (x \cdot x) + (x \cdot \bar{x}) && \text{Postulate 5(b)} \\ &= x \cdot (x + \bar{x}) && \text{Postulate 4(b)} \\ &= x \cdot 1 && \text{Postulate 5(a)} \\ &= x && \text{Postulate 2(b)} \end{aligned}$$

b) By duality ∎

Note that a proof such as this, that follows directly from the basic postulates without enumeration, implies that the result is valid for *any* Boolean algebra, not just the binary Boolean algebra. Once a law has been proven, it can then be used in the proof of subsequent laws.

The laws of Boolean algebra can also be used to derive algebraic expressions which describe the behavior of circuits formed from connections of gates.

Example 1.1 For the circuit of Figure 1.11 (which is identical to that of Figure 1.6) an algebraic expression for the output as a function of the input variables is derived using the basic laws of Boolean algebra as follows: G_i denotes the output value of gate G_i.

$$G_5 = \overline{G_1 \cdot G_4} = \overline{G_1} + \overline{G_4} \tag{1}$$
$$G_4 = G_2 + G_3 \tag{2}$$
$$G_2 = \overline{x_2 \cdot x_3} = \overline{x_2} + \overline{x_3} \tag{3}$$
$$G_3 = x_3 \cdot x_4 \tag{4}$$

Substituting (3) and (4) into (2) we obtain

$$G_4 = \overline{x_2} + \overline{x_3} + x_3 \cdot x_4 = \overline{x_2} + \overline{x_3} + x_4 \text{ (since } \overline{x} + xy = \overline{x} + y)$$
$$G_1 = x_1 + x_2 \tag{5}$$

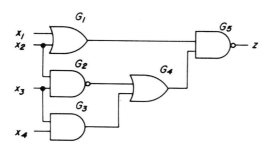

Figure 1.11 A simple circuit

Substituting in (1) we obtain

$$G_5 = \overline{x_1 + x_2} + \overline{\overline{x}_2 + \overline{x}_3 + x_4}$$
$$= \overline{x}_1 \cdot \overline{x}_2 + x_2 \cdot x_3 \cdot \overline{x}_4$$

The output has been expressed as a sum of product terms and the output of the circuit is 1 if and only if all input variables in some product term are 1. Thus, the output of the circuit is 1 if $x_1 = x_2 = 0$ or if $x_2 = x_3 = 1$ and $x_4 = 0$. ∎

1.4 DESIGN HIERARCHY

Conceptually the design of a complex digital system can be treated on different levels depending on the complexity of the elements considered as primitive. These levels are ordered from low level, with very simple elements like gates, to high level, with much more complex elements like processors, memories, etc. The lowest logic level usually considered is *gate or circuit level* where the basic elements, gates and flip-flops, are interconnected to form circuits. In the next higher level, the *register level*, the basic elements are registers (sets of flip-flops) and combinational and sequential circuits which are interconnected to form subsystems. At the highest level the system is formulated from basic elements, corresponding to complex subsystems. These three design levels correspond approximately to levels of integrated circuit technology SSI, MSI, and LSI. With the advent of VLSI, complete microcomputer systems can be incorporated on a single chip.

The microcomputer is a representative of the family of digital computers, the most important class of digital systems. A digital computer can be represented in block diagram form as an interconnection of functional modules as shown in Figure 1.12. The input/output devices are digital devices (such as terminals and printers) which transfer information between the user and the memory unit. The

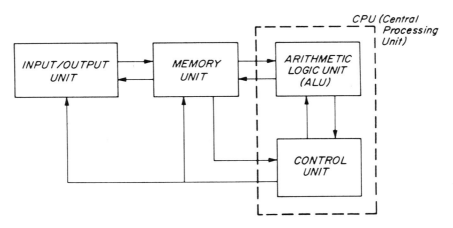

Figure 1.12   Block diagram of a digital computer

memory unit consists of magnetic or semiconductor devices and is used to store programs as well as data and the results of computations. Computations are performed by the arithmetic logic unit (ALU), which consists of logic circuits similar to those with which we will be primarily concerned. The ALU is under the direction of the control unit, a digital circuit which oversees the entire process by interpreting instructions and translating them into an appropriate sequence of signals to perform the intended computation or information transfer from or to memory.

In designing a digital system proceeding from high level to low level design has been referred to as *topdown* or *structured* design. At each level the design progresses to successively greater detail. It is natural for a design to proceed in this order. With the great advances in integrated circuitry, culminating in the development of single chip microcomputers, the higher design levels have become increasingly important. Design at the higher levels is highly heuristic rather than algorithmic and greatly dependent on the designer's ability. However the concepts employed in high level design must be founded on a complete and thorough understanding of the principles of low level design. In the following chapters we will consider the basic principles of gate-level design.

REFERENCES

1. Boole, G., *An Investigation of the Laws of Thought*, Dover Publications, New York, N.Y., 1854.
2. Huntington, E.V., "Sets of Independent Postulates for the Algebra of Logic," *Trans. Am. Math. Soc.*, 5, 288–309, 1904.
3. Shannon, C.E., "A Symbolic Analysis of Relay and Switching Circuits," *Trans. AIEE*, 57, 713–723, 1938.

ADDITIONAL READING

1. Hill, F.J., and G.R. Peterson, *Introduction to Switching Theory and Logical Design,* Third Edition, John Wiley and Sons, New York, N.Y., 1981.
2. Mano, M.M., *Digital Design*, Prentice-Hall, Englewood Cliffs, N.J., 1984.
3. Taub, H., and D. Schilling, *Digital Integrated Electronics,* McGraw-Hill, New York, N.Y., 1977.

PROBLEMS

1.1 For a circuit consisting of binary devices where the two voltage (current) levels are V_H, V_L, $V_H > V_L$, if V_H is represented as 1 and V_L as 0 the circuit is said to have *positive logic* and if V_H is 0, V_L is 1, the circuit is said to have *negative logic*. Consider a device which operates as specified by the following table.

Inputs	Output
x_1 x_2	$f(x_1, x_2)$
V_L V_L	V_H
V_L V_H	V_H
V_H V_L	V_H
V_H V_H	V_L

a) For positive logic what type of gate is this device?

b) For negative logic what type of gate is this device?

c) Define a 2-input 1-output device which realizes the same element for positive and negative logic.

d) Define a *logic insensitive function* as a function which is the same for positive and negative logic. Determine the number of logic insensitive functions of n variables.

1.2 Use the basic laws of Boolean algebra to prove (or disprove) the following equivalences.

a) $xy + \bar{x}\bar{y} + \bar{x}yz = xy\bar{z} + \bar{x}\bar{y} + yz$

b) $xyz + w\bar{y}\bar{z} + wxz = w\bar{y}\bar{z} + wx\bar{y} + xyz$

1.3 For each of the following expressions determine the complement expression using the generalized DeMorgan's Law.

a) $(x_1 + x_2)(\bar{x}_1 x_3 + x_4(x_2 + x_3)(x_3 + x_5)) + \bar{x}_1\bar{x}_2\bar{x}_3(x_4 + x_5x_6)$

b) $\bar{x}_2(x_1 + \bar{x}_3 x_4 (\bar{x}_1 + x_2))$

1.4 Derive Boolean expressions for the outputs of the circuits of Figure 1.13(a) and (b). Are these two output expressions equivalent?

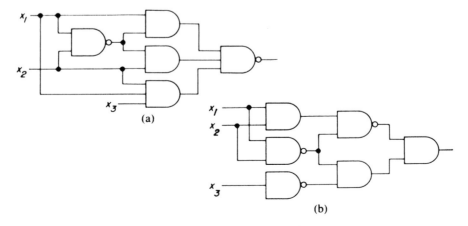

Figure 1.13 Problem 1.4

1.5 A function $f(x)$ is *self dual* if the dual of f, f_d, is such that $f = f_d$.

   a) For each of the functions f_1, f_2, f_3 shown below, determine whether the function is self dual.

   b) Prove that the number of self dual functions of n variables is $2^{2^{n-1}}$.

$$f = x_1 x_2 + \bar{x}_1 \bar{x}_2$$

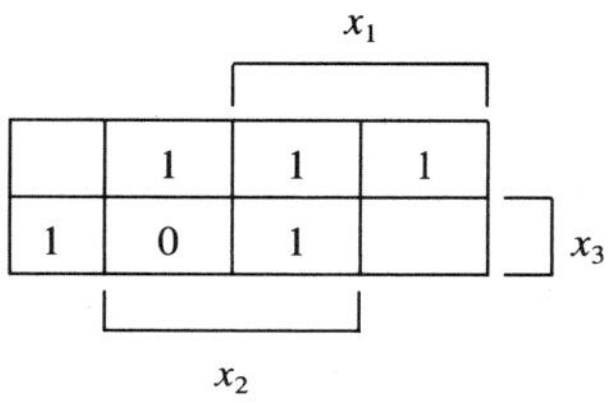

x_1	x_2	x_3	f_3
0	0	0	1
0	0	1	1
0	1	0	0
0	1	1	1
1	0	0	0
1	0	1	0
1	1	0	0
1	1	1	0

Figure 1.14 Problem 1.5

1.6 For the circuit of Figure 1.11, change gates G_2 and G_5 to NOR gates, G_1 and G_4 to AND gates, and G_3 to an OR gate.

   a) Derive a Boolean expression for the resultant circuit.

   b) Using Boolean algebra, simplify the expression derived in (a). From the simplified expression derive an equivalent circuit.

1.7 Consider the following algebra defined on the set $\{0,1,a\}$.

+	0	1	a
0	0	1	a
1	1	1	1
a	a	1	a

·	0	1	a
0	0	0	0
1	0	1	a
a	0	a	a

   a) For each of Huntington's postulates, determine whether or not it is satisfied.

   b) If some postulate is not satisfied attempt to redefine the tables so that all postulates are satisfied. What conclusion can be reached?

   c) Generalize the conclusion reached in (b) to specify for what values of n it is possible to define a Boolean algebra on a set of n elements.

1.8 For each of the laws of Boolean algebra shown in Figure 1.9, other than those which are Huntington's postulates,

   a) Prove the law directly from Huntington's postulates.

   b) For the binary Boolean algebra, prove the law using truth table case enumeration.

c) Define the Boolean algebra on a set of four elements $\{0,1,a,b\}$, then prove the laws for the Boolean algebra defined on this set using truth table case enumeration.

1.9 Prove that any combinational function can be represented as

a) $f(x_1, x_2, \ldots, x_n) = x_1 f(1, x_2, \ldots, x_n) + \bar{x}_1 f(0, x_2, \ldots, x_n)$

b) $f(x_1, x_2, \ldots, x_n) = x_1 x_2 f(1, 1 \, x_3, \ldots, x_n) + \bar{x}_1 x_2 f(0, 1, x_3, \ldots, x_n)$
$+ x_1 \bar{x}_2 f(1, 0, x_3, \ldots, x_n) + \bar{x}_1 \bar{x}_2 f(0, 0, x_3, \ldots, x_n)$

c) Generalize this expansion to i variables. (This result is known as the *Shannon expansion theorem*).

Chapter 2

BINARY REPRESENTATION AND ARITHMETIC

Before proceeding to the design of logic circuits, it will be helpful to first consider the representation of information, both alphabetic and numeric, using an alphabet of only two characters, usually denoted by 0 and 1. This is commonly referred to as *binary* representation of information.

2.1 BINARY NUMBER SYSTEM REPRESENTATION

In binary representation of information each character is referred to as a *bit* (which is a contraction of the term *binary digit*). A sequence of bits $b_n b_{n-1}$, . . . , $b_1 b_0$ in the standard* binary number system represents the integer N where

$$N = b_n \cdot 2^n + b_{n-1} \cdot 2^{n-1} + \cdots + b_1 \cdot 2^1 + b_0 \cdot 2^0.$$

Thus 1101 represents the number

$$1 \cdot 2^3 + 1 \cdot 2^2 + 0 \cdot 2^1 + 1 \cdot 2^0 = 13$$

Given an integer N, we may wish to convert N from decimal (base 10) to binary (base 2) by determining the coefficients $b_k b_{k-1}$, . . . , $b_1 b_0$, $b_i = 0$ or 1, such that $\sum_{i=0}^{k} b_i \cdot 2^i = N$. The integer N can be rewritten as

$$N = \sum_{i=0}^{k} b_i \cdot 2^i = \left(2 \sum_{i=1}^{k} b_i \cdot 2^{i-1} \right) + b_0$$

Dividing N by 2 we obtain

$$\frac{N}{2} = \sum_{i=1}^{k} b_i \cdot 2^{i-1} + \frac{b_0}{2}$$

where the first term is an integer and the second term $(b_0/2)$ is a fraction.

---

*The standard binary number system will be referred to simply as the binary number system.

Hence b_0 is the remainder resulting from dividing N by 2. The quotient of this division will be denoted as Q_1 where $Q_1 = \sum_{i=1}^{k} b_i \cdot 2^{i-1}$. Dividing Q_1 by 2 results in a remainder equal to b_1 and a quotient Q_2. This procedure is iterated, the division of Q_i producing a remainder equal to b_i, and a quotient Q_{i+1}, until $Q_{i+1} = 0$. Thus the following procedure can be used to convert any integer N from base 10 to base 2.

Procedure 2.1   (Binary representation of a decimal number)*

1. Divide N by 2 resulting in a quotient Q_1 and a remainder $P_0 = b_0$, $b_0 = 0$ or 1.
2. Repeat (1) on Q_i resulting in a quotient Q_{i+1} and a remainder $P_i = b_i$, for all $i \geq 1$; terminate when $Q_i = 0$.   ■

Example 2.1   We will represent the integer 116 in base 2. Dividing 116 by 2 yields $Q_1 = 58$, $b_0 = 0$. Dividing Q_1 by 2 yields $Q_2 = 29$, $b_1 = 0$. Dividing Q_2 by 2 yields $Q_3 = 14$, $b_2 = 1$. Repeating we obtain $Q_4 = 7$, $b_3 = 0$; $Q_5 = 3$, $b_4 = 1$; $Q_6 = 1$, $b_5 = 1$; $Q_7 = 0$, $b_6 = 1$. Thus the number 116 is represented in binary as 1110100.

This repeated division can be represented in the following format:

Remainders

2	116	
	58	$0 = b_0$
	29	$0 = b_1$
	14	$1 = b_2$
	7	$0 = b_3$
	3	$1 = b_4$
	1	$1 = b_5$
	0	$1 = b_6$

■

A fractional number $.N$ can be represented in binary by the bit sequence

$$.b_{-1}b_{-2}, \ldots, b_{-p} = b_{-1} \cdot 2^{-1} + b_{-2} \cdot 2^{-2} + \cdots + b_{-p} \cdot 2^{-p}$$

$$= \sum_{i=1}^{p} b_{-i} \cdot 2^{-i}$$

---

*The procedures presented in this chapter can be generalized to apply to any positive integer base r in a straightforward manner.

This can be rewritten as

$$.N = \sum_{i=1}^{p} b_{-1} \cdot 2^{-i} = 2^{-1}\left[\sum_{i=2}^{p} b_{-i} \cdot 2^{-i+1} + b_{-1}\right]$$

Multiplying by 2 yields

$$.N \cdot 2 = \sum_{i=2}^{p} b_{-i} \cdot 2^{-i+1} + b_{-1}$$

the first term of which is a fraction and the second term (b_{-1}) is an integer (0 or 1). Thus the multiplication $N \cdot 2$ results in a number whose integer part I_{-1} is equal to b_{-1} and whose fractional part is defined by

$$F_1 = \sum_{i=2}^{p} b_{-i} 2^{-i+1}$$

Similarly, multiplying F_1 by 2 yields a number whose integer part, I_2, is equal to b_{-2}, and whose fractional part is F_2. This is iterated, the multiplication of F_k by 2 generating $b_{-(k+1)}$, until $F_k = 0$.

Procedure 2.2 (Binary representation of a fractional number)

1. To convert a fractional decimal number $.N$ to base 2, multiply $.N$ by 2, resulting in an integer part $I_1 = b_{-1}$ and a fractional part F_1.
2. Repeat (1) on F_i resulting in an integer part $I_{i+1} = b_{-(i+1)}$ and a fractional part F_{i+1}, for $i = 1, 2, \ldots$. Terminate when $F_i = 0$. ■

However, unlike the integer conversion procedure, the fractional number conversion procedure may not terminate because the number $.N$ may not have a finite representation in base 2. If $F_j = F_k$ for $j > k$, then the base 2 representation of $.N$ repeats the bit sequence $b_{-(k+1)}b_{-(k+2)} \cdots b_{-j}$ indefinitely. Note that a nonterminating fractional number in base 10 may be terminating in base 2. However, the reverse situation may also occur.

Since the representation of fractional numbers may be nonterminating, it is important to determine the maximum error involved in truncation after k bits. That is, if $N = \sum_{i=1}^{\infty} b_{-i} 2^{-i}$ is represented as $N' = \sum_{i=1}^{k} b_{-i} 2^{-i}$, what is the maximum value of $N - N'$. Since $N - N' = \sum_{i=(k+1)}^{\infty} b_{-i} 2^{-i}$, $0 \le b_i \le 1$, the maximum value of $N - N'$ occurs if $b_i = 1$ for all $i > k$. In this case $N - N' < 2^{-k}$. (Exercise)

Example 2.2

a) To convert .4 to base 2, the repeated multiplication of Procedure 2.2 is
   represented as shown below:

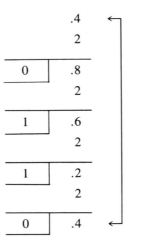

Thus the repeated multiplication yields the result

$$.4_{10} = \underbrace{.01100110}_{\substack{\text{repeated} \\ \text{sequence}}} \ldots \,_2$$

b) To represent .4 in base 2 using a sufficient number of bits so the error is
   $<.01$, the number of bits required is the smallest value of k such that
   $2^{-k}<.01$. This implies $k = 7$. From part (a) $.4 = .0110011_2$.   ∎

There are several ways in which negative numbers can also be represented.
The simplest, conceptually, is to add a sign bit to the number (usually the leftmost
bit). The sign bit is usually assigned the value 0 to represent a positive number
and 1 to represent a negative number. This representation is referred to as *sign
magnitude*. Other representations are useful to simplify binary arithmetic. We
shall consider these later in this chapter.

2.2   BCD AND HEXADECIMAL CODES

In digital systems, signals are restricted to two possible values, so the binary
(base 2) number system is important in representing numbers. However, the
binary system representation of numbers has several disadvantages when used
by individuals who are more familiar with decimal number representation. One
disadvantage is the relative difficulty of converting binary to decimal and back

again. Numerical information can also be represented by a sequence of 0,1 integers in such a way that it is simple to convert between the 0,1 representation and decimal. One such representation is referred to as Binary Coded Decimal (BCD). Each decimal digit is represented by the binary equivalent sequence of 4 bits. Thus 509 is represented as $\underbrace{0101}_{5}\ \underbrace{0000}_{0}\ \underbrace{1001}_{9}$. To convert from BCD to decimal, we simply decode successive 4-bit sequences starting at the right of the word. Thus, 100001110010 represents the decimal number 872.

In BCD code each decimal digit is represented by its 4-bit binary representation. It is possible to use other representations for each digit. One such representation is the *excess-3 code* in which the representation for a digit i corresponds to the binary representation of $i + 3$.

Digit value	Excess-3 representation
0	0011
1	0100
2	0101
3	0110
4	0111
5	1000
6	1001
7	1010
8	1011
9	1100

Note that for this code, the representations for any value i and its 9's complement $9 - i$ are exact complements of each other. This code therefore facilitates the design of circuits to perform arithmetic by the method of complements.

It may also be necessary to represent non-numeric information using the two symbols 0,1. Each element which must be represented can be made to correspond to a unique sequence of bits. If the total number of distinct elements is k and all elements correspond to equal length bit sequences, then the length of the sequence l must be such that $2^l \geq k$ or equivalently $l \geq \lceil \log_2 k \rceil$ where $\lceil X \rceil$ is the smallest integer $\geq X$. In decimal number systems each digit can have 10 values. The number of bits required to represent a digit is hence $l \geq \lceil \log_2 10 \rceil = 4$. Note that six of the sixteen 4-bit sequences do not correspond to digits. It is possible to use these sequences to represent letters so that alphanumeric information can be represented. The *hexadecimal code* represents the ten numbers, 0–9, and the letters A, B, C, D, E, F and is a generalization and extension of the BCD code previously considered. Using this code, $A15$ is represented as $\underbrace{1010}_{A}\ \underbrace{0001}_{1}\ \underbrace{0101}_{5}$ while $\underbrace{1100}_{C}\ \underbrace{1010}_{A}\ \underbrace{1101}_{D}$ represents *CAD*.

The complete alphanumeric list of symbols which it might be desirable to represent includes 26 lower case letters, 26 capital letters, 10 digits, and several special symbols such as $+$, $*$, \$, $=$, etc. A 7-bit code is needed to represent all of these characters. (An n-bit code can uniquely represent at most 2^n characters. Thus $n = 6$ can represent at most $2^6 = 64$ distinct characters). Several such standard codes exist. They usually use 8 bits (referred to as a *byte*) instead of the required 7, with the extra bit being utilized to make it easier to determine the presence of errors should they occur in the system. The use of such codes is briefly considered later in this chapter.

Although it is easy to represent numbers in BCD, arithmetic operations are considerably more difficult for BCD than for binary numbers. Thus it is desirable to be able to convert from BCD to binary and vice versa. The following procedure can be used to convert from BCD to binary.

Procedure 2.3   (Conversion from BCD to binary)

1. Shift the BCD number to the right one bit, shifting in a 0 in the leftmost position. The bit shifted out of the rightmost position becomes the least significant bit of the binary representation.
2. Subtract a correction factor of 3 from each digit (group of 4 bits) whose most significant bit is 1.*
3. Repeat steps 1 and 2 until the remaining BCD number is 0. For an r-digit number there are at most $4r$ iterations.   ■

Example 2.3   The following table illustrates the conversion of the decimal number 107 to the binary representation 1101011.

		BCD Number			
Operation	Iteration	Digit 2	Digit 1	Digit 0	Binary Number
	0	0001	0000	0111	
Shift right	1	0000	1000	0011	1
Subtract 3 from digit 1	1	0000	0101	0011	
Shift right	2	0000	0010	1001	11

---

*This correction is necessary since a 1 in digit k which corresponds to $1 \cdot 10^k$ before shifting, becomes $8 \cdot 10^{k-1}$ after shifting. By subtracting 3, $8 \cdot 10^{k-1}$ is reduced to $5 \cdot 10^{k-1}$ and the net effect of shifting and correcting is equivalent to dividing by two, the same effect shifting has in the binary number representation.

Example 2.3 (continued)

Operation	Iteration	BCD Number Digit 2	Digit 1	Digit 0	Binary Number
Subtract 3 from digit 0	2	0000	0010	0110	11
Shift right	3	0000	0001	0011	011
Shift right	4	0000	0000	1001	1011
Subtract 3 from digit 0	4	0000	0000	0110	1011
Shift right	5	0000	0000	0011	01011
Shift right	6	0000	0000	0001	101011
Shift right	7	0000	0000	0000	1101011

∎

A similar procedure can be used to convert from binary to BCD. In this case the binary number is shifted left and a correction factor of 3 is added to each digit ≥ 5 before each shift. The proof of the validity of these procedures is left as an exercise (Problem 2.3).

2.3 BINARY NUMBER SYSTEM ARITHMETIC

Since arithmetic operations are frequently encountered, the design of binary arithmetic logic circuits is very important in digital system design. We shall now consider algorithms for binary number system arithmetic.

2.3.1 Binary Number System Addition

Let us consider the addition of two binary numbers. As in decimal addition, the numbers to be added are aligned to the rightmost least significant bits which are then added. If the two numbers are $A = a_n a_{n-1} \ldots a_1 a_0$ and $B = b_n b_{n-1} \ldots b_1 b_0$ where $0 \leq a_i$, $b_i \leq 1$ then the result, $A + B = d_{n+1} d_n \ldots d_1 d_0$, $0 \leq d_i \leq 1$, is computed as follows. The addition of the least significant positions a_0, b_0 results in $a_0 + b_0$ where $0 \leq a_0 + b_0 \leq 2$. If $a_0 + b_0 = 2$ the sum can be represented in base 2 by the sequence of two bits, 10. In this case the addition of the least significant position results in a carry of 1 to the next least significant position. If a 1 carry is generated it is then added to the next position addition resulting in $a_1 + b_1 + 1$, which is ≤ 3. If $a_1 + b_1 + 1 \geq 2$ it is represented by $1 d_1$ where $d_1 = (a_1 + b_1 + 1) - 2$, thus generating a 1 carry into the next position. This is repeated for all positions proceeding sequentially from right to left. Note that the carry into any position is always either 0 or 1. The addition of two numbers represented by bit sequences of length n may result in a number represented by a bit sequence of length $n + 1$.

Procedure 2.4   (Binary Addition)

1. The addition of two binary numbers $A = a_n a_{n-1} \ldots a_0$ and $B = b_n b_{n-1} \ldots b_0$ results in $A + B = d_{n+1} d_n \ldots d_1 d_0$. To compute d_0 add $a_0 + b_0$. If $a_0 + b_0 < 2$, $d_0 = a_0 + b_0$, and a carry $C_1 = 0$ is generated for position 1. If $a_0 + b_0 \geq 2$, then $d_0 = a_0 + b_0 - 2$ and a 1 carry is generated into position 1.

2. Add bits a_i, b_i and the carry C_i into position i. If $a_i + b_i + C_i < 2$, then $d_i = a_i + b_i + C_i$ and a carry $C_{i+1} = 0$ is generated for the position $i + 1$. If $a_i + b_i + C_i \geq 2$ then $d_i = (a_i + b_i + C_i) - 2$ and a carry $C_{i+1} = 1$ is generated into position $i + 1$. Repeat sequentially for positions $i = 2, 3, \ldots, n$.

3. The most significant bit of $A + B, d_{n+1} = C_{n+1}$ where C_{n+1} is the carry resulting from the addition of the nth position numbers a_n, b_n, C_n.   ∎

The binary addition of 1001 and 0101 can be represented as follows:

```
          1 0 0 1
          0 1 0 1
          0 0 0 1←      generated carries
          0 1 1 1 0     sum
```

BCD Addition

It is possible to utilize the procedure for binary addition with a slight modification to add two BCD numbers. This process is illustrated in Figure 2.1.

X	0101	0111	0110	576
Y	0100	1000	0010	482
Z	1001	1111	1000	
Second Digit Correction		0110		
	1	0101		
	1010			
Third Digit Correction	0110			
0001	0000			1058

Figure 2.1   Illustration of BCD addition

Addition of the least significant digits denoted as X_0 and Y_0, resulted in the correct computation of Z_0, and the correct carry (0) to the next digit. However, the next digit computation is incorrect. Since $X_1 + Y_1 \geq 10$, it is necessary to generate a 1 carry. Adding 1 to digit 3 is offset by subtracting 10 from digit 2 $(1 \times 10^2 = 10 \times 10^1)$. To generate the correct value for digit 2 it is necessary to subtract 10. By adding a correction factor of $16 - 10 = 6$ to the digit value, the correct second digit and carry are generated. A similar correction is required for the third digit due to the carry from the second digit addition. Thus the following procedure can be used to add BCD numbers using the binary addition procedure.

Procedure 2.5   (BCD Addition)

1. Add the rightmost 4 bits of the two operands and the carry (initial carry is 0) using the algorithm for binary addition. If the result $Z_i \geq 10$ add a correction factor of 6 to generate the correct digit and a 1 carry.
2. Repeat (1) for the next least significant digits and carry until the addition is completed. ∎

2.3.2   Binary Number System Subtraction

Subtraction can be performed in a manner similar to addition, requiring alignment of the least significant positions of the integer parts of the operands, and successive digit subtraction proceeding from least to most significant position. The binary subtraction $A - B$, where $A = a_n \ldots a_1 a_0$, and $B = b_n \ldots b_1 b_0$ results in $D = d_n \ldots d_1 d_0$ where $0 \leq a_i, b_i \leq 1$. Since $-1 \leq a_0 - b_0 \leq 1$ and $0 \leq d_0 \leq 1$, if $a_0 - b_0 < 0$, then we borrow (subtract) a 1 from the rightmost nonzero digit a_k in A, lend (add) 1 to all intermediate digits between a_k and a_0, and add 2 to bit a_0 thus generating $d_0 = (a_0 + 2) - b_0$. (The validity of this borrowing/lending technique stems from the fact that $x \cdot 2^k = (x-1)2^k + \left(\sum_{i=1}^{k-1} 2^i \right) + 2$.) If $a_0 - b_0 \geq 0$ then $d_0 = a_0 - b_0$. We then repeat this procedure for all bit positions proceeding sequentially from right to left.

Procedure 2.6   (Binary Subtraction)

1. If $A = a_n a_{n-1} \ldots a_1 a_0$ and $B = b_n b_{n-1} \ldots b_1 b_0$ are binary numbers then $A - B = d_n d_{n-1} \ldots d_1 d_0$ is derived by successive bit subtraction as follows. If $a_i - b_i \leq 0$ then $d_i = (a_i + 2) - b_i$ and a 1 is borrowed (subtracted) from the rightmost nonzero digit $a_k, k < i$, and a 1 is added to all digits $a_{k-i}, a_{k-2} \ldots, a_{i+1}$.
2. Step (1) is repeated for $i = 1, 2, \ldots, n$ to obtain the binary representation of $A - B$. ∎

If $B > A, A - B$ is a negative number. In this case Procedure 2.6 will not lead to a meaningful result. To rectify this, we must first define a means of representing negative numbers. The simplest manner to accomplish this is to use a separate sign bit to represent the sign of the number (0 corresponding to positive and 1 to negative, usually) and to represent the magnitude of the number using the standard binary system. This is referred to as *sign-magnitude code*. However using another type of code addition and subtraction can be treated in a uniform manner (i.e., subtraction is simply addition of a negative number). Thus it is possible to represent negative numbers in such a manner that subtraction can be performed via the use of the addition algorithm. This is significant from a digital system design viewpoint since it implies that the same circuit can be used for both addition and subtraction. In order to understand this representation we must first introduce the concept of *modulo number representation*.

For any pair of integers x,y where $y>0$ the number x has a unique representation of the form $x = k_1 \cdot y + k_2$ where k_1,k_2 are integers and $0 \le k_2 < y$. For example if $y = 6$ and $x = 28$, $x = 4 \cdot 6 + 4$. The number k_2 in this representation of x in terms of y is referred to as x modulo y or x mod y. If $x = -11$ and $y = 5$, $x = (-3) \cdot 5 + 4$ and hence -11 mod $5 = 4$.

Lemma 2.1 If x,y and k are integers then $(x+k \cdot y)$ mod $y = x$ mod y

Proof Assume x mod $y = k_1$. Then $x = k_2 \cdot y + k_1$. Therefore

$$x + k \cdot y = (k_2 \cdot y + k_1) + k \cdot y$$
$$= (k_2 + k) \cdot y + k_1$$
$$= k' \cdot y + k_1 \quad \text{where } k' = (k_2 + k)$$

Therefore $(x + k \cdot y)$ mod $y = k_1 = x$ mod y. ∎

In performing addition the sum of two numbers may be greater than either of the numbers. If the two operands A,B in an addition are represented as k-digit binary numbers, then $A,B \le 2^k - 1$ and the sum $A + B \le 2^{k+1} - 2$ which may require a $(k+1)$-bit representation. If only the k least significant bits are used to represent $A + B$ the resulting number is $(A + B)$ mod 2^k since if $A + B > 2^k - 1$ the most significant bit, which was deleted, is 1 and the result is $A + B - 2^k = (A+B)$ mod 2^k. For instance, assuming 4-digit representation, if $A = 1001$ and $B = 0111$, the addition of A and B yields

$$
\begin{array}{r}
1\ 0\ 0\ 1 \\
0\ 1\ 1\ 1 \\
\underline{1\ 1\ 1\ 1} \\
1\ 0\ 0\ 0\ 0
\end{array}
\qquad \text{carries}
$$

4-bit representation

Deleting the most significant bit of $A + B$ the result becomes 0000. This is because $A + B = 16$ and (16) mod $2^4 = 16$ mod $16 = 0$. Thus the operation of addition when performed with k-digit operands and k-digit result is actually modulo 2^k addition.

2's Complement Arithmetic

The operation of subtraction $A - B$, for $A,B < 2^k$ can be expressed as an addition operation involving a negative operand, $A + (-B)$. Assuming addition is modulo 2^k, then, by Lemma 2.1, $(A + (-B)) \bmod 2^k = [(A + (-B)) + 2^k] \bmod 2^k$. Thus the modulo 2^k addition can be performed with two positive operands, A and $2^k - B$. The term $2^k - B$ is called the *2's complement representation of* $-B$.

A number can be converted to 2's complement form without using subtraction. The 2's complement $2^k - B$ can be represented as $(2^k - 1) - B + 1$. The number $2^k - 1$ is represented as $\underbrace{111. \ . \ .1}_{k \text{ times}}$. Hence $2^k - 1 - B$ can be generated by simply changing all 0 bits of B to 1 and all 1 bits of B to 0. The resulting number is called the *complement of B*. To form $2^k - B$ we thus complement B and then add 1.

Procedure 2.7   (Generation of 2's Complement)   To compute the 2's complement of a binary number $B = b_{k-1} \ . \ . \ . \ b_1 b_0$
1. Complement all bits of B.
2. Add 1 to the resulting number.   ■

Example 2.4   The 2's complement representation of -13 is formed by complementing the binary representation of 13, which is 01101, resulting in 10010, and adding 1, resulting in 10011. Note that adding first and then complementing yields the incorrect result of 10001.   ■

The 2's complement of a number B can also be obtained by complementing all bits to the left of the least significant (rightmost) 1 bit in B. (See Problem 2.12.) For example if $B = 011001$ we complement the leftmost 5 bits to form the 2's complement of B which is 100111. Similarly if the number is 10011100 the 2's complement is 01100100.

In order to ensure that $A + B < 2^k$ we assume that $A,B < 2^{k-1}$. If $B < 2^{k-1}$, then the 2's complement of B will always have a 1 in bit b_k. We will therefore use this bit as a sign bit. A sign bit equal to 1 indicates a negative number and a sign bit equal to 0 indicates a positive number. Given a 2's complement representation of a number B, if $B' = 2^k - B$, the 2's complement of B' is equal to $2^k - (2^k - B) = B$. Thus if $k = 4$, the number 10110 represents a negative number, since the most significant bit is 1. Taking the 2's complement of this number we obtain 01010 which is the binary representation of 10. Thus 10110 is the 2's complement representation of -10. Subtraction can now be performed by converting all negative operands to 2's complement representation and then performing addition. In order that we obtain the correct result mod 2^k, each of the operands A,B is restricted to be within the range of values $-2^{k-1} < A,B < 2^{k-1}$. If the sign bit addition is performed as specified in the following procedure the sign bit of the result will always be correct.

Procedure 2.8   (2's Complement Addition)

1. Convert any negative operands to 2's complement form.
2. Add the operands as specified in Procedure 2.4 treating the sign bit in the same manner as all other bits and permitting a carry into the (high order) sign bit position, while ignoring a carry out of the sign bit position into bit position $k + 1$.   ∎

It remains to be proven that the sign bit of the result is always correct.

Theorem 2.1   If addition and subtraction are performed as specified in Procedure 2.8, the result sign bit will be 0 if the result is ≥ 0 and the sign bit will be 1 if the result is < 0.

Proof   We must consider three distinct cases, corresponding to addition of two positive numbers, one positive and one negative number, and two negative numbers.

Case #1   Assume both numbers are non-negative. Then if these numbers are $A = a_{k-1} \ldots a_1 a_0$ and $B = b_{k-1} \ldots b_1 b_0$ they are represented as $0a_{k-1} \ldots a_1 a_0$ and $0b_{k-1} \ldots b_1 b_0$. Assuming the addition is such that $A + B < 2^k - 1$ (which is required for modulo 2^k addition) then there will be no carry into the sign bit position and therefore the result sign bit is 0, which is correct since $A + B \geq 0$.

Case #2   Assume A is non-negative and B is negative. Then A is represented as $0B_A$ where B_A is the binary representation of A, and B is represented as $1B_C$ where B_C is the binary representation of $C = 2^k - B$. If $A \geq B$ then this addition will result in a carry into the sign position since $B_C + B_A = 2^k - B + A \geq 2^k$. Therefore the result sign bit will be $0 + 1 + 1 = 0$ mod 2 which is correct since if $A \geq B, A - B \geq 0$. If $A < B$ then $B_C + B_A = 2^k - B + A < 2^k$ and there is no carry into the sign position. The result sign bit will be $0 + 1 + 0 = 1$ which is correct since if $A < B$, $A - B < 0$.

Case #3   Assume both A and B are negative. Then A is represented as $1B_D$ where $D = 2^k - A$ and B is represented as $1B_C$. Then $B_D + B_C = (2^k - A) + (2^k - B) = 2^{k+1} - (A + B)$. But $-(A + B)$ is restricted to be $\geq -(2^k - 1)$ for correct modulo 2^k addition and hence $B_D + B_C \geq 2^k$. Therefore there will always be a carry into the sign position and the sign bit of the result will be $1 + 1 + 1 = 1$ mod 2 which is correct since $A + B < 0$.   ∎

Example 2.5   a) Consider the addition 4 + 6 (where $k = 4$). Since neither operand is negative, we add the corresponding binary numbers with 0 in the sign bit position

sign bit

↙

0 0 1 0 0

0 0 1 1 0

  1   Carry

0 1 0 1 0

↖

sign bit

The result is + 10 (since the sign bit is 0 and the magnitude bits are 1010).

   b) Consider the addition 6 + (− 4). The negative number is represented by its two complement, 11100. The addition is:

sign bit

↙

0 0 1 1 0

1 1 1 0 0

1 1   Carry

0 0 0 1 0

↖

sign bit

The result is + 2. (Note the carry into the sign bit position.)

   c) Consider the addition − 6 + 4. This addition is represented as:

sign bit

↙

1 1 0 1 0   (2's complement representation of − 6)

0 0 1 0 0

1 1 1 1 0

↖

sign bit

The result is a negative number, since the sign bit is 1. The number can be determined by taking the 2's complement of the result yielding 00010. Thus the result is − 2.

d) Consider the addition $-6 + (-4)$. Both numbers are represented in 2's complement form and added as follows:

sign bit

↙

1 1 0 1 0

1 1 1 0 0

1   Carry

1 0 1 1 0

↖

sign bit

The result is negative. The 2's complement of the result is 01010. Thus the result is -10. ∎

In the preceding it was necessary to assume that $-(2^k-1) \leq A + B \leq 2^k - 1$ in order for the computation to be correct. If this condition is violated then *overflow* is said to have occurred when $A + B > 2^k - 1$ and *underflow* if $-(2^k-1) < A + B$. Overflow and underflow in addition can easily be determined from the sign bits of A and B and the carry into the sign position. Specifically, if A and B are both positive (sign bit 0) and there is a carry into the sign bit then overflow has occurred and if A and B are both negative and there is no carry into the sign position then underflow has occurred.

1's Complement Arithmetic

The *1's complement* representation of a negative number B is defined as $2^k - B - 1$. It can be obtained from B by simply complementing all bits. It is also possible to perform subtraction using an addition procedure and 1's complement representation. However the advantage over 2's complement arithmetic in deriving the 1's complement is offset by the necessity to correct the result by adding 1 when adding two negative numbers or when adding a negative number to a larger positive number as shown below:

$$A + (2^k - B - 1) = 2^k + (A - B) - 1$$

Must add 1 for correct
answer if $A > B$

$$(2^k - A - 1) + (2^k - B - 1) = 2^{k+1} - A - B - 2$$

Must add 1 to obtain correct
answer corresponding to 1's
complement of $-A - B$

2.3.3 Binary Number System Multiplication

Consider the multiplication of two binary numbers $A = a_n a_{n-1} \ldots a_1 a_0$ and $B = b_n b_{n-1} \ldots b_1 b_0$:

$$A \cdot B = \left(\sum_{i=0}^{n} a_i \cdot 2^i \right) \cdot B = a_0 \cdot B + a_1 \cdot 2^1 B + \cdots + a_n \cdot 2^n B$$

If $Y = y_n y_{n-1} \ldots y_1 y_0$ the product $2^i \cdot Y = y_n y_{n-1} \ldots y_1 y_0 \underbrace{00 \ldots 0}_{i \text{ zeros}}$. (The

proof of this is left to the student as an exercise.) Thus the multiplication of $A \cdot B$ can be expressed as a sum of n such simpler multiplications of the form $a_i \cdot (y_n y_{n-1} \ldots y_1 y_0 \underbrace{00 \ldots 0}_{i \text{ zeros}})$. Furthermore $a_i = 0$ or 1 and $0 \cdot B \cdot 2^i = 0$ and $1 \cdot B \cdot 2^i = B \cdot 2^i$. Hence binary multiplication consists of adding all terms of the form $2^i \cdot B$ for all i such that $a_i = 1$.

Procedure 2.9   (Binary Multiplication)   To multiply $A = a_n a_{n-1} \ldots a_1 a_0$, by $B = b_n b_{n-1} \ldots b_1 b_0$

1. Set $Z = 0$, $i = 0$
2. If $a_i = 1$ add $2^i B = (b_n b_{n-1} b_0 \underbrace{0 \ldots 0}_{i})$ to Z
3. Increment i by 1
4. Repeat (2) and (3) for all i, $0 \leq i \leq n$. At completion Z contains the binary representation of $A \cdot B$. If A and B are n-bit numbers, $A \cdot B$ has at most $2n$ bits. ∎

Example 2.6   Let $A = 01011$ and $B = 11000$. Initially $Z = 0$. Since $a_0 = 1$ we add B to Z resulting in $Z = 11000$. Since $a_1 = 1$ we add $2B = (110000)$ to Z resulting in $Z = (1001000)$. Since $a_3 = 1$ we add $2^3 \cdot B = (11000000)$ to Z resulting in $Z = (100001000) = A \cdot B$. Multiplication can be represented as follows:

$$
\begin{array}{rl}
B = 1\,1\,0\,0\,0 & \\
A = 0\,1\,0\,1\,1 & \\
\hline
1\,1\,0\,0\,0 & = 2^0 \cdot B \\
1\,1\,0\,0\,0\,0 & = 2^1 \cdot B \\
1\,1\,0\,0\,0\,0\,0\,0 & = 2^3 \cdot B \\
\hline
1\,1\,1\,1 \quad\quad & \text{Carries} \\
\hline
A \cdot B = 1\,0\,0\,0\,0\,1\,0\,0\,0 &
\end{array}
$$

∎

2's Complement Multiplication

Multiplication can also be performed using the concept of 2's complement. Since the product of two k bit numbers may be a $2k$ bit number, certain modifications must be made. The multiplication $A \cdot (-B)$ corresponds to $A \cdot (2^k - B) \bmod 2^k$ $= (2^k \cdot A - A \cdot B) \bmod 2^k = (2^k - AB) \bmod 2^k$ which is the 2's complement of $A \cdot B$. Similarly the multiplication $(-A) \cdot (-B)$ corresponds to $(2^k - A) \cdot (2^k - B) \bmod 2^k = [2^k(2^k - A - B) + AB] \bmod 2^k = AB$. The following example illustrates the operation of 2's complement multiplication.

Example 2.7   a) We shall first multiply $2 \cdot (-3)$ in 2's complement, assuming $k = 5$:

$$
\begin{array}{ll}
1\ 1\ 1\ 1\ 0\ 1 & \text{2's complement of 3} \\
\underline{0\ 0\ 0\ 0\ 1\ 0} & \\
1\ 1\ 1\ 1\ 0\ 1\ 0 & \text{2's complement of } -6
\end{array}
$$

b) We shall now illustrate the multiplication $(-2) \cdot (-3)$:

$$
\begin{array}{ll}
1\ 1\ 1\ 1\ 1\ 0 & \text{2's complement of 2} \\
\underline{1\ 1\ 1\ 1\ 0\ 1} & \text{2's complement of 3} \\
1\ 1\ 0\ 1\ 1\ 1\ \underbrace{0\ 0\ 0\ 1\ 1\ 0} &
\end{array}
$$

6-bit representation   ∎

2.3.4 Binary Number System Division

The operation of division is somewhat more complex due to the fact that for two integers $A, B, A \div B$ may not be an integer. Suppose

$$
A \div B = \sum_{i=0}^{n} C_i\, 2^i + R/B
$$

where R, the remainder, is such that $0 \leq R < B$.
Then

$$
A = B \cdot \sum_{i=0}^{n} C_i\, 2^i + B
$$

In this case $C_n = 1$ if $A - 2^n B = A - b_n b_{n-1} \ldots b_1 b_0 \underbrace{0 \ldots 0}_{n} \leq 0$, otherwise $C_n = 0$. If $C_n = 1$, the remaining bits $C_{n-1} \ldots C_0$ must be such that $A = 2^n \cdot B + \sum_{i=0}^{n-1} C_i \cdot 2^i \cdot B$. These remaining bits are generated by first subtracting $2^n \cdot B$ from A resulting in $A' = A - 2^n B$ which is then used to define the succeeding bits $C_{n-1}, C_{n-2}, \ldots, C_0$.

Procedure 2.10   (Binary Division)

1. Set $i = n$, the remainder $= A$
2. If $R - 2^i B \geq 0$ then set $C_i = 1$ and subtract $2^i \cdot B$ from A. If $R - 2^i \cdot B < 0$ then set $C_i = 0$

3. Repeat (2) for $i = n - 1, n - 2, \ldots, 1,0$ to generate the bits C_{n-1}, $C_{n-2}, \ldots, C_1 C_0$. At completion the binary representation of $A \div B$ is $C_n C_{n-1} \ldots C_i C_0$ and the remainder is R. ∎

Example 2.8 We will divide $A = 11101_2$ by $B = 00101_2$. The result $C = C_4 C_3 C_2 C_1 C_0$ is obtained as follows: Since $A - 2^4 B = A - 001010000 < 0$, $C_4 = 0$. Similarly $C_3 = 0$ since $A - 2^3 B < 0$. However, $A - 2^2 B > 0$. Therefore $C_2 = 1$ and $A' = A - 2^2 B = 11101 - 10100 = 01001$. $A' - 2^1 \cdot B = 01001 - 01010 < 0$. Therefore $C_1 = 0$. Finally $A' - 2^0 \cdot B = 01001 - 00101 = 00100$. Thus $C_0 = 1$. The binary representation of $A \div B$ is $C = 00101$ and the remainder is $R = 00100$. This division can be represented as follows:

$$
\begin{array}{r}
00101 \\
00101 \,\overline{\big)\, 11101} \\
-10100(2^2 \cdot B) \\
\hline
01001 \\
-00101(2^0 \cdot B) \\
\hline
00100
\end{array}
$$
∎

In succeeding chapters we shall design digital circuits and systems which perform binary arithmetic computations as specified in the algorithms presented in this section.

2.4 FLOATING POINT ARITHMETIC

Until now we have limited our discussion to *fixed point representation* of numbers in which all of the digits of a number must be represented. In many applications the numbers to be represented may require many digits. These numbers can frequently be represented with fewer digits using *floating point notation*. For example the number 5,000,000 can be represented as 5×10^6. In digital systems, binary floating point numbers may be represented in the *normalized* form $M \cdot 2^{\pm E}$ where M, the *mantissa*, is constrained to be, $1/2 \leq M < 1$ and E is the *exponent* of the number, and both M and E are represented in binary. Thus 1011000 would be represented as $(.1011) \cdot 2^{111}$ and .00001 would be represented as $(.1) \cdot 2^{-100}$.

Arithmetic operations for floating point numbers are quite simple. Thus if

$$X = M_x \cdot 2^{E_x}$$

and

$$Y = M_y \cdot 2^{E_y}$$

then

$$X \cdot Y = M_x \cdot M_y \cdot 2^{E_x + E_y}$$

and

$$X \div Y = (M_x \div M_y) \cdot 2^{E_x - E_y}$$

The 2's complement representation can be used for both the mantissas and exponents. In this way floating point multiplication (division) corresponds to fixed point multiplication (division) of the mantissas and fixed point addition (subtraction) of the exponents. To perform addition or subtraction on floating point numbers the numbers must have the same exponent. (This corresponds to proper alignment of the numbers.) If $E_x > E_y$ then Y is represented as $M_y' = \underbrace{.00\ldots.0}_{E_x - E_y} b_{-1} b_{-2} \ldots b_{-n}$ where $.b_{-1} b_{-2} \ldots b_{-n}$ corresponds to M_y and $E_y' = E_y + (E_x - E_y) = E_x$. Then $X + Y = (M + M_y') \cdot 2^{E_x}$. Thus the addition $(.1)2^1 + (.1)2^{10}$ is performed as $(.01)2^{10} + (.1)2^{10} = (.11)2^{10}$.

2.5 OTHER CODES

The binary representation of numbers which we have considered so far is important because of its simplicity for representing information and of performing arithmetic computations. In certain applications, however, other properties become important and *codes* with special properties have been developed for these applications.

For example the binary representation of numbers has the property that an error (change of value) in any bit converts one number to another number. Thus an error in bit b_1 of the representation of 6 (110) changes the number to 4 (100). Now consider a code in which we augment the standard binary code with an extra *check bit*, Pc, the value of the check bit being defined so that the total number of 1-bits in the entire word is even. Figure 2.2 shows the representation of the numbers 0–7 and their respective values of the check bit. Now an error

b_2	b_1	b_0	Pc
0	0	0	0
0	0	1	1
0	1	0	1
0	1	1	0
1	0	0	1
1	0	1	0
1	1	0	0
1	1	1	1

Figure 2.2   Binary code with even parity bit

in bit b_1 of 6 converts 1100 to 1000. The resultant word has an odd number of 1's whereas all of the valid code words have an even number of 1's. Thus it can easily be determined an error has occurred. This code is called a *parity check code* [1]. It has the property that an error affecting any single bit will always produce a word with an odd number of 1's (odd parity) and hence all single bit errors can be detected.

It is not possible, however, to determine which bit is in error and hence the word cannot be corrected. Many more sophisticated and complex codes have been developed which have greater fault detecting and correcting capabilities [2,3].

The common binary code representations for alphanumeric characters are frequently augmented by an additional parity check bit to form an 8-bit code. A group of 8-bits is usually called a *byte*.

We shall now consider another example of a code with a special property which has application to digital system design. In normal binary number representation two consecutive numbers may have representations which have different values in many bits. In some applications it is desirable to have a k-bit representation of the numbers 0 to $2^k - 1$ in which all successive code words differ in only one variable as do the codes for $2^k - 1$ and 0. For example this would prevent possible problems in a counting application which might occur if multiple bit changes did not occur exactly in synchronism. The *Gray code* is one such code which has had applications in design of counting circuits. The 2-bit and 3-bit Gray codes are shown in Figure 2.3.

	x_1	x_2			x_1	x_2	x_3
0	0	0		0	0	0	0
1	0	1		1	0	0	1
2	1	1		2	0	1	1
3	1	0		3	0	1	0
				4	1	1	0
	(a)			5	1	1	1
				6	1	0	1
				7	1	0	0

(b)

Figure 2.3 Gray codes (a) 2-bit (b) 3-bit

A k-bit Gray code G can be obtained from a $(k-1)$-bit Gray code G' as shown in Figure 2.4, by adding a bit x_1, which is 0 for the numbers 0 through $(2^{k-1} - 1)$, and the remaining bits of the code are identical to G' for these numbers. The remaining numbers (2^{k-1} through ($2^k - 1$)) have $x_1 = 1$ and the other bits are defined by G'_r, which is obtained by reversing the rows of G, (i.e., first row becomes last and vice versa).

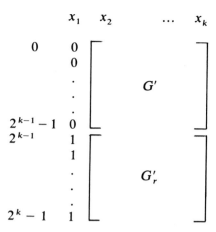

Figure 2.4   Defining k-bit Gray code from $(k-1)$-bit Gray code

The adjacency properties of codes play an important role in the design of asynchronous circuits which we shall consider in Chapter 6. The error detecting and correcting properties of codes are very important considerations in the design of computer and communication systems. These topics, however, are beyond the scope of this book. Having introduced the fundamental concepts related to Boolean algebra and binary representation of information, in the next chapter we will consider the use of Boolean algebra in the design of combinational circuits.

REFERENCES

1. Hamming, R.W., "Error Detecting and Error Correcting Codes," *Bell System Technical Journal*, 29, 147–160, April 1950.
2. Peterson, W.W., and E.J. Weldon, *Error-Correcting Codes*, (2nd Ed.), MIT Press, Cambridge, Mass., 1972.
3. Sellers, F.F., Jr., Hsiao, M.Y., and Bearnson, L.W., *Error Detecting Logic for Digital Computers*, McGraw-Hill, New York, N.Y., 1968.

ADDITIONAL READING

1. Flores, I., *The Logic of Computer Arithmetic*, Prentice-Hall, Englewood Cliffs, N.J., 1963.
2. Hwang, K., *Computer Arithmetic, Principles, Architecture, and Design*, John Wiley & Sons, N.Y., 1979.

PROBLEMS

2.1 For each of the following pairs of decimal numbers, convert to 2's complement form and add.

a) $17 + 5$
b) $-14 - 12$
c) $-8 + 18$
d) $12 - 6$

2.2 For each of the decimal numbers 543 and 777:

a) generate the BCD representation.
b) Convert to binary representation using Procedure 2.3.
c) Add the two numbers in BCD representation.

2.3 Prove the validity of Procedure 2.3.

2.4 Formulate a procedure (similar to Procedure 2.3) for conversion of a standard binary code number to BCD representation.

2.5 Prove that the maximum error resulting from trunction after k bits of a fraction in standard binary code is bounded by 2^{-k}.

2.6 Formulate a procedure (similar to Procedure 2.5) for subtraction of BCD numbers.

2.7 If $A = .101 \cdot 2^{101}$ and $B = .11 \cdot 2^{-11}$ find $A + B$, $A - B$, and $A \cdot B$. Express your answer in normalized floating point form.

2.8 Perform the following operations using 2's complement arithmetic.

a) $39 \cdot 18$
b) $-17 \cdot 52$
c) $-41 \cdot -28$
d) $39 \div -6$
e) $-52 \div -7$

2.9 A weighted code associates a fixed value w_i with the bit in position i. The standard binary code is a weighted code with $w_i = 2^i$. In the standard binary code each number has a unique representation.

a) Consider a weighted binary code with weights $w_{n-1}, \ldots, w_1, w_0$. What relationship must exist among the weights in order that no two codes represent the same number?

b) Consider the weighted binary code with weights $8,4,3,-2$. Derive representations of the numbers 0 through 15.

c) How many different sets of weights w_3, w_2, w_1, w_0 exist which define unique binary codes for the 16 numbers 0, . . . , 15?

2.10 Assume that a digital system has all registers having n bits and addition and subtraction is done in 2's complement form. If the result R is not in the range $-2^n < R < 2^n$, then R cannot be stored in a n-bit register. In this case an *overflow error* is said to have occurred. Specify a combinational function of variables A_0, . . . , A_{n-1}, B_0, . . . , B_{n-1}, R_0, . . . , R_{n-1} whose value is 1 if and only if an overflow error has occurred. (*Hint:* The function can be defined so as to be independent of all variable other than the sign bits of the operands A_{n-1}, B_{n-1}, and the sign bit of the result R_{n-1}.)

2.11 From the Gray codes of Figure 2.3, derive 4 and 5-bit Gray codes.

2.12 Prove that the 2's complement of a binary number N can be formed by complementing all bits to the left of the least significant 1 bit.

2.13 Assume that the words of a digital system are encoded in an even parity check code of 4 bits. Which of the outputs 0011, 1011, 1110, if received would indicate an error.

2.14 a) Modify Procedure 2.8 to perform one's complement addition and subtraction and use this procedure to perform the computations specified in Example 2.5.

b) For each of the decimal numbers in Problem 2.1 convert to 1's complement form and add.

2.15 A weighted BCD code represents each decimal digit N by a sequence of four binary bits $b_3b_2b_1b_0$ with weights w_3, w_2, w_1, w_0 such that $N = w_3 \cdot b_3 + w_2 \cdot b_2 + w_1 \cdot b_1 + w_0 \cdot b_0$.

a) Define a BCD code with weights $(4,3,2,1)$ so that the coding for each decimal digit N, $0 \le N \le 9$, is the complement of the coding for the digit $9-N$.

b) How many sets of weights exist which have the complementing property if none of the weights can be negative?

Chapter 3

FUNDAMENTALS OF COMBINATIONAL FUNCTIONS AND CIRCUITS

3.1   INTRODUCTION

Consider a digital circuit C with inputs $(x_1, x_2, \ldots, x_n)$ and output Z. If the output value of the circuit only depends on the current value of the inputs and is completely independent of previous (past) values of the inputs, the circuit is called a *combinational circuit*. Such a circuit defines a mapping from the set of 2^n possible values of the input set $(x_1, x_2, \ldots, x_n)$, which may be referred to as *input states*, to the possible output values $(0,1)$. This mapping is called a *combinational function*, $f(x_1, x_2, \ldots, x_n)$, and C is said to realize f. If the output depends on previous values of the inputs as well as the current values, the circuit is called a *sequential circuit* and the corresponding function is a *sequential function*.

It is easily shown that an *acyclic** circuit of gates is combinational. Although it is possible for a cyclic circuit to realize combinational functions also, this case is unusual and we will not consider it here. We shall use the term combinational circuit to imply acyclic.

A *completely specified* combinational function $f(x_1, x_2, \ldots, x_n)$ is a mapping from the set of 2^n possible values of the set of n inputs into $K = \{0,1\}$. Since each of the 2^n n-tuples can be mapped into either of two possible values there are 2^{2^n} possible completely specified combinational functions.

It is also desirable to define *incompletely specified* combinational functions which map a proper subset of the 2^n input n-tuples into $K = \{0,1\}$. The value of the function for the remaining n-tuples is left *unspecified*. An unspecified value for a particular input state is used to indicate that that input state will never occur or that the value of the function for that input state can be defined to be either 0 or 1 and is sometimes referred to as a *don't care*.

A combinational function f (or a set of functions defined on the same set of input variables) can be represented by a truth table with 2^n rows, one for each

---

*A circuit C is *cyclic* if there exists an ordered set of gates $G_1, G_2, \ldots, G_r$ in C such that the output of G_i is an input to G_{i+1} for all i, $1 \leq i \leq r - 1$, and the output of G_r is an input to G_1. Informally, there is a directed path from the output of a gate G_1 in C to an input to G_1.

possible input state. Associated with each such row is the corresponding value of the function (or functions). Unspecified values are denoted by a dash (-) in the table. Figure 3.1 shows one such truth table, this one with 3 input variables x_1, x_2, x_3 and 3 functions f_1, f_2, and f_3. The function f_1 is completely specified while f_2 and f_3 are incompletely specified.

x_1	x_2	x_3	f_1	f_2	f_3
0	0	0	1	1	1
0	0	1	0	0	0
0	1	0	1	-	1
0	1	1	0	-	0
1	0	0	1	1	-
1	0	1	1	1	0
1	1	0	0	0	1
1	1	1	0	0	0

Figure 3.1   A truth table of combinational functions

A combinational circuit C is said to *realize* a function $f(x)$ if for every specified value x_i of f the corresponding output of the circuit is 1 for any input corresponding to a 1-point, and the output is 0 for any input corresponding to a 0-point. The output corresponding to a don't care point can be either 0 or 1.* The circuit of Figure 3.2 with output $F(x_1, x_2, x_3)$ realizes f_1 of Figure 3.1 (since $F(x_1, x_2, x_3) = f_1(x_1, x_2, x_3)$) and also f_2 (since $f_2(x_1, x_2, x_3)$ and $F(x_1, x_2, x_3)$ are equal for all input states for which f_2 is specified). However the circuit does not realize f_3 since $f_3(1,0,1) = 0$ and $F(1,0,1) = 1$.

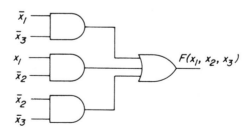

Figure 3.2   A combinational logic circuit

In this chapter we will consider the problem of deriving a digital circuit to realize a combinational function specified by a word description. The first step in this *synthesis* problem is often the derivation of a truth table describing the

---

*Although a combinational function may be unspecified for an input state **x**, the output of any digital circuit is always 0 or 1 for any input state. Thus the output of a combinational circuit always corresponds to a completely specified combinational function.

function to be realized. (This is not *always* done as we shall demonstrate later in this chapter.) The derivation of the truth table may involve the necessity of formulating a binary representation of the inputs and outputs of the function, and can usually be formulated as the following 3-step process.

1. Represent the function *inputs* as binary valued variables x_i.
2. Represent the function *output* as binary valued variables z_i.
3. For each input combination, specify the value each output should assume.

Although there exists no systematic procedure to generate a truth table (due to the vague concept of what constitutes a word description of a function) it can usually be accomplished without great difficulty as illustrated in the following example.

Example 3.1 A combinational circuit is to be used to control a seven segment display of LED's (Light Emitting Diodes). The circuit inputs represent a single BCD digit and its outputs are used to control the display so that for each input the appropriate set of LED's are activated so as to visually represent the BCD input digit.

The circuit and display are represented in Figure 3.3(a). The visual representation of the digits 0–9 are shown in Figure 3.3(b). It is assumed that an output $z_i = 1$ will activate the corresponding LED segment while $z_i = 0$ deactivates the segment.

Figure 3.3(c) shows the 16 possible values of the four input bits, the corresponding BCD digits, and the values of $z_1, \ldots, z_7$ corresponding to each of the BCD digits. Note that the output entries are unspecified for the six rows which do not correspond to BCD digits since it is assumed that those inputs will not occur. ■

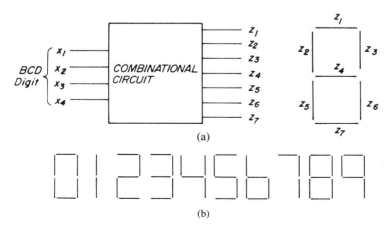

(a)

(b)

Figure 3.3 Seven segment LED display example

x_1	x_2	x_3	x_4	Corresponding BCD digit	z_1	z_2	z_3	z_4	z_5	z_6	z_7
0	0	0	0	0	1	1	1	0	1	1	1
0	0	0	1	1	0	0	1	0	0	1	0
0	0	1	0	2	1	0	1	1	1	0	1
0	0	1	1	3	1	0	1	1	0	1	1
0	1	0	0	4	0	1	1	1	0	1	0
0	1	0	1	5	1	1	0	1	0	1	1
0	1	1	0	6	0	1	0	1	1	1	1
0	1	1	1	7	1	0	1	0	0	1	0
1	0	0	0	8	1	1	1	1	1	1	1
1	0	0	1	9	1	1	1	1	0	1	0
1	0	1	0	None	-	-	-	-	-	-	-
1	0	1	1	None	-	-	-	-	-	-	-
1	1	0	0	None	-	-	-	-	-	-	-
1	1	0	1	None	-	-	-	-	-	-	-
1	1	1	0	None	-	-	-	-	-	-	-
1	1	1	1	None	-	-	-	-	-	-	-

(c)

Figure 3.3   (continued)

Once a truth table corresponding to the circuit to be designed has been specified, the next task is to design a gate level circuit to realize the truth table. We assume the truth table has n input variables $(x_1, x_2, \ldots, x_n)$.

For an n-dimensional cube defined by variables $(x_1, x_2, \ldots, x_n)$ each point can be represented as a product term in which each of the n variables appears complemented or uncomplemented. For example, if $n = 3$ the product term $x_1 \bar{x}_2 x_3$* represents the point $(x_1, x_2, x_3) = (1,0,1)$. Such a product term is called a *minterm*, since it defines a Boolean function which has the value 1 for only one point in the n-dimensional space. It is convenient to label minterms as m_i where i is the integer defined by treating the product term as a binary number sequence of 0's (for each complemented variable) and 1's (for each uncomplemented variable) where x_1 defines the most significant bit. Thus $x_1 \bar{x}_2 x_3$ defines the number 101 which represents m_5, since 101 is a binary representation of the integer 5. Similarly m_3 corresponds to $\bar{x}_1 x_2 x_3$ which defines the binary number 011.

A combinational function $f(x_1, \ldots, x_n)$ can be realized by a circuit of the form shown in Figure 3.4. This circuit has several n-input AND gates and one OR gate. The AND gates are used to realize the minterms which correspond to 1-points of f. This realization is called a *canonical sum of minterms* realization.

The function f_1 of Figure 3.1 can be expressed as the sum of minterms

$$f_1 = \bar{x}_1 \bar{x}_2 \bar{x}_3 + \bar{x}_1 x_2 \bar{x}_3 + x_1 \bar{x}_2 \bar{x}_3 + x_1 \bar{x}_2 x_3$$
$$= m_0 + m_2 + m_4 + m_5 .$$

---

*Since no ambiguity results we will represent product terms by concatenating literals without interspersing the product sign between the literals.

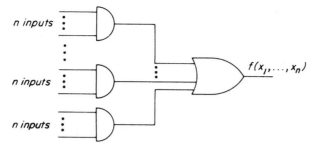

Figure 3.4 Canonical sum of minterms circuit

Incompletely specified functions can be represented by specifying the minterms for which the function is 1 and those for which it is unspecified separately. Thus for the function f_2 of Figure 3.1

$$f_2 = \underset{\text{1-pts}}{\Sigma}\; m_0, m_4, m_5 \;+\; \underset{\substack{\text{don't}\\\text{cares}}}{\Sigma}\; m_2, m_3.$$

The dual canonical realization is the *product of maxterms*. If we represent a function $\bar{f}$ as a sum of minterms we obtain $\bar{f} = \underset{i \epsilon I_0}{\Sigma}\; m_i$ where I_0 is the set of integer labels corresponding to 0-points of f (or 1-points of $\bar{f}$). Applying DeMorgan's Law to the sum of minterms expression for $\bar{f}$, we obtain an expression for f as

$$f = \underset{i \epsilon I_0}{\Pi}\; M_i$$

where $M_i = \bar{m}_i$ is a sum term containing each variable complemented or uncomplemented. M_i represents a function which has the value 0 only for the point m_i, and hence is called a *maxterm*. The circuit of Figure 3.5 can be used to realize a canonical product of maxterms.

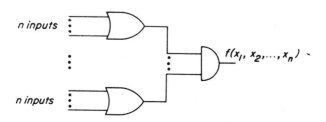

Figure 3.5 Canonical product of maxterms circuit

Example 3.2   For the function f_1 of Figure 3.1, $\overline{f}_1$ can be expressed as a sum of minterms

$$\overline{f}_1 = m_1 + m_3 + m_6 + m_7.$$

By DeMorgan's Law this is converted to a product of maxterms expression for f

$$f = M_1 \cdot M_3 \cdot M_6 \cdot M_7$$
$$= (x_1 + x_2 + \overline{x}_3) \cdot (x_1 + \overline{x}_2 + \overline{x}_3) \cdot (\overline{x}_1 + \overline{x}_2 + x_3) \cdot (\overline{x}_1 + \overline{x}_2 + \overline{x}_3)$$

which is realized by the circuit of Figure 3.6. Note that by interpreting complemented variables as 1's and uncomplemented variables as 0's (the opposite convention as for minterms), the maxterm M_j defines a 0, 1 sequence corresponding to the binary number representation of j.   ∎

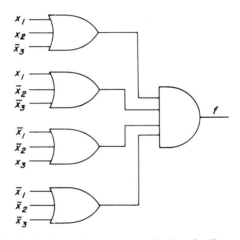

Figure 3.6   Product of maxterms realization for Example 3.2

The number of *levels* of a combinational circuit is the maximum number of gates from any input signal to any output. These two canonical realizations are two level circuits. This assumes that each of the variables x_i and its complement $\overline{x}_i$ can be used as circuit inputs. Such inputs are sometimes referred to as *double rail inputs*. (If only the uncomplemented variables can be used as circuit inputs, then inverters may be required and the number of levels in the resultant circuit may exceed two. Such inputs are called *single rail*.)

Since there is usually a delay associated with each gate, the speed of a circuit (i.e., the elapsed time for an input change to cause an output change to occur) is proportional to the number of levels. Hence two level circuits have the desirable property of being relatively fast. However in general there exist other two level realizations for a combinational function which require fewer gates than either of the two canonical realizations we have considered.

The fundamental combinational circuit design is as follows:

For a given combinational function f (or set of functions) design a combinational circuit which realizes f and optimizes some parameter (or set of parameters) subject to constraints on other parameters.

Classically the parameters optimized have been total number of gates or total number of gate inputs. The rationale behind such an optimization goal was the cost associated with hardware in earlier technologies. The primary constraint considered is that l, the number of levels in the circuit, be at most two (two-level circuits).

Relatively simple procedures have been developed to design minimal gate (or gate-input) two level circuits. The basic tool in these procedures is described in the next section.

3.2   COMBINATIONAL FUNCTION MINIMIZATION

For the combinational function f, specified by the truth table of Figure 3.7, f can be expressed as a sum of minterms, $f = \bar{x}_1 \bar{x}_2 \bar{x}_3 + x_1 \bar{x}_2 x_3 + x_1 x_2 x_3$. Using the laws of Boolean algebra, this expression can be simplified since $\bar{x}_1 \bar{x}_2 x_3 + x_1 \bar{x}_2 x_3 + x_1 x_2 x_3 = (\bar{x}_1 + x_1) \bar{x}_2 x_3 + x_1 x_2 x_3$ (by postulate 4(b)) and since $(\bar{x}_1 + x_1) = 1$, this expression simplifies to $\bar{x}_2 x_3 + x_1 x_2 x_3$. Thus two of the three minterms (m_1 and m_5) can be replaced by a single product term in an equivalent Boolean expression. The original expression could also be simplified by combining minterms m_5 and m_7 as follows:

$$\bar{x}_1 \bar{x}_2 x_3 + x_1 \bar{x}_2 x_3 + x_1 x_2 x_3 = \bar{x}_1 \bar{x}_2 x_3 + x_1 x_3 (\bar{x}_2 + x_2)$$
$$= \bar{x}_1 \bar{x}_2 x_3 + x_1 x_3.$$

Both of these simplifications can be utilized if we represent the original expression as $m_1 + m_5 + m_5 + m_7$ (m_5 can be repeated since $m_5 + m_5 = m_5$) resulting in the equivalent expression $\bar{x}_2 x_3 + x_1 x_3$.

In this section we will consider the problem of deriving two level realizations of a combinational function which are minimal in some respect. There are several criteria of optimality which could be used. The relevance of these criteria is of

x_1	x_2	x_3	f
0	0	0	0
0	0	1	1
0	1	0	0
0	1	1	0
1	0	0	0
1	0	1	1
1	1	0	0
1	1	1	1

Figure 3.7   A combinational function truth table

course dependent on costs associated with the technology which will be used to design the associated circuit. In this chapter we will consider the following two criteria of optimality [1,2,3]:

1. A two level circuit which requires the minimal total number of gate inputs.
2. A two level circuit which requires the minimal number of gates, and has the fewest gate inputs amongst all minimal gate circuits.

In general there may be more than one minimal circuit and therefore we consider the design of "*a* minimal" rather than "*the* minimal" circuit. The procedures we will utilize may be extended to derive realizations which are optimal with respect to related criteria of optimality.

We first consider two level realizations referred to as *sum of product* realizations in which the first level consists of AND gates and the second level consists of a single OR gate as shown in Figure 3.8. In such a circuit the AND gates generate products of *literals* where a *literal* is defined to be an input variable x_i or its complement $\bar{x}_i$. The OR gate sums these product terms. Thus the output of this circuit is a sum of product terms.

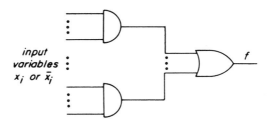

Figure 3.8   Sum of products circuit

In an n-dimensional space defined by variables $x_1, x_2, \ldots, x_n$, a product term in which each variable or its complement appears, represents a single point in the space as we mentioned previously. Such a term is referred to as a *complete product term*. A product term in which some variable does not appear, either complemented or uncomplemented, represents several points in the n-dimensional cube in the following sense. Suppose P is a product term which contains each variable except x_n. Then by the law of distributivity, $P = P (x_n + \bar{x}_n) = Px_n + P \bar{x}_n$. Thus P can be expressed as the sum of two complete product terms. Hence for either of these two points in the n-cube, P will take the value 1 and hence P is said to *cover* (i.e., represent) these two points. Thus for the set of variables x_1, x_2, x_3 the product term $\bar{x}_1 x_3$ covers the two points $(0,0,1)$ ($x_1 = 0, x_2 = 0, x_3 = 1$) and $(0,1,1)$.

In an exactly analogous manner a product term of k literals covers 2^{n-k} points in the n-dimensional space. (Such a product term is said to represent a cube of dimension $(n - k)$ or simply an $(n - k)$-*cube*. Thus a minterm represents a *cube* of dimension 0. For the set of variables x_1, x_2, x_3, the product term $\bar{x}_2$ (a product of one literal) covers 4 points, $(0,0,0)$, $(0,0,1)$, $(1,0,0)$, $(1,0,1)$.

For a combinational function $f(x_1, x_2, \ldots, x_n)$ a product term P is an *implicant of f* if P covers at least one 1-point of f and P does not cover any 0-points of f.* Thus if P is an implicant of f, for every point covered by P, f has the value 1 or f is unspecified. An implicant P of a combinational function f is a *prime implicant* of f if for any other implicant of f, P', there exists a point which is covered by P but not covered by P'.

Example 3.3   Consider the combinational function $f(x_1, x_2, x_3)$ specified by the truth table of Figure 3.9. The product term $P_1 = \bar{x}_1\bar{x}_2$ covers the points $(0,0,0)$ and $(0,0,1)$. Since f has the value 1 for both of these points, P_1 is an implicant of f. Similarly $P_2 = x_1\bar{x}_2$ covers the points $(1,0,0)$ and $(1,0,1)$. Since $f(1,0,0)$ is unspecified and $f(1,0,1) = 1$, P_2 is also an implicant of f. The product term $P_3 = \bar{x}_1x_2$ covers points $(0,1,0)$ and $(0,1,1)$. Since $f(0,1,0) = 0$, P_3 is not an implicant of f. The product term $P_4 = \bar{x}_2$ covers 4 points and is an implicant of f. Since P_4 is an implicant and P_1 does not cover any point not covered by P_4, P_1 is not a prime implicant of f. Similarly P_2 is not a prime implicant of f. However P_4 is a prime implicant of f since it is the only implicant of f covering 4 points.   ■

x_1	x_2	x_3	f
0	0	0	1
0	0	1	1
0	1	0	0
0	1	1	1
1	0	0	-
1	0	1	1
1	1	0	0
1	1	1	0

Figure 3.9 Combinational function truth table

The importance of implicants in a sum of products realization of a combinational function f is easily seen by referring to the prototype circuit of Figure 3.8. This circuit will have an output $f = 1$ for any point covered by any product term realized by an AND gate. Hence each such product term must be an implicant of f. Since $f = 0$ for any point not covered by some product term, each 1-point of f must be covered by some such product term. Hence in a sum of products realization of f each product term must be an implicant of f and each 1-point of f must be covered by some such product term. The concept of prime

---

*Product terms covering only unspecified points have also been defined as implicants in the literature but such terms are superfluous in any sum of products realization.

implicant is important in sum of products realizations which are optimal with respect to total number of gate inputs or total gates. In such a circuit the output of every AND gate must be a prime implicant of the function being realized as we shall now prove.

Theorem 3.1   In a sum of products realization of a combinational function f, if the realization is optimal with respect to total gate inputs, or total gates, then the output of every AND gate is a product term which is a prime implicant of f.

Proof   (Our proof is based on the mathematical concept of contradiction, i.e., assume the theorem is false and from that derive a contradiction.) Suppose there exists such an optimal realization of f in which the output of some AND gate G is a product term P_1 which is *not* a prime implicant of f. Then there must be another implicant of f, P_2, which covers all points covered by P_1. If we replace the AND gate G realizing P_1 by an AND gate G' realizing P_2, the circuit will still realize f since every point covered by P_2 is either unspecified or a 1-point of f. If P_1 is a product of k literals then P_2 is a product of $k' < k$ literals since P_2 covers more points then P_1. Thus this circuit modification reduces the total number of gate inputs with the same number of gates. This contradicts the assumption that the original circuit was optimal in this respect and hence proves the theorem.   ∎

Thus a sum of products realization of a combinational function f which is optimal with respect to gate inputs or gates, is a sum of prime implicants in which each 1-point of f is covered by some prime implicant of the sum. However this optimal realization is not in general equal to the sum of *all* prime implicants of f. For instance for the function specified by the truth table of Figure 3.10(a), the set of all prime implicants is $x_1 x_2, \bar{x}_1 x_3, x_2 x_3$. The circuit of Figure 3.10(b) corresponds to the sum of all prime implicants of f. However the prime implicants $x_1 x_2$ and $\bar{x}_1 x_3$ cover all 1-points of f. Thus $f = x_1 x_2 + \bar{x}_1 x_3$ and the corresponding circuit (Figure 3.10(c)) has fewer inputs (and fewer gates) than the sum of all prime implicants. From the preceding we can formulate a general procedure for

x_1	x_2	x_3	f
0	0	0	0
0	0	1	1
0	1	0	0
0	1	1	1
1	0	0	0
1	0	1	0
1	1	0	1
1	1	1	1

(a)

Figure 3.10   (a) Truth table (b) Sum of all prime implicants (c) Optimal circuit realization

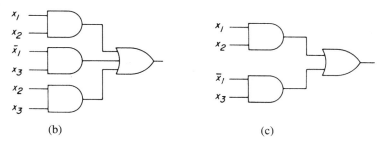

(b)   (c)

Figure 3.10   (continued)

obtaining the minimal gate-input (or minimal gate) sum of products realization of a combinational function f.

Procedure 3.1

1. Find the complete set of prime implicants of f.
2. From the set of all prime implicants of f, select a "minimal cost" subset which covers all 1-points of f, and realize f as a sum of this minimal cost subset of prime implicants of f.

■

The "cost" of a prime implicant P_k is, of course, related to the optimization goal. A prime implicant of l literals requires an l-input AND gate (if $l > 1$) and one input to the OR gate. If $l = 1$ no AND gate is required. Therefore the cost $C(P_k)$ of such a prime implicant is equal to $l + 1$ (if $l > 1$) and the cost is 1 if $l = 1$ assuming the optimization goal is total gate-input minimization. If the optimization goal is to minimize gates, the cost of a prime implicant is 1 if $l > 1$ and the cost is 0 if $l = 1$. The cost of a set of prime implicants is equal to the sum of the individual costs.

We have now formulated the problem of minimal sum of products combinational circuit synthesis in terms of two well defined subproblems. We shall now consider solutions to these two subproblems.

3.2.1   Generation of Prime Implicants—Tabular Method

A product term covering two points (i.e., a 1-cube) can be formed by combining two product terms covering one point each (i.e., two 0-cubes) if these two terms differ in only one literal. Suppose these two terms are $x_1 P$ and $\bar{x}_1 P$ where P is a product of literals. Then since $x_1 P + \bar{x}_1 P = (x_1 + \bar{x}_1) P = P$ these two terms are combined by deleting the literal x_1 and $\bar{x}_1$ (in which the two terms differ), thus resulting in a product term of n-1 literals which covers both points. In a completely analogous manner two product terms of n-k literals (each covering 2^k points) can be combined if they contain the same set of variables and differ in only one literal, into a composite product term covering 2^{k+1} points and having $(n-k-1)$ literals. Thus $x_2 x_3 \bar{x}_4$ and $x_2 \bar{x}_3 \bar{x}_4$ are combined by deleting x_3 and $\bar{x}_3$ into the product term $x_2 \bar{x}_4$. However $x_1 x_2 x_3$ and $x_2 x_3 x_4$ cannot be combined in this manner since the product terms are defined on different sets of variables.

The prime implicants of a combinational function f can be obtained by combining sets of 1-points and unspecified points in this manner. The procedure is iterated until no further combinations are possible at which time the terms which could not be further combined are the complete set of prime implicants of f.

For a function containing k points which are 1-points or unspecified, there are $\binom{k}{2}$ possible pairs of points which can be combined to form implicants covering two points. As k gets large this function grows very rapidly. The Quine-McCluskey procedure [1,2,3] is a systematic method of generating all prime implicants efficiently with relatively few combinations of points required to the considered.

Procedure 3.2   (Quine-McCluskey procedure)

1. List all 1-points and don't care points of $f(x_1, x_2, \ldots, x_n)$ in a table, representing a minterm m_i by the binary number i arranged as a sequence of 0 and 1 bits in columns labeled $x_1, x_2, \ldots, x_n$. Partition this list into classes $S_0, S_1, S_2, \ldots, S_n$ where S_i consists of all such points with i variables equal to 1, and $(n-i)$ variables equal to 0 in the respective binary representations.

2. A point in a set S_i and a point in a set S_j where $j > i + 1$ will differ in at least two variables and hence cannot be combined. For all $i = 0,1,2, \ldots, n-1$, compare each element in set S_i with each element in set S_{i+1}. For those pairs of points which differ in a single literal x_j, create a new implicant which agrees with both points in the $(n-1)$ literals in which they agree and is unspecified $(-)$ in x_j and place it in a new set S_i' containing 1-cubes with i variables equal to 1. To indicate that the two individual points which were combined are not prime implicants, flag ($\surd$) each point when it is combined with another point. Repeat this for all pairs of points of which one is in S_i and the other in S_{i+1} for all $i = 0,1,2, \ldots, n-1$.

3. After completing (2) apply the same procedure to the sets S_0', S_1', S_{n-1}', to combine implicants. Note that implicants with don't cares must have the don't cares in the same variables in order to be combined. Implicants are flagged ($\surd$) when combined with other implicants. This results in sets $S_0'', S_1'', \ldots, S_{n-2}''$. The procedure is then iterated on these sets continually until no further combinations are possible, at which time all unflagged elements represent prime implicants of f.* ∎

---

*For some of these terms all points covered may be unspecified, and hence these are not actually prime implicants. Such terms will be discarded during step (2) of Procedure 3.1, the selection of a minimal cost set of prime implicants which cover all 1-points of f.

The representation of minterms as binary numbers enables the determination of the number of bits in which terms differ by inspection, and is attractive for computer implementations of this procedure. Alternatively it is possible to represent minterms as decimal numbers. Such terms differ in one variable only if the difference between their decimal representations is 2^k for some integer k. Implicants representing a set of 2^r points can be represented by a set of decimal minterms. Two implicants can be combined only if each element of one set differs from some element of the other set by 2^k for the same value of k. For functions of many variables, the decimal procedure for determination of prime implicants may result in fewer errors of a mechanical nature for hand computations.

Examples 3.4   Consider the combinational function $f(x_1, x_2, x_3, x_4)$, specified by the truth table of Figure 3.11(a). The 1-points and the don't care point of f are listed in a table and partitioned into sets S_0, S_1, S_2, S_3, S_4 as shown in Figure 3.11(b). Set S_0' is formed by combining elements in S_0 and S_1. The first row in S_0' results from combining the points (0000) and (0001), the second row from combining (0000) and (0010), and the third from (0000) and (1000). Note that the same row is combined with several other rows. Similarly S_1' is formed from S_1 and S_2, S_2' from S_2 and S_3, and S_3' from S_3 and S_4. The 3rd row of S_0' and the 2nd row of S_1' are combined to form S_0''. Combining row 2 of S_0' and row 3 of S_1' results in the same implicant. The unflagged rows are the prime implicants of f: $\bar{x}_1 \bar{x}_2 \bar{x}_3, \bar{x}_1 \bar{x}_3 x_4, \bar{x}_1 x_2 x_4, x_1 x_3 \bar{x}_4, x_2 x_3 x_4, x_1 x_2 x_3, \bar{x}_2 \bar{x}_4$. ∎

Figure 3.11(c) shows the procedure for determining prime implicants, using a decimal notation. Associated with each row of each set S_i' and S_i'', etc. is the set of points covered by the corresponding implicant and the decimal difference Δ between these elements. The rows (m_0, m_2) of S_0' and (m_8, m_{10}) of S_1' have constant difference $\Delta = 8 = 2^3$ and are combined to form a set of 4 elements (m_0, m_2, m_8, m_{10}) with 2 differences $\Delta_1 = 2$ (the difference for the original combinations (m_0, m_2) and (m_8, m_{10})) and $\Delta_2 = 8$ (the constant difference between these 2 sets). A row in S_i' can be combined with a row of S_{i+1}' if and only if the difference (or set of differences) of these two rows is identical.

3.2.2   Generation of Prime Implicants—Map Method

Another method of generating prime implicants for functions of a relatively small number of variables involves the use of a Karnaugh map [4]. A Karnaugh map for n input variables $(x_1, x_2, \ldots, x_n)$ is effectively a 2-dimensional pictorial representation of the n-cube represented by the n inputs. Such a map contains 2^n cells, one representing each of the 2^n points in the n-cube (i.e., each of the 2^n possible values of the inputs $(x_1, x_2, \ldots, x_n)$). In Figure 3.12(a) the 2-dimensional space defined by variables x_1, x_2 is represented. The corresponding Karnaugh map is shown in Figure 3.12(b). Note that the Karnaugh map has one

x_1	x_2	x_3	x_4	f
0	0	0	0	1
0	0	0	1	1
0	0	1	0	1
0	0	1	1	0
0	1	0	0	0
0	1	0	1	1
0	1	1	0	0
0	1	1	1	-
1	0	0	0	1
1	0	0	1	0
1	0	1	0	1
1	0	1	1	0
1	1	0	0	0
1	1	0	1	0
1	1	1	0	1
1	1	1	1	1

(a)

	x_1	x_2	x_3	x_4	
S_0 {	0	0	0	0✓	m_0
	0	0	0	1✓	m_1
S_1 {	0	0	1	0✓	m_2
	1	0	0	0✓	m_8
S_2 {	0	1	0	1✓	m_5
	1	0	1	0✓	m_{10}
S_3 {	0	1	1	1✓	m_7
	1	1	1	0✓	m_{14}
S_4	1	1	1	1✓	m_{15}

	x_1	x_2	x_3	x_4	
S_0' {	0	0	0	-	$(m_0,m_1) \Delta = 1$
	0	0	-	0✓	$(m_0,m_2) \Delta = 2$
	-	0	0	0✓	$(m_0,m_8) \Delta = 8$
S_1' {	0	-	0	1	$(m_1,m_5) \Delta = 4$
	-	0	1	0✓	$(m_2,m_{10}) \Delta = 8$
	1	0	-	0✓	$(m_8,m_{10}) \Delta = 2$
S_2' {	0	1	-	1	$(m_5,m_7) \Delta = 2$
	1	-	1	0	$(m_{10},m_{14}) \Delta = 4$
S_3' {	-	1	1	1	$(m_7,m_{15}) \Delta = 8$
	1	1	1	-	$(m_{14},m_{15}) \Delta = 1$
S_0'' {	-	0	-	0	$(m_0,m_2,m_8,m_{10}) \Delta_1 = 2, \Delta_2 = 8$

(b)　　　　　　　　　　　(c)

Figure 3.11 (a) Truth table (b) Binary prime implicant generation (c) Decimal prime implicant generation

box corresponding to each point in the space and orthogonal adjacent cells in the map differ in only one variable.

Figure 3.13(a) shows a pictorial representation of a 3-dimensional space defined by variables x_1, x_2, x_3. In order to represent this space as a 2-dimensional

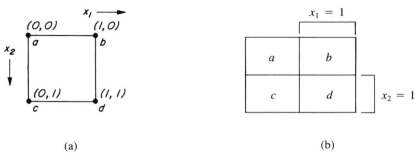

(a)   (b)

Figure 3.12   Representations of a 2-dimensional space

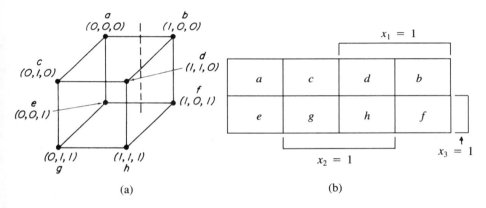

(a)   (b)

Figure 3.13   Representations of a 3-dimensional space

Karnaugh map it is necessary to imagine the 3-dimensional space being cut and folded open along the dotted line of Figure 3.13(a). This leads to the Karnaugh map shown in Figure 3.13(b).

As a result of this cut points a and b, as well as e and f, which are adjacent in Figure 3.13(a), are on opposite sides in Figure 3.13(b). Thus in the three variable Karnaugh maps orthogonally adjacent points as well as points on opposite sides of the map represent points which differ in only a single variable.

As the number of variables defining the space increases the representation becomes more complex. Figure 3.14 shows the representation of a 5-dimensional space. To define the corresponding Karnaugh maps it is necessary to increase the number of cuts and folds, thus creating more complex patterns to represent points which differ in a single variable.

Karnaugh maps for functions of three, four, and five variables are shown in Figure 3.15. Note that there are several different maps possible for each of these. For example, two different four-variable maps are shown in Figure 3.15(b) and (c). The input combination represented by each cell of the map can be determined by examining the column and row labels. For example, the point labeled a in

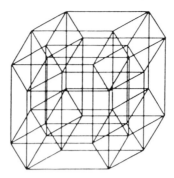

Figure 3.14   Representation of a 5-dimensional space

the maps of Figure 3.15(b) and (c) represents the input combination 0010, since it is not within either of the two columns labeled $x_1 = 1$, not in either of the two columns labeled $x_2 = 1$, or in the two rows labeled $x_4 = 1$, but is in a row labeled $x_3 = 1$. Note that exactly one half of the cells in each map correspond to $x_i = 1$ and the remaining cells to $x_i = 0$ for each of the n variables x_1, x_2, . . . , x_n. The $x_i = 0$ and $x_i = 1$ parts of the map are separated by lines called *axes*.

For each point q in an n-dimensional space (n-cube) there are exactly n points which differ from q in only one variable. From the maps of Figure 3.15 it is obvious that each cell can have at most four orthogonal neighbor cells. Thus it is apparent that non-adjacent cells in the map represent points that differ in only one variable. In order for the maps to be useful for determining prime implicants, it should be possible to determine points that differ in a single variable by inspection. For example, the points a and c in Figure 3.15(b) (and (c)) differ only in the variable x_3. In this map, the first and fourth columns may be treated as being adjacent and likewise, the top and bottom rows. The usefulness of Karnaugh maps is limited to a small number of variables, because of our inability to represent larger cubes in such a way that neighboring input combinations can be determined by inspection.

A combinational function can be represented on a Karnaugh map by filling in the 1 and don't care entries of the map with the understanding that the function has the value 0 at the other points. The function specified by the table of Figure 3.11(a) (Example 3.4) can thus be represented by the Karnaugh map of Figure 3.16.

Since implicants of a function are formed by combining 1-points of a function which differ in only one input variable, such terms will appear in a Karnaugh map as a cluster of "adjacent" 1-points, where points such as a and c in Figure 3.15(b) are considered to be adjacent. With a little experience, it becomes easy to visually identify such clusters of 2^k adjacent points which represent implicants. In general, k-cubes can be determined by their symmetry with respect

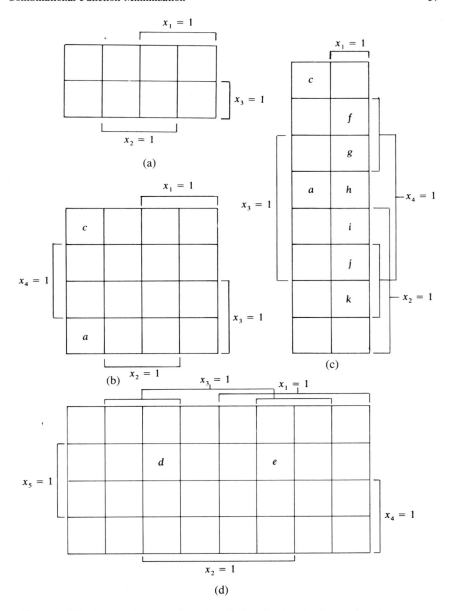

Figure 3.15 Karnaugh maps of (a) 3 variables (b) 4 variables (c) 4 variables (d) 5 variables

to k axes in the map. Thus a and c in Figure 3.15(b) are symmetric with respect to the axis separating the $x_3 = 1$ and $x_3 = 0$ spaces, and d and e in Figure 3.15(d) are symmetric with respect to the axis separating the $x_1 = 1$ and $x_1 = 0$ spaces. In Figure 3.15(c) the set of points $\{f,g,j,k\}$ forms a cube of four points (a 2-

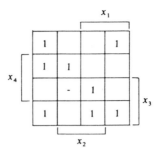

Figure 3.16   Karnaugh map of a combinational function

cube) that is symmetric with respect to the x_2 and x_3 axes. Since $x_1 = 1$ and $x_4 = 1$ for all four points, they represent the implicant $x_1 x_4$.

The prime implicants of a function can be determined by finding all k-cubes that are not contained in larger cubes.

Example 3.5   The combinational function specified in the truth table of Figure 3.11(a) (Example 3.4) is represented by the Karnaugh map of Figure 3.16. In Figure 3.17(a) and (b), clusters of 1-points defining prime implicants are encircled and labelled. These prime implicants are

$$A: \bar{x}_1 \, \bar{x}_2 \, \bar{x}_3$$
$$B: \bar{x}_1 \, \bar{x}_3 \, x_4$$
$$C: \bar{x}_1 \, x_2 \, x_4$$
$$D: x_2 \, x_3 \, x_4$$
$$E: x_1 \, x_2 \, x_3$$
$$F: x_1 \, x_3 \, \bar{x}_4$$
$$G: \bar{x}_2 \, \bar{x}_4$$

which is identical to the set of prime implicants obtained in Example 3.4 using the tabular procedure. The prime implicant $\bar{x}_2 \, \bar{x}_4$ is defined by the four corner cells.   ■

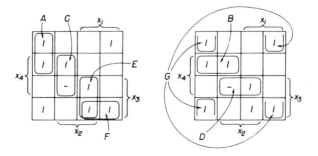

Figure 3.17   Karnaugh map of prime implicants of a function

The ability to "spot" prime implicants is a skill which is developed with practice. One aid in helping spot prime implicants is to look at 1-points which are relatively isolated (i.e., surrounded by 0-points) since such 1-points will have relatively few candidate points with which they can be combined. We will expand on this problem later in the next section, in which we consider the problem of selecting a minimal cost set of prime implicants.

3.2.3 Selection of a Minimal Covering Set of Prime Implicants

The problem of selecting a minimal cost set of prime implicants which cover all 1-points of a function f, is referred to as the *prime implicant covering problem* [5,6,7]. The covering relationship between prime implicants and 1-points can be represented by a *prime implicant covering table*, in which there is one row corresponding to each prime implicant, one column corresponding to each min-term which is a 1-point of f, and the entry in row i and column j is 1 if and only if the prime implicant represented by row i covers the 1-point represented by column j. Associated with each row (prime implicant) is a cost, which reflects the cost of the hardware associated with realizing that prime implicant as part of a sum of products circuit. Cost functions for minimal gate inputs and for minimal gates as optimality objectives have been previously discussed. These or other cost functions can be associated with the rows of a covering table. For the combinational function of Example 3.5, the prime implicant covering table is shown in Figure 3.18, where column C_1 reflects the cost function associated with minimization of gate inputs and C_2, the cost function associated with minimization of gates. Note that the unspecified entry of f, m_7, does not define a column of the covering table since it is not necessary to cover that point.

	m_0	m_1	m_2	m_5	m_8	m_{10}	m_{14}	m_{15}	C_1	C_2
(P_1) $\bar{x}_1 \bar{x}_2 \bar{x}_3$	1	1							4	1
(P_2) $\bar{x}_1 \bar{x}_3 x_4$		1		1					4	1
(P_3) $\bar{x}_1 x_2 x_4$				1					4	1
(P_4) $x_1 x_3 \bar{x}_4$						1	1		4	1
(P_5) $x_1 x_2 x_3$							1	1	4	1
(P_6) $x_2 x_3 x_4$								1	4	1
(P_7) $\bar{x}_2 \bar{x}_4$	1		1		1	1			3	1

Figure 3.18 Prime implicant covering table

The *prime implicant covering problem* is to select a minimal cost set of rows (prime implicants) such that for every column (1-point) m_j, at least one row in the selected set has a 1 in column m_j (i.e., covers m_j), where the cost of a set of rows is the arithmetic sum of the costs of the individual rows in the set.

Informally it is not difficult to solve this problem for the table of Figure 3.18. Looking at the table we see that column m_8 is covered by only one prime implicant, P_7, which *must* therefore be chosen as part of the minimal cover. P_7 covers m_0, m_2, m_8, m_{10} leaving only m_1, m_5, m_{14}, and m_{15} remaining. Each of these 1-points is covered by two different prime implicants. Let us consider the two prime implicants, P_1 and P_2, which cover m_1. Both P_1 and P_2 have cost 4, and cover m_1. In addition P_2 covers m_5 and P_1 covers m_0. However m_0 has already been covered by P_7. Therefore it is preferable to cover m_1 with P_2 rather than with P_1. In a similar way it is preferable to cover m_{15} with P_5 than with P_6. Thus a minimal cost cover for the table is P_2, P_5, P_7.

We shall now formalize the procedures we have applied to this table to develop some rules which are frequently helpful in solving the covering problem.

These rules may determine some rows which can be selected as part of a minimal cost cover, and may simplify the table via elimination of rows and/or columns in such a way that any minimal cost covering set for the simplified (reduced) table is also a minimal cost covering set for the original table.

Reduction Rule 1 (Essential Prime Implicant)

A prime implicant P_i of a combinational function f is *essential with respect to a 1-point m_j* of f if P_i is the only prime implicant which covers m_j. An essential prime implicant corresponds to a row P_i of the covering table such that the only 1-entry in column m_j occurs in row P_i. Any cover of the table must contain P_i. Therefore, row P_i can be selected as a member of the minimal cost covering set. The table can then be simplified by deleting row P_i and all columns covered by P_i.

For the table of Figure 3.18, P_7 is essential with respect to m_8 (and m_2). This row can be selected as part of the minimal covering set and along with columns m_0, m_2, m_8, m_{10} can be deleted from the table. The reduced table is shown in Figure 3.19. This table cannot be further simplified by Reduction Rule 1.

	m_1	m_5	m_{14}	m_{15}	C_1	C_2
P_1	1				4	1
P_2	1	1			4	1
P_3		1			4	1
P_4			1		4	1
P_5			1	1	4	1
P_6				1	4	1

Figure 3.19   Reduced prime implicant covering table

Reduction Rule 2 (Row Dominance)

Let C (P_k) be the cost of row (prime implicant) P_k. A row P_i *dominates* a row P_j if C $(P_i) \leqq C$ (P_j) *and* P_i covers all 1-points covered by P_j (i.e., P_i has 1's in all columns in which P_j has 1's). If row P_i dominates P_j, there exists a minimal cost cover which does not contain P_j (Exercise). Therefore, we can eliminate P_j from the table since any minimal cost cover for the reduced table will also be a minimal cost cover for the original table.

The table reduction resulting from application of this rule may cause a row of the table to become essential. Rule 1 can then be applied to further simplify the table. For the table of Figure 3.19 for either cost function, row P_5 dominates both P_4 and P_6 and row P_2 dominates both P_1 and P_3. Thus rows P_1, P_3, P_4 and P_6 can be eliminated from the table, resulting in the reduced table of Figure 3.20. In this table P_2 is essential with respect to m_1 and m_5 and P_5 is essential with respect to m_{14} and m_{15}. Hence the minimal covering set for the table of Figure 3.20 consists of P_2 and P_5 and the minimal covering set for the table of Figure 3.18 consists of P_7, P_2 and P_5.

	m_1	m_5	m_{14}	m_{15}	C_1	C_2
P_2	1	1			4	1
P_5			1	1	4	1

Figure 3.20   Reduced covering table

These two reduction rules may not be sufficient to determine a minimal covering set for some covering tables, if the original table or a reduced version of the original table has no essential or dominating rows. Such tables are called *cyclic tables*. A procedure called *branching* is useful for obtaining a minimal cover for such tables. The procedure consists of selecting a column m_j of the table and the set of rows R which cover m_j. Any covering set must contain one or more of these rows. We arbitrarily choose one row in R as part of the cover, simplify the table accordingly by deleting this row and all columns covered by it, and obtain the optimal cover containing this row. We then repeat this operation for each row in the set R. We compare all of these "optimal" covers and select the lowest cost one as the minimal cost cover of the original cyclic table. Thus as the name implies, the branching procedure consists of exhaustive examination of a set of different rows one of which is required to be part of a cover.

Branching can be performed with respect to any column of the cyclic table. However, in general, it is computationally more efficient to branch around the column with the fewest number of 1-entries. Several levels of branching may be required to obtain a minimal cost cover. That is in obtaining the minimal cover containing a particular row of a set R, where R is defined by a column m_j, it may be necessary to branch around another set R' defined by another column m_p. The following example demonstrates the application of the branching procedure to a cyclic table.

Example 3.6   In the cyclic table of Figure 3.21 all rows have cost k. From column m_a, we can determine that any cover contains P_1 and/or P_3. We apply

	m_a	m_b	m_c	m_d	m_e	C
P_1	1	1		1		k
P_2		1	1			k
P_3	1		1			k
P_4				1	1	k
P_5			1		1	k
P_6				1		k

Figure 3.21   A cyclic table

the branching procedure and first determine the optimal cover containing P_1. Eliminating row P_1 and columns m_a, m_b, and m_d, which are covered by P_1, results in the reduced table of Figure 3.22. In this table row P_5 dominates P_2, P_3, P_4, and P_6. Hence the optimal cover containing P_1 for the table of Figure 3.21 is P_1 and P_5 which has cost $2k$.

	m_c	m_e	C
P_2	1		k
P_3	1		k
P_4		1	k
P_5	1	1	k
P_6		1	k

Figure 3.22   The reduced table, branch 1

We now determine the optimal cover containing P_3 for the cyclic table of Figure 3.21. In this case P_3 is selected and the table is reduced to that of Figure 3.23. For this table P_1 dominates P_2, and P_4 dominates P_5. After this reduction the table is again cyclic. An optimal cover containing P_3 for the cyclic table of Figure 3.21 consists of P_3 and any 2 of the rows (P_1, P_4, P_6) and has cost $3k$.

	m_b	m_d	m_e	C
P_1	1	1		k
P_2	1			k
P_4		1	1	k
P_5			1	k
P_6	1		1	k

Figure 3.23   The reduced table, branch 2

Since the first selection of the branch generated a cover of cost $2k$, the minimal cost cover for the original table consists of P_1 and P_5 and is of cost $2k$.   ∎

One additional reduction rule for a covering table is that of *column dominance*.

Reduction Rule 3 (Column Dominance)

A *column m_i of a covering table dominates a column m_j* if every row which covers m_j also covers m_i (i.e., column m_i has 1's in all rows in which column m_j has 1's). Any row which covers m_j will also cover m_i. Column m_i can thus be eliminated from the table since any covering set of rows for the reduced table will cover m_j and hence will also cover m_i.

However any table which is cyclic with respect to the first two rules will also be cyclic with respect to all three rules. Small prime implicant table covering problems can also be solved by a method developed by Petrick [8]. Each column of the table can be covered by any prime implicant which has a 1 in that column. For each prime implicant we define a Boolean variable p_i such that $p_i = 1$ if the prime implicant P_i is a member of the covering set, and $p_i = 0$ otherwise. Then the condition that a column m_j be covered by some prime implicant can be represented by the Boolean expression $\Sigma_{i \in I_j} p_i = 1$, where I_j is the set of rows covering the column m_j. For example, column m_a of the table of Figure 3.21 will be covered if $(p_1 + p_3) = 1$. Similarly covering column m_b requires $(p_1 + p_2 + p_6) = 1$. The set of prime implicants covering both columns m_a and m_b must satisfy the condition

$$(p_1 + p_3) \cdot (p_1 + p_2 + p_6) = 1.$$

Since all the p_i's are Boolean variables, this condition can be written as:

$$p_1 + p_2 p_3 + p_3 p_6 = 1.$$

In general, the condition for covering all columns of an m-column table can be written as the Boolean expression

$$\prod_{j=1}^{m} \left(\sum_{i \in I_j} p_i \right) = 1.$$

If the left hand side of this equation is written in a sum of products form, each term will represent a set of prime implicants that cover all 1-points and the expression will represent *all covers* which are not subsets of other covers. The cost of each set is the sum of the costs of the individual prime implicants contained in the set. If all prime implicants have equal cost the product term with the fewest number of variables represents a minimal cover. Otherwise a minimal cover is defined by the lowest cost product term.

For the table of Figure 3.21, this procedure generates the expression

$$(p_1 + p_3)(p_1 + p_2 + p_6)(p_2 + p_3 + p_5)(p_1 + p_4)(p_4 + p_5 + p_6)$$
$$= p_1 p_5 + p_1 p_2 p_4 + p_1 p_2 p_6 + p_2 p_3 p_4 + p_3 p_4 p_6 + p_1 p_3 p_4$$
$$+ p_1 p_3 p_6.$$

The minimal cost cover is defined by the product term $p_1 p_5$.

3.2.4   Selection of Minimal Covers from Karnaugh Maps

The concepts of essentiality and dominance can frequently be visually applied to derive essential prime implicants and *good* prime implicants directly from a Karnaugh map representation of a function f. A prime implicant P is *good* with respect to a 1-point m_j of a combinational function f if P covers m_j and P dominates all other prime implicants which cover m_j (i.e., P covers all (previously uncovered) 1-points covered by any other prime implicant P' which covers m_j, and $C(P) \le C(P')$). For any prime implicant P which is good with respect to a 1-point m_j of a function f, a minimal sum of products realization can be obtained containing P and hence, P can be selected as part of a minimal realization. Once an essential or good prime implicant has been selected as part of the minimal cover, the 1-points covered by this term are changed to unspecified entries in the Karnaugh map and other good prime implicants can be selected from the resulting map. Thus the Karnaugh map can sometimes be used to combine the two steps of prime implicant generation and selection in the derivation of minimal sum of products realizations. Of course, branching may sometimes be required.

In attempting to find "essential" or "good" prime implicants it is convenient to consider 1-points which are primarily surrounded by (i.e., adjacent to) 0-points. For such 1-points there will be relatively few possible points with which they can be combined, thus leading to a more likely possibility of an essential or good prime implicant.

Example 3.7   For the combinational function f specified by the Karnaugh map of Figure 3.24, the 1-point 0010, which is adjacent to three 0-points and one unspecified point, is covered by only one prime implicant $\bar{x}_2 x_3 \bar{x}_4$ which is therefore essential with respect to m_2 of f. The 1-point 0111, which is adjacent to two 0-points, one 1-point, and a don't care, is covered by two prime implicants, $\bar{x}_1 x_2 x_4$ and $x_2 x_3 x_4$. However $x_2 x_3 x_4$ does not cover any other 1-points of f.

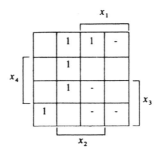

Figure 3.24   A combinational function map

Therefore $\bar{x}_1 x_2 x_4$ is good with respect to m_7 of f and is selected as a product term in the minimal gate input sum of products of f. (Note that $\bar{x}_1 x_2 x_4$ is not good with respect to the other 1-point it covers, m_5). The 1-point 0100 is covered by two prime implicants, $x_2 \bar{x}_3 \bar{x}_4$ and $\bar{x}_1 x_2 \bar{x}_3$ each of which covers two 1-points of f. However the other 1-point covered by $\bar{x}_1 x_2 \bar{x}_3$, 0101, has already been covered by the previously selected prime implicant $\bar{x}_1 x_2 x_4$. Therefore $x_2 \bar{x}_3 \bar{x}_4$ is good with respect to m_4 of f. (Note that $x_2 \bar{x}_3 \bar{x}_4$ is not good with respect to the 1-point 1100 since the prime implicant $x_1 \bar{x}_4$ covers this point and has fewer literals.) At this stage all 1-points have been covered and the minimal cost sum of products expression is $f = \bar{x}_2 x_3 \bar{x}_4 + \bar{x}_1 x_2 x_4 + x_2 \bar{x}_3 \bar{x}_4$. The three prime implicants comprising this covering set are depicted by the circled sets of points in the Karnaugh map of Figure 3.25.   ∎

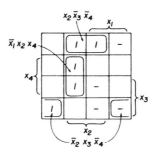

Figure 3.25   Prime implicants of covering set

In the following examples we consider some additional Karnaugh maps for which we derive minimal sum of products realizations.

Example 3.8   For the combinational function specified by the Karnaugh map of Figure 3.26, the minimal gate input sum of products realization is obtained as follows:
The 1-point 0110, which is adjacent to one 1-point and one unspecified point, is covered by two prime implicants, $\bar{x}_1 x_2 x_3$ and $\bar{x}_1 x_2 \bar{x}_4$. Since $\bar{x}_1 x_2 x_3$ does

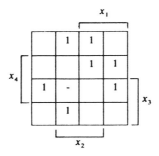

Figure 3.26   A combinational function map

not cover any other 1-point of f, $\bar{x}_1 \, x_2 \, \bar{x}_4$ is good with respect to m_6 of f. The 1-point 1100 is covered by $x_1 \, x_2 \, \bar{x}_3$ and $x_2 \, \bar{x}_3 \, \bar{x}_4$. However $x_2 \, \bar{x}_3 \, \bar{x}_4$ does not cover any other 1-point except 0100 and that was previously covered by $\bar{x}_1 \, x_2 \, \bar{x}_4$. Therefore $x_1 \, x_2 \, \bar{x}_3$ is good with respect to m_{12} of f. Similarly $x_1 \, \bar{x}_2 \, x_4$ is then good with respect to m_9 and $\bar{x}_2 \, x_3 \, x_4$ is good with respect to m_3. Thus a minimal sum of products expression is $f = \bar{x}_1 \, x_2 \, \bar{x}_4 + x_1 \, x_2 \, \bar{x}_3 + x_1 \, \bar{x}_2 \, x_4 + \bar{x}_2 \, x_3 \, x_4$. The corresponding realization has four 3-input AND gates and one 4-input OR gate, thus requiring 16 gate inputs.　　　■

Example 3.9　　For the Karnaugh map of Figure 3.27 the 1-point 1111 is adjacent to four 0-points. The prime implicant $x_1 \, x_2 \, x_3 \, x_4$ is essential with respect to this 1-point. The 1-points m_0, m_5, and m_{12} are all adjacent to three 0-points and one 1-point. For these points

$$\bar{x}_1 \, \bar{x}_3 \, \bar{x}_4 \text{ is essential with respect to } m_0$$
$$\bar{x}_1 \, x_2 \, \bar{x}_3 \text{ is essential with respect to } m_5$$
$$x_2 \, \bar{x}_3 \, \bar{x}_4 \text{ is essential with respect to } m_{12}$$

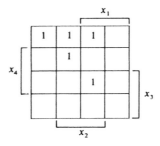

Figure 3.27　　The function of Example 3.9

The minimal sum of products $x_1 \, x_2 \, x_3 \, x_4 + \bar{x}_1 \, \bar{x}_3 \, \bar{x}_4 + \bar{x}_1 \, x_2 \, \bar{x}_3 + x_2 \, \bar{x}_3 \, \bar{x}_4$ requires 5 gates (4 ANDS, 1 OR) and 17 gate inputs (13 AND inputs, 4 OR inputs).　　　■

It is conjectured that for completely specified functions, a minimum gate input sum of products realization is also a minimum gate sum of products realization. However this is not always true for incompletely specified functions, as illustrated by the following example.

Example 3.10　　Consider the function $f(x_1, x_2, \ldots, x_{10})$, which is defined as follows:

$$f(0,0,0,0,0,0,0,0,0,0) = f(1,1,0,0,0,0,0,0,0,0) = 1$$
$$f(0,1,0,0,0,0,0,0,0,0) \text{ and } f(1,0,0,0,0,0,0,0,0,0) \text{ are unspecified}$$

$$f(0,1,x_3, x_4, \ldots, x_{10}) = 0 \text{ if } x_3 + x_4 + \ldots + x_{10} = 1$$
$$f(1,0,x_3, x_4, \ldots, x_{10}) = 0 \text{ if } x_3 + x_4 + \ldots + x_{10} = 1$$

For all other points f is unspecified. This function has 3 prime implicants. $P_1 = \bar{x}_1 \bar{x}_2$, $P_2 = x_1 x_2$, $P_3 = \bar{x}_3 \bar{x}_4 \bar{x}_5 \bar{x}_6 \bar{x}_7 \bar{x}_8 \bar{x}_9 \bar{x}_{10}$.

The covering table is as shown in Figure 3.28, where column C_1 is the cost function to minimize gate inputs and C_2 is the cost function to minimize gates. The minimal cost gate-input realization is $f = \bar{x}_1 \bar{x}_2 + x_1 x_2$, defined by the covering set $\{P_1, P_2\}$. The minimal cost gate realization is $f = \bar{x}_3 \bar{x}_4 \bar{x}_5 \bar{x}_6 \bar{x}_7 \bar{x}_8 \bar{x}_9 \bar{x}_{10}$ which is defined by the covering set $\{P_3\}$.

■

	m_0	m_2	C_1	C_2
P_1	1		3	1
P_2		1	3	1
P_3	1	1	8	1

Figure 3.28 The covering table of Example 3.10

3.2.5 Minimal Product of Sums Realizations

We have thus shown how a minimal sum of products realization can be derived for a function f. A product of sums realization (OR/AND) of f can be derived from a sum of products realization of $\bar{f}$ by DeMorgan's Law as follows

$$\text{If} \quad \bar{f} = \sum_{i \in I} P_i \quad \text{then} \quad f = \prod_{i \in I} \bar{P}_i$$

where if $P_i = \prod x_k^*$ then $\bar{P}_i = \sum \bar{x}_k^*$ (where x_k^* is x_k or $\bar{x}_k$). (If P_i is a prime implicant of $\bar{f}$, then $\bar{P}_i$ is called a *prime implicate* of f.)

If this transformation is applied to a *minimal cost* sum of products realization of $\bar{f}$, the resulting circuit is a minimal cost product of sums realization of f (for either of the two cost functions being considered).

Theorem 3.2 The expression derived by applying DeMorgan's Law to a minimal sum of products realization of a function $\bar{f}$ is a minimal product of sums realization of f.

Proof Suppose there is a product of sums expression for f, E', with cost C' and the cost of the product of sums expression E derived from G, the minimal sum of products expression of $\bar{f}$, is $C > C'$. Then applying DeMorgan's Law to E' we derive a sum of products expression of $\bar{f}$ with cost C' (Exercise). This contradicts the assumption that G is a minimal sum of products expression of $\bar{f}$ and proves the theorem. ■

Hence the following procedure can be used to generate a minimal product of sums realization for a combinational function f.

Procedure 3.3

1. Define the combinational function $\bar{f}$ as follows:
   For a point m_i in the n-cube

$$\text{if } f(m_i) = 1 \text{ then } \bar{f}(m_i) = 0,$$
$$\text{if } f(m_i) = 0 \text{ then } \bar{f}(m_i) = 1,$$
$$\text{if } f(m_i) \text{ is unspecified then } \bar{f}(m_i) \text{ is unspecified.}$$

2. Using Procedure 3.1 find a minimal cost sum of products realization of $\bar{f}$, $\bar{f} = \Sigma_{i \in J} P_i$.

3. Apply DeMorgan's Law to this expression to obtain $f = \Pi_{i \in J} \bar{P}_i$. The resulting expression is a minimal cost product of sums realization of f. ∎

   In general the minimal cost sum of products realization of a function f, and the minimal cost product of sums realization of f will not have equal costs. Thus to determine a *minimal cost two level realization of* f we would determine both the minimal cost sum of products and the minimal cost product of sums realizations. The two level realization of minimal cost is the less costly of these two realizations.

Example 3.11   For the function f considered in Example 3.8 (Figure 3.26), $\bar{f}$ is shown in Figure 3.29. The minimal sum of products of $\bar{f}$ is derived in order to determine the minimal product of sums of f. In the map of Figure 3.29, the only prime implicant which covers the 1-point 1000 is $\bar{x}_2 \bar{x}_4$. Therefore $\bar{x}_2 \bar{x}_4$ is essential with respect to m_8. (It is also essential with respect to m_2 but not with respect to m_0 or m_{10}). The 1-point 1111 is covered by two prime implicants, $x_1 x_2 x_3$ and $x_2 x_3 x_4$. However since $x_2 x_3 x_4$ does not cover any other 1-points, $x_1 x_2 x_3$ is good with respect to m_{15}. Similarly $\bar{x}_1 \bar{x}_3 x_4$ is good with respect to m_5. The minimal sum of products expression for $\bar{f}$ is $\bar{f} = \bar{x}_2 \bar{x}_4 + x_1 x_2 x_3 +$

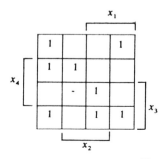

Figure 3.29   The map of $\bar{f}$

$\bar{x}_1 \bar{x}_3 x_4$. By applying DeMorgan's Law to this expression we obtain the minimal product of sums expression, $f = (x_2 + x_4) \cdot (\bar{x}_1 + \bar{x}_2 + \bar{x}_3) \cdot (x_1 + x_3 + \bar{x}_4)$. This requires one 2-input OR gate, two 3-input OR gates, and one 3-input AND gate, 11 gate inputs in all. Hence for this function, the minimal cost product of sums is superior to the minimal cost sum of products realization found in Example 3.8.   ■

The minimum gate-input two level realization may not be a minimum gate two level realization even for completely specified functions as illustrated in the following example.

Example 3.12   For the function f considered in Example 3.9 $\bar{f}$ is shown in Figure 3.30.

$$x_1 \bar{x}_2 \text{ is essential with respect to } m_8$$
$$x_1 \bar{x}_3 x_4 \text{ is essential with respect to } m_{13}$$
$$x_3 \bar{x}_4 \text{ is essential with respect to } m_{14}$$
$$\bar{x}_2 x_4 \text{ is essential with respect to } m_1$$
$$\bar{x}_1 x_3 \text{ is essential with respect to } m_7$$

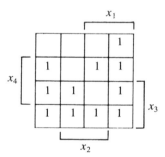

Figure 3.30   Combinatorial function for Example 3.12

The minimal sum of products of $\bar{f}$ is

$$\bar{f} = x_1 \bar{x}_2 + x_1 \bar{x}_3 x_4 + x_3 \bar{x}_4 + \bar{x}_2 x_4 + \bar{x}_1 x_3$$

The minimal product of sums of f is

$$f = (\bar{x}_1 + x_2) \cdot (\bar{x}_1 + x_3 + \bar{x}_4) \cdot (\bar{x}_3 + x_4) \cdot (x_2 + \bar{x}_4) \cdot (x_1 + \bar{x}_3)$$

which requires 5 OR gates and 1 AND gate for a total of 6 gates and 16 gate inputs. Comparing these results with those of Example 3.9, we see that the sum of products realization is minimal with respect to number of gates while the product of sums is minimal with respect to number of gate inputs.   ■

3.2.6   Minimal Two Level *NAND* and *NOR* Realizations

It is also possible to realize an arbitrary combinational function as a two level NAND circuit. A two level NAND circuit realization of a function f can be obtained directly from a sum of products realization of f by the sequence of transformations depicted in Figure 3.31.

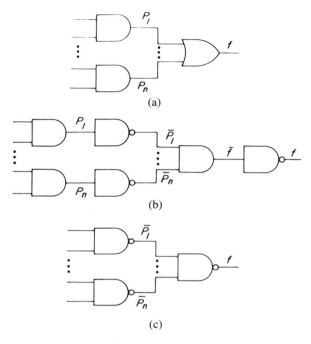

(a)

(b)

(c)

Figure 3.31   Transformation to NAND realization

The circuit of Figure 3.31(b) is obtained from that of Figure 3.31(a) by DeMorgan's Law, $P_1 + P_2 + \ldots + P_n = \overline{\overline{P}_1 \cdot \overline{P}_2 \ldots \overline{P}_n}$. Since a NAND gate is trivially equivalent to an AND gate followed by an inverter, the circuit of Figure 3.31(c) is derived from that of Figure 3.31(b). Note that the inputs to the first level gates have not been changed. Hence simply changing all gates in the sum of products realization of f to NAND gates results in a two level NAND realization of f. The minimal cost two level NAND realization is obtained by applying this transformation to the minimal cost sum of products realization. (The proof of this statement is virtually identical to that of Theorem 3.2 and is left as an exercise.)

A two level NOR gate realization of a combinational function f can be obtained from a product of sums realization of f by the sequence of transformations depicted in Figure 3.32. The circuit of Figure 3.32(b) is obtained from that of Figure 3.32(a) by DeMorgan's Law,

$$P_1 \cdot P_2 \cdot \ldots \cdot P_n = \overline{\overline{P}_1 + \overline{P}_2 + \ldots + \overline{P}_n}$$

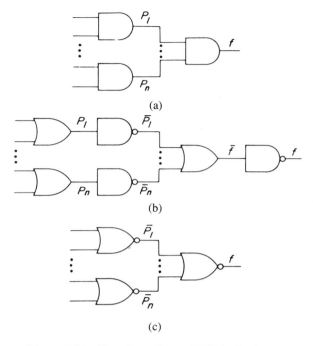

(a)

(b)

(c)

Figure 3.32 Transformation to NOR realization

The circuit of Figure 3.32(c) is generated by recognizing that an OR gate followed by an inverter is equivalent to a NOR gate. Note that the inputs to the first level gates have not been changed by this transformation. Thus a product of sums realization of f is converted to a two level NOR realization of f by changing all gates to NOR gates. Applying this transformation to the minimal cost product of sums realization results in the minimal cost two level NOR realization (Exercise).

Example 3.13 For the functions of Examples 3.8 and 3.11 minimal NAND and NOR realizations (Figure 3.33) are obtained from the minimum sum of products and product of sums realizations respectively. ■

3.2.7 Multiple Output Combinational Circuit Minimization

In the previous section we developed procedures for the design of minimal two level realizations of arbitrary single output (i.e., binary valued) combinational functions. In many situations circuits are designed to realize a set of outputs. In this section we shall consider the design of minimal two level realizations of circuits which realize a set $F = \{f_1, f_2, \ldots, f_r\}$ of binary valued combinational functions. Such circuits will be called *multiple output combinational circuits*.

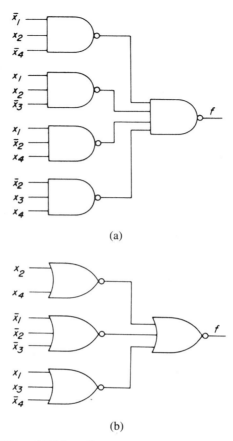

(a)

(b)

Figure 3.33   NAND and NOR realizations of function of Examples 3.9 and 3.12

Assuming that an AND-OR (sum of products) circuit is to be designed to realize F, each function f_i corresponds to the output of an OR gate, the inputs of which are AND gates. If the output of each AND gate is only permitted to be an input of a single OR gate then the problem reduces to realizing each individual function f_i in a minimal two level realization as in the previous section. In this case we say that the *sharing* of logic gates between functions is prohibited. However if logic sharing is permitted then it becomes necessary to generalize the single function minimization procedure [9,10].

Consider the two functions of Figure 3.34. Considered individually the minimal sum of products realizations are

$$f_1 = \bar{x}_2\, x_4 + x_3\, x_4$$
$$f_2 = x_2\, x_3 + x_2\, \bar{x}_4$$

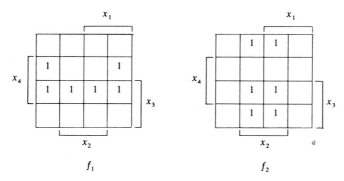

Figure 3.34   A multiple output combinational function

However, the multiple output two level AND-OR (sum of products) circuit realization which minimizes the total number of gate inputs for this pair of functions is shown in Figure 3.35. The term $x_2 x_3 x_4$ is *not* a prime implicant of either f_1 or f_2 as we can see from the Karnaugh maps of Figure 3.34. However, it is a prime implicant of the product of these two functions $f_1 \cdot f_2$ as seen from

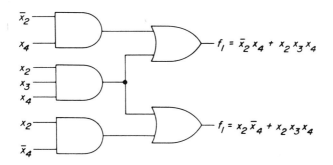

Figure 3.35   The minimal sum of products realization

the Karnaugh map of Figure 3.36. We will account for the use of such a product term in a minimal cost circuit by generalizing the concept of prime implicant to *multiple output prime implicant* as follows:

Given a set of combinational functions $F = \{f_1, f_2, \ldots, f_r\}$, a product term P is a *multiple output prime implicant* of a subset F' of F if P is a prime implicant of $G = \Pi_{f_i \in F'} f_i$ (G is the product of all functions in the subset F'). The product of two functions $f_1(x_1, \ldots, x_n)$ and $f_2(x_1 \ldots x_n)$ is defined as follows:

$$f_1 \cdot f_2(x_i) = 0 \text{ if } f_1(x_i) \text{ or } f_2(x_i) \text{ is equal to } 0$$
$$f_1 \cdot f_2(x_i) = 1 \text{ if } f_1(x_i) \text{ and } f_2(x_i) \text{ are equal to } 1$$
$$f_1 \cdot f_2(x_i) = - \text{ if neither } f_1(x_i) \text{ nor } f_2(x_i) \text{ is equal to } 0 \text{ and }$$
$$f_1(x_i) \text{ and/or } f_2(x_i) \text{ is unspecified.}$$

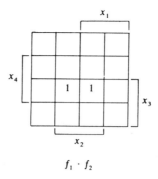

$$f_1 \cdot f_2$$

Figure 3.36   Karnaugh map of $f_1 \cdot f_2$

The following theorem shows that minimal two level AND-OR (sum of product) realizations of sets of combinational functions can be obtained in which the output of each AND gate is a multiple output prime implicant.

Theorem 3.3   Given a set of combinational fractions $F = \{f_1, f_2, \ldots, f_r\}$ there exists a multiple output two level sum of products realization which is minimal with respect to total gate inputs and in which the output of every AND gate is a multiple output prime implicant.

Proof   Consider a minimal AND-OR realization of a set of functions $F = \{f_1, f_2, \ldots, f_r\}$ and suppose the output of some AND gate A is a product term P which is not a multiple output prime implicant. Assume the output of A is an input to the OR gates realizing the subset of combinational functions $F' \subseteq F$. Let $G = \Pi_{f_i \epsilon F'} f_i$. Since P is not a multiple output prime implicant of G there must exist a multiple output prime implicant P' of G such that (1) P' covers every 1-point of each $f_i \epsilon F'$ covered by P, (2) every point covered by P' is a 1-point or is unspecified for each $f_i \epsilon F'$, and (3) the number of literals in P' does not exceed the number of literals in P. Hence we can replace gate A by a gate A' which realizes the multiple-output prime implicant P' and the circuit remains a realization of F. This can be repeated until all such AND gates are replaced and the output of every AND gate is a multiple output prime implicant.   ■

It can also be shown that there exists a sum of products realization which is optimal with respect to number of gates in which the output of each AND gate is a multiple output prime implicant.

Thus the problem of generating a minimal two level AND-OR realization for a set of combinational functions reduces to the following general procedure.

Procedure 3.4

1. Generate the set of all multiple output prime implicants of $F = \{f_1, f_2, \ldots, f_r\}$. (Note that prime implicants of an individual function f_i are also multiple output prime implicants where the subset F' contains only f_i.)
2. Select a "minimal cost" set of multiple output prime implicants to realize the set of combinational functions $F = \{f_1, f_2, \ldots, f_r\}$. Such a set must cover all 1-points of each function $f_i \in F$. If a selected term P is a multiple output prime implicant of $G = \Pi_{f_i \in F'} f_i$ then this term will be used as an implicant for each $f_i \in F'$, (i.e., P will be realized by an AND gate, the output of which will be an input to the OR gates realizing each of the functions $f_i \in F'$). ∎

Both the Quine-McCluskey tabular procedure and the Karnaugh map technique can be extended to the generation of multiple-output prime implicants. The covering table for selecting a minimal cost set of prime implicants must contain a column for each 1-point of each of the sets of functions being realized. These procedures are considerably more complex than the corresponding single function cases. As we shall see in the next chapter, in many circumstances, two level realizations are rather impractical. Consequently we shall not consider the solution procedures for multiple output two level realizations in greater detail.

REFERENCES

1. McCluskey, E.J., Jr., "Minimization of Boolean Functions," *Bell System Technical Journal*, 6, pp. 1417–1444, November 1956.
2. Quine, W.V., "The Problem of Simplifying Truth Functions," *Am. Math. Monthly*, 8, pp. 521–531, October 1952.
3. Quine, W.V., "A Way to Simplify Truth Functions," *Am. Math. Monthly*, 62, 9, pp. 627–631, November 1955.
4. Karnaugh, M., "The Map Method for Synthesis of Combinational Logic Circuits," *Trans. AIEE*, Part I, 72, 9, pp. 593–598, 1953.
5. Gimpel, J.F., "A Reduction Technique for Prime Implicant Tables," *IEEE Trans. on Electronic Computers*, vol. EC-14, pp. 535–541, August 1965.
6. Luccio, F., "A Method for the Selection of Prime Implicants," *IEEE Trans. on Electronic Computers*, vol. EC-15, pp. 205–212, April 1966.
7. Friedman, A.D., "Comment on 'A Method for the Selection of Prime Implicants'," *IEEE Trans. on Electronic Computers*, vol. EC-16, pp. 221–222, April 1967.
8. Petrick, S.R., "On the Minimization of Boolean Functions," *Proc. Symposium on Switching Theory*, ICIP, Paris, France, June 1959.
9. Bartee, T.C., "Computer Design of Multiple Output Logical Networks," *IRE Trans. Electronic Computers*, vol. EC-10, pp. 21–30, March 1961.
10. McCluskey, E.J., Jr. and H. Schorr, "Essential Multiple-Output Prime Implicants," *Mathematical Theory of Automata*, Proceedings Polytechnic Institute of Brooklyn Symposium, 12, pp. 437–457, April 1962.

ADDITIONAL READING

1. Hill, F.J., and G.R. Peterson, *Introduction to Switching Theory and Logical Design*, 3rd Ed., John Wiley & Sons, New York, N.Y., 1981.
2. McCluskey, E.J., Jr., *Introduction to the Theory of Switching Circuits*, McGraw-Hill, New York, N.Y., 1965.

PROBLEMS

3.1 Design two level minimal gate-input NAND and NOR realizations for the following functions

a) $f(x_1, x_2, x_3, x_4) = \Sigma\ m_3, m_4, m_5, m_7, m_9, m_{13}, m_{14}, m_{15}$

b) $f(x_1, x_2, x_3, x_4) = \Sigma\ m_2, m_5, m_6, m_8, m_{12}, m_{15}$
$$+ \underset{\substack{\text{don't}\\\text{cares}}}{\Sigma}\ m_1, m_3, m_{11}, m_{14}$$

c) $f(x_1, x_2, x_3, x_4) = \Sigma\ m_3, m_4, m_6, m_8, m_{12}, m_{13}, m_{14}$

d) $f(x_1, x_2, x_3, x_4) = \Sigma\ m_0, m_2, m_7, m_8, m_9, m_{10}, m_{13}$
$$+ \underset{\substack{\text{don't}\\\text{cares}}}{\Sigma}\ m_3, m_6, m_{11}, m_{15}$$

3.2 We wish to design a combinational circuit to operate in the following manner.

a) The circuit has four inputs (x_1, x_2, x_3, x_4) and 1 output (z)
b) If three or more of the inputs are 1 then $z = 1$ unless $x_1 = 0$
c) If $x_1 = 0$ and exactly two of the inputs are 1 then $z = 0$
d) If exactly one input is 1 then $z = 1$ unless $x_2 = 1$
e) If $x_1 = 1$ and one other input is 1 then $z = 0$
f) If all inputs are 0 then $z = 1$
g) All other input conditions are don't cares

Derive a truth table for the function and express f as a product of *maxterms* with all unspecified entries interpreted as 1's.

3.3 a) For the combinational function of Figure 3.37 find a minimal two level NOR realization.

b) Is there any prime implicate (prime implicant of $\overline{f}$) not included in your solution?

3.4 a) For the combinational function of Figure 3.38 the entities indicated by a and b are *partial don't cares* in that a may be equal to 0 or 1 but b must take the opposite value. Thus either point is a don't care but when one of them is specified the other point is no longer a don't care.

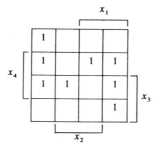

Figure 3.37 Problem 3.3

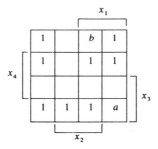

Figure 3.38 Problem 3.4

Find a minimal gate-input two level AND-OR (sum of products) realization.

b) What is the optimal solution if both *a* and *b* are don't cares?

3.5 Assume that information is transferred in a digital system using a 4-bit code in which 3 bits are information bits (which can have any value) and the 4th bit is a parity check bit which is chosen so that the total number of 1 bits in a word is odd. For instance if the information bits are 101 the check bit is 1 resulting in the word 1011. Design a minimal two level NAND circuit whose output is 1 if the word has a single bit in error. Will your circuit detect errors in two bits? Characterize the class of errors your circuit will detect.

*3.6 What is the largest number of prime implicants a combinational function of *n* variables can have?

---

*Unsolved research problem

3.7 a) For the circuit of Figure 3.39 if $f_1 = A + B$, f_3 is an AND gate, and $Z = A$, is f_2 uniquely determined?

b) If $Z = A$ can you specify a function f_3 which depends on both inputs and enables f_2 to be uniquely determined?

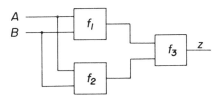

Figure 3.39 Problem 3.7

3.8 Prove or give a counterexample for each of the following statements.

a) For every prime implicant P of $f(x_1, \ldots, x_n)$ there exists a minimal two level realization of f containing P.

b) For a completely specified combinational function there is a unique minimal sum of products expression.

c) For a completely specified combinational function the costs of the minimal sum of products and product of sums expressions are equal.

d) If a combinational function $f(x_1, x_2, \ldots, x_n)$ has a unique minimal sum of products expression then it also has a unique minimal product of sums expression and the two expressions have equal cost.

3.9 Use a Karnaugh map to find a minimal two level realization of the function

$$f(x_1, x_2, x_3, x_4) = \Pi\ M_0, M_4, M_6, M_7, M_{10}, M_{12}, M_{13}, M_{14}$$

3.10 Use the Quine-McCluskey method to find a minimal two level sum of products realization of the function

$$f(x_1, x_2, x_3, x_4) = \underset{\text{1-points}}{\Sigma}\ m_4, m_5, m_7, m_{12}, m_{14}, m_{15}$$
$$+ \underset{\substack{\text{don't} \\ \text{cares}}}{\Sigma}\ m_3, m_8, m_{10}$$

3.11 Design a minimal two level combinational circuit whose input is a number with four bits $b_3\ b_2\ b_1\ b_0$, and whose output is the 2's complement of the input.

3.12 Design a minimal two level comparator as a combinational circuit that behaves as follows:

1. There are four inputs $y_1\ y_0$ and $x_1\ x_0$ representing two 2-bit numbers where y_1 and x_1 are the most significant bits.

b) There are two outputs z_1 z_2 such that $z_1 = 1$ if and only if binary number $x_1 x_0 >$ binary number $y_1 y_0$, and $z_2 = 1$ if and only if $x_1 x_0 < y_1 y_0$.

3.13 For the following combinational circuit:

a) Derive the truth table for the output z.

b) Derive a minimal two level circuit realization.

c) Change all gates to NAND gates and repeat (a) and (b).

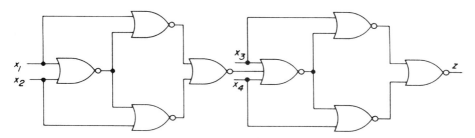

Figure 3.40   Problem 3.13

3.14 Design a combinational circuit to translate a 4 bit BCD digit $b_3 b_2 b_1 b_0$ to an excess-3 code digit $e_3 e_2 e_1 e_0$.

3.15 Design a majority detector as a minimal two level combinational circuit which functions as follows:

a) There are six inputs grouped into three pairs a_1, a_2, b_1, b_2, c_1, c_2 and three outputs z_1, z_2, z_3.

b) If at least two of the three input pairs have identical values, then $z_1 = 1$ and z_2, z_3 have the values associated with the identical pairs. If two or more pairs do not have identical values then $z_1 = 0$, and z_2 and z_3 can assume any value.

3.16 Design a two bit multiplier as a minimal two level combinational circuit with inputs x_1, x_0, y_1, y_0 representing two 2-bit binary numbers x and y, and outputs z_2, z_1, z_0 representing the arithmetic product $x \cdot y$.

3.17 Find minimal NAND or NOR realizations for the following function.

$$F(x_1, x_2, x_3, x_4, x_5) = \Sigma\ m_2, m_3, m_7, m_8, m_9, m_{12}, m_{13}, m_{14},$$
$$m_{18}, m_{19}, m_{21}, m_{28}, m_{29}, m_{30}$$

3.18 A circuit receives two 3-bit binary numbers $A = A_2 A_1 A_0$, $B = B_2 B_1 B_0$. Design a minimal sum of products circuit to produce an output $z = 1$ if and only if A is greater than B.

3.19 Five men vote in a contest. Their votes are indicated on inputs x_i, $i = 1, \ldots, 5$ to a logic circuit C. If the vote is 5-0 or 4-1 to pass ($x_i = 1$) the circuit outputs should be $z_1 z_2 = 11$. If the vote is 5-0 or 4-1 to fail the circuit outputs should be $z_1 z_2 = 00$. If the vote is 3-2 or 2-3 the output should be $z_1 z_2 = 01$. Design C to be a minimal sum of products circuit.

3.20 For the function shown in the Karnaugh map of Figure 3.41 you are permitted to change any single entry to a don't care. Do so in such a manner as to produce the simplest two level realization.

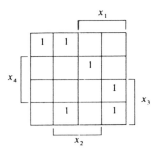

Figure 3.41   Problem 3.20

3.21 Define the *majority function* $M(x, y, z) = xy + yz + xz$. Prove or disprove the following.

a) $M(x_1, y_1, z_1) + M(x_2, y_2, z_2) = M(x_1 + x_2, y_1 + y_2, z_1 + z_2)$
b) $M(x_1, y_1, z_1) \cdot M(x_2, y_2, z_2) = M(x_1 \cdot x_2, y_1 \cdot y_2, z_1 \cdot z_2)$
c) $M(M(a, b, c), d, e) = M(M(a, d, e), b, M(c, d, e))$

3.22 Define the function $S_i(x_1, x_2, \ldots, x_n)$ to have the value 1 if and only if exactly i of the n input variables have the value 1.

a) How many prime implicants does S_i have?
b) How many essential prime implicants does S_i have?

3.23 Define the function $T_i(x_1, x_2, \ldots, x_n)$ to have the value 1 if and only if i or more of the input variables have the value 1.

a) How many prime implicants does T_i have?
b) How many essential prime implicants does T_i have?

3.24 a) Specify a truth table for the following
    i) There are two functions $f(x_1, x_2, x_3, x_4)$ and $g(x_1, x_2, x_3, x_4)$

ii) $f = 1$ when 2 or more of the input signals are 1, otherwise $f = 0$.

iii) $g = 1$ when the number of inputs with a 1 applied is even; in all other cases $g = \bar{f}$.

b) Find minimal sum-of-products and product-of-sums expressions for the functions f and g.

3.25 Find a minimal sum of products using a Karnaugh map and a minimal product of sums using a table technique for each of the following functions, considered individually

$$f(x_1, x_2, x_3, x_4) = \Sigma\ m_1, m_4, m_5, m_6, m_{11}, m_{12}, m_{13}, m_{14}, m_{15}$$
$$g(x_1, x_2, x_3, x_4) = \Sigma\ m_0, m_2, m_4, m_9, m_{12}, m_{15}$$
$$+ \underset{\substack{\text{don't} \\ \text{cares}}}{\Sigma}\ m_1, m_5, m_7, m_{10}$$

3.26 Consider a digital system in which all registers have n bits, and addition and subtraction are done in 2's complement form. If the addition of $\mathbf{X} = x_{n-1}\ x_{n-2}\ \cdots\ x_0$ and $\mathbf{Y} = y_{n-1}\ y_{n-2}\ \cdots\ y_0$ results in an output $\mathbf{Z} = z_{n-1}\ z_{n-2}\ \cdots\ z_0$ then if $\mathbf{X} + \mathbf{Y} \geq 2^{n-1}$ or $\mathbf{X} + \mathbf{Y} \leq -2^{n-1}$ an overflow occurs. Design a simple circuit which generates an output $g = 1$ if overflow has occurred.

3.27 Consider the ring sum function $A \oplus B = A\bar{B} + \bar{A}B$, where A and B are $\bar{f}$Boolean expressions.

a) Show that this function is commutative and associative.

b) Show that the function $x_1 \oplus x_2 \oplus \ldots \oplus x_n$ has the value 1 if and only if an odd number of input variables are 1.

c) Given a function $f(x_1, \ldots, x_n) = \Sigma_{i \in I}\ m_i$ show that $f = \Sigma_{\oplus i \in I}\ m_i$ (Ring sum of minterms is equal to logical OR of minterms).

d) Show that $1 \oplus A = \bar{A}$

e) Show that $A \cdot (B \oplus C) = AB \oplus AC$

f) Show that $A \oplus A = 0$

g) Prove that any completely specified combinational function can be expressed uniquely in the following canonical form.

$$f(x_1, x_2, \ldots, x_n) = a_0 \oplus a_1\ x_1 \oplus a_2\ x_2 \oplus \ldots \oplus a_n\ x_n$$
$$\oplus a_{n+1}\ x_1\ x_2 \oplus a_{n+2}\ x_1\ x_3 \oplus \ldots$$
$$\oplus a_{2^n-1}\ x_1\ x_2 \ldots x_n$$

where $a_i = 0$ or 1. (There is one term for each subset of the variables $(x_1, \ldots, x_n)$. This representation is referred to as the Reed-Muller* representation.)

†3.28 Prove or present a counterexample to the following: For completely specified functions a minimum gate-input sum of products realization is also a minimum gate sum of products realization.

---

*Muller, D.E., "Application of Boolean Algebra to Switching Design and to Error Detection," *IRE Transactions on Electronic Computers*, vol. EC-3, pp. 6–12, September 1954; and Reed, I.S., "A Class of Multiple-Error-Correcting Codes and the Decoding Scheme," *IRE Transactions on Information Theory*, vol. IT-4, pp. 38–49, 1954.

†Unsolved research problem

Chapter 4
MULTIPLE LEVEL AND MSI
COMBINATIONAL CIRCUITS

4.1 INTRODUCTION

In the previous chapter we presented procedures for solving the classical switching theory problem of deriving minimal cost, two level combinational circuits. If a delay is associated with each gate in a circuit, the circuit speed is proportional to the number of levels. Hence two level circuits have the advantage of being relatively fast. As is frequently the case, however, when a design is optimized with respect to one parameter, it may become grossly suboptimal with respect to others, sometimes making the design impractical. In particular two level circuits may have very high (and unfeasible) gate fan-in and the number of gates (and gate inputs) required may be orders of magnitude greater than that required by multiple level circuits as illustrated in the following example.

Example 4.1 A striking example of the trade-off between logic complexity and number of levels (i.e., speed) is the *parity check* function. There are two classes of parity check functions, *odd parity* and *even parity*. The odd parity function has the value 1 if and only if an odd number of input variables have the value 1. The even parity function has the value 1 if and only if an even number of input variables have the value 1. Thus for the input (x_1, x_2, x_3, x_4) = (0, 1, 1, 1), since an odd number of inputs have the value 1, the even parity function would be 0 for this input and the odd parity function would have the value 1. The 4-variable (even) parity check function is shown in Figure 4.1. This family of functions is sometimes referred to as the *checkerboard* function, for obvious reasons.

For the parity check function each 1-point is only adjacent to 0-points and hence each 1-point defines an essential prime implicant corresponding to a product of n variables. Since the function has 2^{n-1} 1-points the two level sum of products realization of an n-variable parity function has 2^{n-1} n-input AND gates and a single 2^{n-1}-input OR gate. The product of sums realization has the same complexity. Even for $n = 10$, the OR gate required would have over 500 inputs and for $n = 32$ it would require in excess of two billion inputs. The parity check

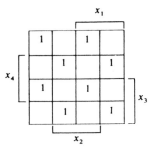

Figure 4.1   Even parity check function

function can also be realized by connecting $(n-1)$ 2-input parity check circuits in the form of a tree with $\lceil \log_2 n \rceil$ levels of these 2-input modules as shown in Figure 4.2. Such a circuit has $3\lceil \log_2 n \rceil$ levels but only has $3(n-1)$ inverters, and has fanout and fan-in indices equal to 2. We will discuss the derivation of such realizations later in this chapter.   ■

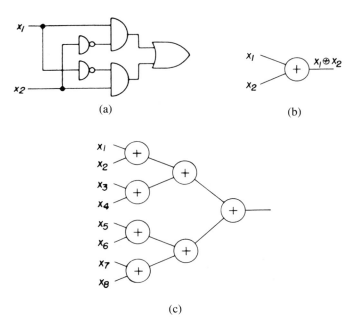

Figure 4.2   (a) A 2-input parity check cell (b) A schematic representation of a 2-input parity check cell (c) A multi-level realization of an 8-bit parity check function

Two level realizations have also become less important due to technological advances. With the development of MSI and LSI logic devices, design using standardized components has in many ways become more important than design using minimal number of components. We shall also consider this aspect of design later in this chapter.

4.2 MULTIPLE LEVEL DESIGN OF RANDOM LOGIC

We use the term random logic to indicate logic that has no mathematical pattern or apparent mathematical function, in contrast, for instance, to the obvious pattern of a parity check function or the obvious mathematical function of binary addition.

Let us consider for example the function defined by the minimal sum of products expression

$$f = x_1 x_2 + x_1 \bar{x}_3 + x_2 x_3 x_4.$$

The corresponding minimal product of sums expression for the same function is

$$f = (x_2 + \bar{x}_3) \cdot (x_1 + x_4) \cdot (x_1 + x_3).$$

Both of these realizations require gates with three inputs.

If we wish to realize the function using no gate with more than two inputs we might attempt to factor common literals from the different product terms. Either x_1 or x_2 can be factored resulting in the expressions

$$x_1(x_2 + \bar{x}_3) + x_2 x_3 x_4$$

or

$$x_2(x_1 + x_3 x_4) + x_1 \bar{x}_3.$$

The second expression corresponds to the circuit of Figure 4.3 and does not require any gate with more than two inputs. The realization requires five gates and has four levels of logic. Since there are no other apparent factorings, it might appear that this was the optimal circuit with respect to number of gates and number of levels of logic; however, a better realization can be derived as follows:

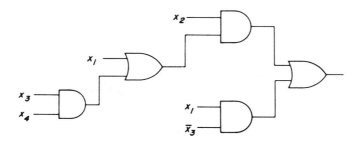

Figure 4.3 A multiple level circuit realization

$$f = x_1 x_2 + x_1 x_3 + x_2 \bar{x}_3 x_4$$
$$= x_1 x_2 + x_1 x_3 + x_2 \bar{x}_3 x_4 + x_3 \bar{x}_3 x_4$$
$$= x_1(x_2 + x_3) + (x_2 + x_3) \bar{x}_3 x_4$$
$$= (x_1 + \bar{x}_3 x_4) (x_2 + x_3)$$

By adding the term $x_3 \bar{x}_3 x_4$ (which is equal to 0) we have derived the factoring corresponding to the circuit of Figure 4.4 requiring only four gates and having three levels of logic.

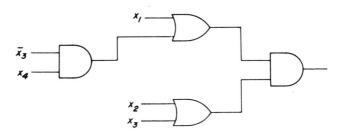

Figure 4.4   A simplified realization

A similar factoring:

$$f = (x_1 + x_3 x_4) (x_2 + \bar{x}_3)$$

can be derived directly from the product of sums expression since $(x_1 + x_4) \cdot (x_1 + x_3) = (x_1 + x_3 x_4)$

The general problem of obtaining realizations which are optimal with respect to number of gates and/or levels of gates with restricted fan-in-gates has not been solved. Relatively complex mathematical procedures for systematically designing multiple level circuits have been developed [1,2]. However the significance of this problem has been reduced by technological advances so we will not consider these procedures here. Before considering the design of random logic using standardized MSI components we will first consider some approaches to the realization of non-random logic.

4.3 MODULAR REALIZATIONS OF COMBINATIONAL FUNCTIONS

Although it may be necessary to realize functions as multiple level circuits there are no systematic procedures for obtaining good multiple level realizations, other than decomposition procedures which are essentially exhaustive in nature and heuristic procedures which may sometimes fail to find good realizations. Many circuits which frequently occur in practical systems, however, are functional rather than random in nature and can be realized in a regular manner from interconnections of identical (or similar) smaller modules. Such realizations can frequently be derived directly from a word description of the function they perform without generating a truth table, and in such a way that they define a circuit (or family of circuits) which is relatively independent (in structure) of the number of input variables upon which the function is computed. Such realizations are said to be *modular*. The realization of the parity check function of Figure 4.2 is such a circuit. We shall now consider some examples of functions which have such a multilevel modular decomposition.

4.3.1 A Comparison Circuit

Consider the design of a comparison circuit (*comparator*) whose inputs are two numbers **X** and **Y**, and whose output **Z**, is equal to 1 if **X** > **Y** and is equal to 0 if **X** ≤ **Y**. Let us consider the procedure by which two numbers would actually be compared. If

$$\mathbf{X} = 1\ 0\ 0\ 1\ 1\ 0\ 1\ 0\ 1\ 1\ 1\ 0\ 0\ 1\ 0\ 1$$

and

$$\mathbf{Y} = 1\ 0\ 0\ 0\ 1\ 0\ 1\ 1\ 0\ 1\ 0\ 1\ 0\ 1\ 0\ 0$$

we could compare these numbers and determine that **X** > **Y** without determining what the corresponding numbers were. Effectively, we would scan the two numbers from left to right (i.e., most significant bit first) until we reached a position in which they were unequal. If in that position $y_i > x_i$ then **Y** > **X**, and if $x_i > y_i$ then **X** > **Y**, independent of the remaining less significant bits of **X** and **Y**. We will now design a circuit which in effect implements this algorithm.

In effect the algorithm can be formulated as a simple procedure repeated consecutively on bit n, $n-1$, $n-2$, etc. It is therefore possible to realize the circuit in the form shown in Figure 4.5.

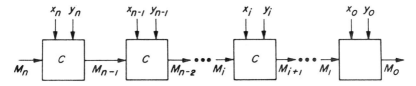

Figure 4.5   A one-dimensional unilateral iterative array

Such a circuit is called a *one-dimensional unilateral iterative array* [3]. The "dimension" refers to the linear array of identical cells. A two dimensional array would have identical cells arranged in rows and columns; conceptually, arrays can also be of dimensions greater than two. The "unilateral" refers to the fact that intercell connections are only from left to right. "Bilateral" arrays have intercell connections from left to right and also right to left.

In this circuit the same cell (i.e., subcircuit) C is used to examine each pair of bits. Cell i receives a message input M_i from its predecessor, and on the basis of that input in addition to x_i, y_i generates a message output M_{i+1} to the next cell. The input message must indicate whether on the basis of bits $i+1, \ldots, n$, $X > Y$, $X < Y$ or $X = Y$ and the output message indicates the same three possibilities based on bits $i, \ldots, n$. To represent three possibilities the intercell messages require two binary signals Z_{i1}, Z_{i2}. We will represent the three messages as shown in the table of Figure 4.6.

Z_{i1}	Z_{i2}	
0	0	$X = Y$ based on cells $i, \ldots, n$
1	0	$X > Y$ based on cells $i, \ldots, n$
0	1	$X < Y$ based on cells $i, \ldots, n$
1	1	not used

Figure 4.6 Intercell information for comparator cell

It is now possible to derive a truth table for a typical cell C with inputs $Z_{(i+1)1}$, $Z_{(i+1)2}$, x_i, y_i and outputs Z_{i1}, Z_{i2}, as shown in Figure 4.7(a); the corresponding Karnaugh maps are shown in Figure 4.7(b).

The circuit consists of a linear cascade of n identical cells with the basic cell as shown in Figure 4.7(c). The outputs of the rightmost cell Z_{o1}, Z_{o2} indicate

$Z_{(i+1)1}$	$Z_{(i+1)2}$	x_i	y_i	z_{i1}	z_{i2}	Explanation
1	0	–	–	1	0	If $X > Y$ ($X<Y$) in bits $i+1$,
0	1	–	–	0	1	$\ldots, n$ then $X > Y$ ($X<Y$) in bits $i, \ldots, n$ independent of x_i, y_i
0	0	0	0	0	0	If $X = Y$ in bits $i+1, \ldots, n$ and
0	0	1	1	0	0	$x_i = y_i$ then $X = Y$ in bits $i, \ldots, n$
0	0	1	0	1	0	If $X = Y$ in bits $i+1, \ldots, n$ and
0	0	0	1	0	1	$x_i > y_i$ ($x_i < y_i$) then $X > Y$ ($X<Y$) in bits $i, \ldots, n$
1	1	–	–	–	–	The input message $Z_{(i+1)1}$, $Z_{(i+1)2}$ = 1, 1 will never occur and hence the output is unspecified

(a)

Figure 4.7 Realization of comparator array

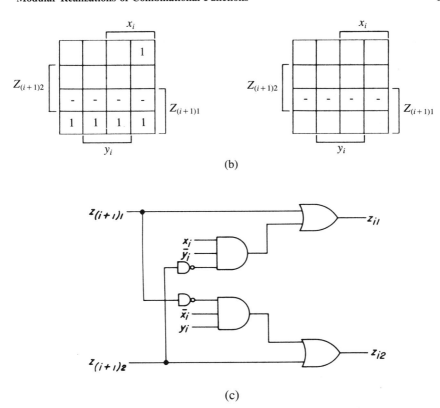

(b)

(c)

Figure 4.7   (continued)

if $X = Y$ ($Z_{o1} = Z_{o2} = 0$), $X > Y$ ($Z_{o1} = 1$, $Z_{o2} = 0$) or $X < Y$ ($Z_{o1} = 0$, $Z_{o2} = 1$).

4.3.2   Parallel Adder

The concept of designing a circuit to implement an algorithm can also be used to design a parallel adder. This circuit will be designed to implement the binary addition algorithm defined in Chapter 2. The addition of two n-bit numbers $X = x_{n-1} \, x_{n-2} \ldots x_1 \, x_0$ and $Y = y_{n-1} \ldots y_1 \, y_0$ is performed by adding the numbers bit by bit proceeding from the least to the most significant bits (right to left). The ith bit of the sum Z_i is generated by adding x_i, y_i and the carry, C_i, from the $(i-1)^{st}$ bit addition. This is repeated for all positions proceeding sequentially from right to left.

The typical cell has three inputs (x_i, y_i, C_i) and two ouputs (Z_i, C_{i+1}) and its behavior is defined by the table of Figure 4.8(a). A two level realization of this basic cell is shown in Figure 4.8(b). Connecting n such circuits results in an n-bit parallel adder where $C_0 = 0$.

x_i	y_i	C_i	Z_i	C_{i+1}
0	0	0	0	0
0	0	1	1	0
0	1	0	1	0
0	1	1	0	1
1	0	0	1	0
1	0	1	0	1
1	1	0	0	1
1	1	1	1	1

(a)

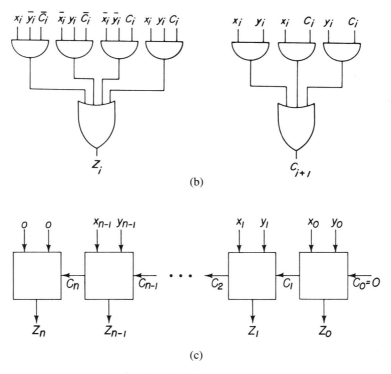

(b)

(c)

Figure 4.8 Realization of adder array

The parallel adder* and the comparator we have designed require much less logic than the comparable two level combinational circuits would require, but they are much slower, again demonstrating the possible trade-off between speed and hardware requirements.

*The parallel adder has been called a *ripple carry* adder since the effect of a carry from module i will propagate (ripple) to cell j if all intermediate cells have the x and/or y input equal to 1.

Modular realizations can frequently be derived for functions specified on sets of related input bits, which can be thought of as words, if the function effectively requires the same computation on each of the bits.

4.3.3 Speedup Techniques

The two level adder and the parallel adder are the two extreme cases in the speed/complexity trade-off. It is possible to design adders which are faster than the parallel adder and require less logic than the two level combinational circuit adder. One such circuit can be designed as a cascade of $n/2$ modules, each of which is a 2-bit adder designed as a two level combinational circuit. The basic module has five inputs $(x_{i-1}, x_i, y_{i-1}, y_i, C_{i-1})$ and three outputs (Z_{i-1}, Z_i, C_{i+1}). The minimal two level multiple output realization of this basic cell has cost in excess of twice the cost of the basic cell of the parallel adder. However, an n-bit adder designed from such 2-bit adder modules will have n levels ($n/2$ two level modules) of logic compared with $2n$ levels for the parallel adder assuming the modules are two level circuits in both cases. Thus this circuit is approximately twice as fast as the parallel adder. This design concept can be generalized to design an n-bit adder as a cascade of k n/k-bit two level combinational circuit adders. The two level n-bit adder and the parallel adder represent the extreme cases $k = 1$ and $k = n$ respectively.

In a $3n$-bit adder circuit designed as a cascade of n two level 3-bit adders, a typical cell has seven inputs $(x_i, y_i, x_{i-1}, y_{i-1}, x_{i-2}, y_{i-2}, C_{i-2})$ and four outputs $(Z_i, Z_{i-1}, Z_{i-2}, C_{i+1})$. The speed of the adder A depends on the number of levels of A which depends on the number of levels in the 3-bit adder cell of the output C_{i+1}. By realizing C_{i+1} as a two level circuit the adder A has $2n$ levels, and is thus about three times as fast as the ripple carry (parallel) adder. Note that the outputs (Z_i, Z_{i-1}, Z_{i-2}) can be realized as multilevel circuits in the same manner as the parallel adder. If C_{i+1} is realized as a four level circuit, as shown in Figure 4.9, the total amount of logic required is greatly reduced while the total number of levels of A is only increased to $2n + 2$ since the number of levels from C_{i-2} to C_{i+1} in each cell is two. The circuit has been referred to as a *carry lookahead adder* [4].

For the two examples, we have considered we were able to derive realizations as linear cascades of identical cells, which are referred to as *one-dimensional iterative arrays*, based on a functional arithmetic algorithm which was repeated (iterated) on successive bits. We shall now consider two examples in which we can derive efficient multiple level circuits based on decompositions.

4.3.4 Decoders

A (complete) decoder is an n input circuit with 2^n outputs such that for each of the 2^n possible input configurations exactly a single output has the value 1. Thus the input serves as an address which is used to select one of the outputs. (An

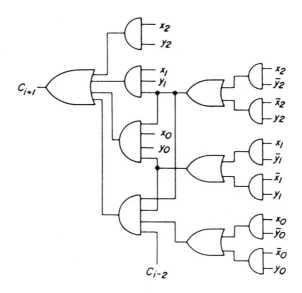

Figure 4.9 Module of carry lookahead adder

enable line E can be added such that whenever $E = 0$ then all outputs z_i will be 0.)

An n-bit decoder can be realized as a one level circuit consisting of 2^n n-input AND gates. This cost can be considerably reduced, however, by realizing the decoder as a multiple level circuit. Consider the design of a 4-bit decoder. The single level 4-bit decoder circuit is shown in Figure 4.10(a) and is represented schematically in Figure 4.10(b). This circuit is easily generalized to an n-bit decoder having 2^n n-input AND gates.

Each of the 16 product terms formed is a combination of one of the four subproducts $(x_1 x_2, x_1 \bar{x}_2, \bar{x}_1 x_2, \bar{x}_1 \bar{x}_2)$ with a second subproduct chosen from the set $(x_3 x_4, x_3 \bar{x}_4, \bar{x}_3 x_4, \bar{x}_3 \bar{x}_4)$. These two sets of subproducts correspond to the outputs of 2-bit decoders with inputs (x_1, x_2) and (x_3, x_4) respectively. Thus the 4-bit decoder can be realized from the two 2-bit decoders as shown in Figure 4.11(a). The circuit labelled (4×4) is as shown in Figure 4.11(b). This circuit is just a collection of sixteen 2-input AND gates arranged in a matrix form to generate all sixteen possible products from each of two sets of four inputs.

The first line of Figure 4.12 compares the complexity of the realizations of Figure 4.10 and 4.11(a).

This type of decomposition can be generalized to realize a 2^p input decoder as a p level circuit. The 8-bit decoder is formed from two decomposed 4-bit decoders cascaded with a 16×16 product matrix as shown in Figure 4.11(c).

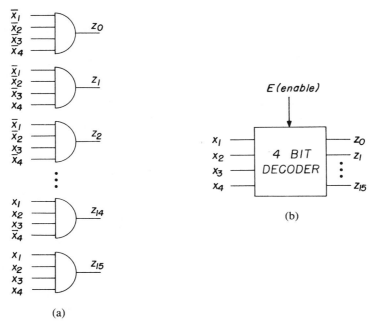

(a)

Figure 4.10   One level 4-bit decoder and its schematic representation

Similarly the 16-bit decoder would be realized from two decomposed 8-bit decoders. The substantial reduction in gate inputs is apparent from Figure 4.12.

A decoder can be utilized to route data from the enable line to the address specified by the inputs x_i. Such a circuit is frequently referred to as a *demultiplexer* since it routes data from a single source to one of several outputs, the

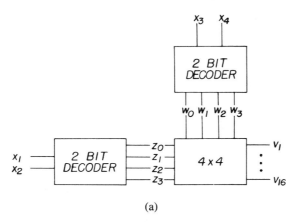

(a)

Figure 4.11   Multiple level decoder realizations

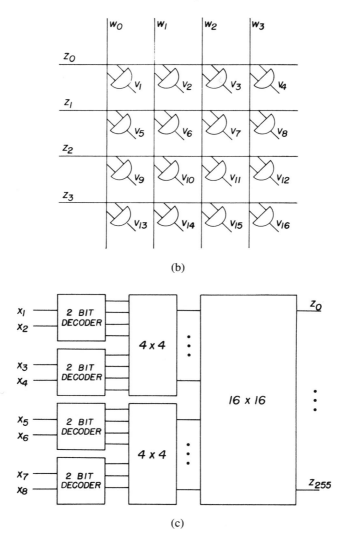

(b)

(c)

Figure 4.11   (continued)

opposite functional behavior of the *multiplexer*, which we shall consider in the next section.

4.3.5   Parity Check Circuit

Our final example of the derivation of multiple level realizations will be the parity check circuit, which we used initially to motivate the necessity for multiple level realizations.

	One level realization		Decomposed realization		
n	Gates	Gate inputs	Gates	Gate inputs	Levels
4	$2^4 = 16$	$2^4 \cdot 4 = 64$	24	48	2
8	$2^8 = 256$	$2^8 \cdot 8 = 2048$	304	608	3
16	2^{16}	$2^{16} \cdot 16 = 2^{20}$	$1216 + (256)^2$	$2(1216 + 256^2)$	4
. . .					
2^p	2^{2^p}	$2^{2^p} \cdot 2^p$	$\sim (2^{p-1})^2$	$\sim 2 \cdot (2^{p-1})^2$	p

Figure 4.12   Logic complexity of decoders

Let us first consider the even parity check function P_e defined on the set of four variables x_1, x_2, x_3, x_4. $P_e (x_1, x_2, x_3, x_4)$ is 1 if and only if there are an *even* number of 1's in the set (x_1, x_2, x_3, x_4). However the set (x_1, x_2, x_3, x_4) can be decomposed into two disjoint sets (x_1, x_2) and (x_3, x_4). There are an even number of 1's in (x_1, x_2, x_3, x_4) if and only if (x_1, x_2) and (x_3, x_4) both have an even number of 1's or both have an odd number of 1's. We can thus derive the expression:

$$P_e (x_1, x_2, x_3, x_4) = P_e (x_1, x_2) P_e (x_3, x_4) + \overline{P}_e (x_1, x_2) \overline{P}_e (x_3, x_4)$$

and the circuit of Figure 4.13(a). The subcircuit P_e is as shown in Figure 4.13(b) and is identical to the subcircuit formed by gates G_3, G_4, G_5 of Figure 4.13(a). Thus the 4-bit parity check circuit can be redrawn as shown in Figure 4.13(c). Similarly an 8-bit parity check circuit can be realized from two 4-bit parity check circuits as shown in Figure 4.13(d) (for even parity) and previously in Figure

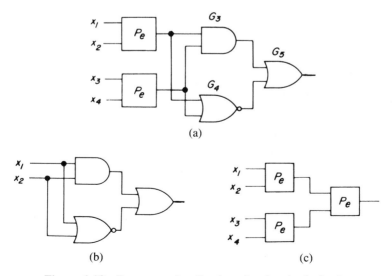

(a)

(b)   (c)

Figure 4.13   Decomposed realization of parity check circuit

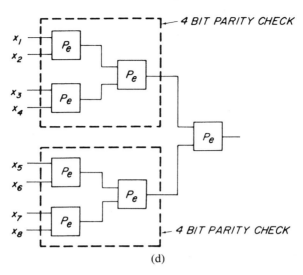

(d)

Figure 4.13   (continued)

4.2(c) (for odd parity). The resulting circuit complexity as compared to the two level realization is shown in Figure 4.14 .

	Two level		Decomposed		
n	Gates	Gate inputs	Gates	Gate inputs	Levels
4	9	40	$3.3 = 9$	$9 \cdot 2 = 18$	4
8	129	$128 \cdot 8 + 128$	$7 \cdot 3 = 21$	$21 \cdot 2 = 42$	6
16	$2^{15} + 1$	$2^{15}(16) + 2^{15}$	$15 \cdot 3 = 45$	$45 \cdot 2 = 90$	8
. . .					
2^p	$2^{p-1} + 1$	$2^{p-1}(p+1)$	$(2^{p-1}) \cdot 3$	$(2^{p-1}) \cdot 6$	$2 \cdot p$

Figure 4.14   Logic complexity of parity function

4.4   MSI DESIGN CONCEPTS

With the advent of MSI and LSI, design based on component minimization has been superseded to a great extent by design based on standardization (i.e., from relatively few different types of standard components) and regularity (i.e., components in which the interconnection structure forms a simple geometrical structure such as a matrix or array). Many of the circuits considered in the previous section can be considered as components or modules in MSI design. As we shall see in Chapter 7, it is frequently conceptually simpler to design complex systems from MSI modules used as basic elements. In this section we will consider another MSI device called a multiplexer which can be used to interconnect MSI devices into a system. We will also consider the use of standardized and regular devices, ROM's (Read Only Memories) and PLA's (Planar Logic Arrays) to realize random logic.

4.4.1 Multiplexers

Frequently in digital systems information is routed to a common destination from one of several sources, the exact source being specified by the values of certain special signals called *control* (*select*) *signals*. The *multiplexer* is a family of devices which can be used to connect several sources to a common destination. The circuit of Figure 4.15(a) is a 2-input multiplexer which connects Z to S_1 if control signal $x = 0$ and connects Z to S_2 if control signal $x = 1$. The enable signal E must be 1 for the connection to occur. This circuit can be generalized to a k-input multiplexer with $S_k = \lceil \log_2 k \rceil$ control signals. Such a circuit would have k AND gates each having S_{k+2} inputs. A 4-input multiplexer is shown in Figure 4.15(b). A k-input r-bit multiplexer would consist of r k-input multiplexers in parallel, and would be represented schematically as shown in Figure 4.15(c), where each S_i represents a group of r bits.

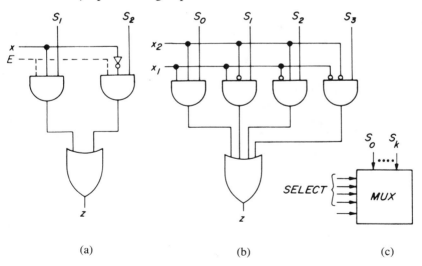

(a)   (b)   (c)

Figure 4.15 Multiplexer logic devices

For large k the amount of logic required can be considerably reduced by realizing a k-input multiplexer in the form of a binary tree of 2-input multiplexers as was done for the parity check circuit. Here each level of the tree has a single distinct control signal. For $k = 4$ such a realization is as shown in Figure 4.16.

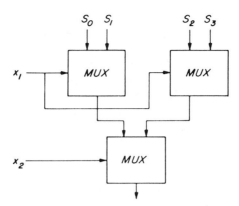

Figure 4.16   A multiple level multiplexer circuit

A 2^p-input multiplexer can be used to realize an arbitrary p-input combinational function f simply by connecting each of the inputs corresponding to 0-points of f to a 0 input and each of the inputs corresponding to 1-points of f to a 1 input. Thus the circuit of Figure 4.15(b) can be used to realize $f = x_1 x_2 + \bar{x}_1 \bar{x}_2$ by connecting inputs S_0 and S_3 to a 1 input and connecting S_1 and S_2 to a 0 input.

4.4.2   ROM's and PLA's

With the advent of LSI technology the concern with component minimization has been replaced to a substantial extent by a desire for circuit *modularity* (using a small number of uniform components) and *regularity* (the desire for simple regular interconnection structures). The uniform and regular structure enable efficient mass production of these devices in LSI technology. The basic structure is modified during manufacture to enable a designer to realize an arbitrary function. This customization of regular highly structured universal devices enables random logic functions to be efficiently realized in LSI technologies.

We shall consider two classes of devices, *Planar Logic Arrays* (PLA's) and *Read Only Memory Arrays* (ROM's). Both of these devices can be derived from a regular rectangular array of diodes as shown in Figure 4.17.

The PLA can be realized as a rectangular grid of conductors with a diode connecting the horizontal and vertical conductors at each cross point. To realize a set of r n-variable functions, $2n$ columns are chosen as input columns with one column for each input variable x_i and one column for its complement $\bar{x}_i$, and r columns to realize the set of r functions.

The set of $2n$ input columns are used to realize product terms of the sum of products realization of the set of r functions. The diodes in each row of this subarray behave as AND gates with each row generating one product term. These product terms are input to the subarray defined by the r output columns. The diodes in each column of this subarray behave as OR gates thus generating the sum of all product terms connected to an output column.

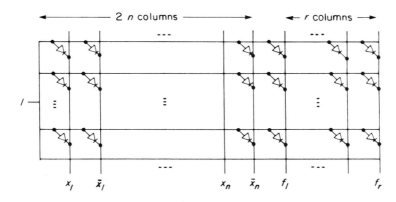

Figure 4.17 A diode logic array

Conceptually the PLA can be represented as shown in Figure 4.18. The functions to be realized are programmed into the array by eliminating diode connections in both the input and output subarrays.

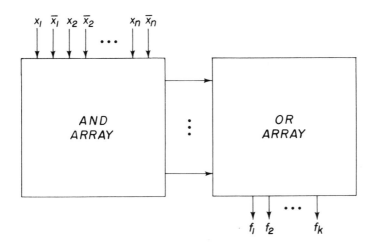

Figure 4.18 Programmable logic array

The AND matrix is programmed to generate product terms of the set of r functions, and the OR matrix is used to OR together the appropriate product terms to generate the functions as a sum of product terms. The set of functions is directly implemented as a sum of product terms with sharing. Figure 4.19(a) shows a PLA realization for the set of functions, $f_1 = x_1 \bar{x}_2 x_3 + x_2 \bar{x}_3$, $f_2 = x_1 x_2 x_3, f_3 = x_1 x_3 + x_2 \bar{x}_3$. A more economical realization may sometimes be obtained as a multiple output minimal sum of products as shown in Figure 4.19(b).

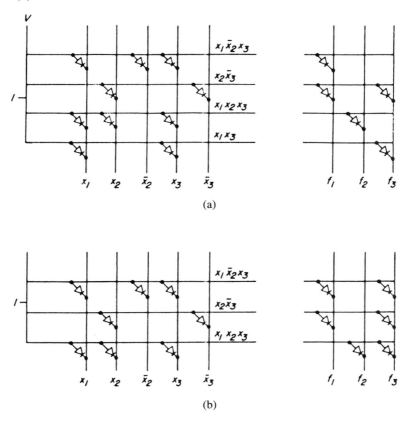

(a)

(b)

Figure 4.19   PLA design of a set of functions

Note that both the AND and OR subarrays are customized. A ROM array may be considered as a slight modification of the PLA in which the AND subarray need not be customized.

A Read-Only Memory (ROM) operates in a similar manner to a conventional memory unit in the sense that when a word is addressed, the data contained in that word is read out. However the contents of a ROM, once initialized, are not easily altered. Because they are relatively inexpensive, ROM's have been utilized to perform logical functions. A combinational function $f(x_1, x_2, \ldots, x_n)$ of n variables can be realized by a ROM consisting of 2^n 1-bit words. Each of the 2^n possible values of $\mathbf{x}^*$ causes a distinct word of the ROM to be accessed, and that word should be specified (*programmed*) as the value of f for that particular

---

*The bold face **x** represents the set of inputs and $\mathbf{x}_i$ represents a particular input state.

input. Thus for any input $\mathbf{x}_i$, the output of the ROM would be $f(\mathbf{x}_i)$. A set of k combinational functions of n variables can be realized in a similar manner by a ROM consisting of 2^n k-bit words. Effectively the ROM stores the truth tables of the functions to be realized and upon receiving any input $\mathbf{x}_i$, outputs the corresponding function values listed in the truth table. Thus a ROM realization corresponds to a sum of *minterms* realization. The subarray generating the minterms can be standardized at the expense of a much more rapidly growing requirement for array size. Figure 4.20 shows a ROM realization for the same set of functions realized by the PLA of Figure 4.19. Note that the AND subarray which realizes all minterms is actually a decoder, which was considered earlier.

So far we have considered procedures for realizing combinational circuits that in effect define simple mappings from inputs to outputs. In the next chapter we shall consider sequential circuits, which define mappings from *input sequences* to *output sequences*. As we shall see sequential circuits can be conceptualized as a modification of one-dimensional iterative arrays discussed earlier in this chapter.

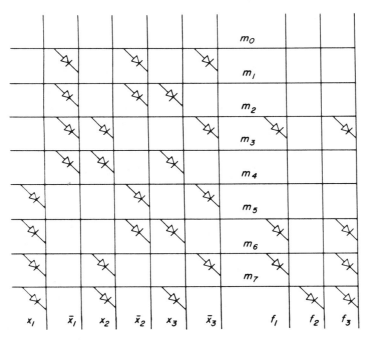

Figure 4.20   ROM realization of a set of combinational functions

REFERENCES

1. Ashenhurst, R.L., "The Decomposition of Switching Functions," *Proceedings of International Symposium on the Theory of Switching*, April 1957, Ann. Computation Lab. Harvard University, *29*, pp. 74–116, 1959.

2. Curtis, H.A., *A New Approach to the Design of Switching Circuits*, D. Van Nostrand Co., Inc., Princeton, N.J., 1962.
3. McCluskey, E.J., "Iterative Combinational Switching Networks: General Design Considerations," *IRE Transactions on Electronic Computers*, vol. EC-7, pp. 285–291, December 1958.
4. MacSorley, O.L., "High-Speed Arithmetic in Binary Computers," *Proc. IRE*, 49, pp. 67–91, Jaunary 1961.

ADDITIONAL READING

1. Blakeslee, T.R., *Digital Design with Standard MSI and LSI*, John Wiley & Sons, New York, N.Y., 1975.
2. Hayes, J.P., *Computer Architecture and Organization*, McGraw-Hill, New York, N.Y., 1977.
3. Mano, M.M., *Digital Design*, Prentice-Hall, Englewood Cliffs, N.J., 1984.

PROBLEMS

4.1 For the combinational function $f(x_1, x_2, x_3) = \Sigma\ m_3, m_5, m_6, m_7$ find a factored realization with fan-in index equal to 2.

4.2 a) Find a modular realization of a parallel subtractor.
   b) Discuss the possible applicability of the techniques for high speed adder design.

4.3 Design a modular realization of a circuit which examines a word for the bit patterns consisting of three successive 0's or 1's and generates a 1 output if and only if the word contains such a pattern.

4.4 a) Prove that a number $X = x_n\, x_{n-1}, \ldots, x_1\, x_0$ can be incremented by 1 by complementing all bits to the right of and including the least significant 0, assuming $X < 2^{n+1} - 1$.
   b) Find a modular realization of this function, and compare its complexity with that of a parallel adder.
   c) Find a similar algorithm for decrementing by 1 and a corresponding modular realization.

4.5 If a 1-dimensional iterative array corresponds to a sequential circuit to what would a 2-dimensional array (identical cells with two outputs interconnected in geometrically uniform rectangular manner) correspond?

4.6 For the following combinational function, derive a realization using only NOR gates with fan-in not exceeding three.

$$f(x_1, x_2, x_3, x_4) = \Sigma\ m_0, m_3, m_4, m_7, m_9, m_{12}, m_{15}$$

4.7 Show in block diagram form how to use four 4-bit decoders to construct a 6-bit decoder.

4.8 Consider an array type decoder as shown below. The cells are not identical. Each cell has a single level of two input AND gates. Cell i has 2^{i+1} outputs. Derive an expression for the total number of gates as a function of i.

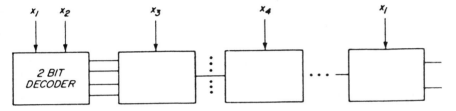

Figure 4.21   Problem 4.8

4.9 Derive a multiplexer realization of the following pair of combinational functions.

$$f_1(x_1, x_2, x_3, x_4) = \Sigma\ m_0, m_1, m_2, m_4, m_6, m_7, m_8, m_{10}, m_{12}$$
$$f_2(x_1, x_2, x_3, x_4) = \Sigma\ m_0, m_1, m_4, m_6, m_{10}, m_{12}$$

4.10 Derive a PLA and a ROM realization for the following set of these combinational functions

$$f_1(x_1, x_2, x_3, x_4) = \Sigma\ m_1, m_3, m_4, m_8, m_{12}, m_{14}, m_{15}$$
$$f_2(x_1, x_2, x_3, x_4) = \Sigma\ m_0, m_1, m_5, m_8, m_{12}$$
$$f_3(x_1, x_2, x_3, x_4) = \Sigma\ m_2, m_4, m_5, m_8, m_{13}, m_{15}$$

4.11 Derive a one-dimensional unilateral iterative array to operate as follows. Each cell has a single external input x_i and a single external output Z_i. The output Z_i is 1 if and only if x_i is 1 and $x_j = 0$ for all $j \leq i$. Thus the array outputs indicate the first (lowest subscript) input which has the value 1. This circuit is referred to as a *priority encoder*.

4.12 a) Specify an iterative array in which the basic cell is a 2-bit adder with inputs $(x_{i-1}, x_i, y_{i-1}, y_i)$, input carry C_{i-2}, output carry C_i, and outputs (Z_{i-1}, Z_i).

 b) Realize the cell derived above using only 2-bit multiplexers.

Chapter 5

FUNDAMENTALS OF SEQUENTIAL MACHINES AND SYNCHRONOUS SEQUENTIAL CIRCUITS

5.1 INTRODUCTION

In the previous chapters we have considered many types of realizations of combinational functions including modular realizations that consist of linear cascades of identical cells of combinational logic and have been referred to as *one-dimensional iterative arrays*. For functions which have such modular realizations, the general speed/complexity trade-off can often be made more dramatic by realizing such functions as sequential circuits.

Consider a typical iterative array shown in Figure 5.1(a). Here an array of identical combinational cells labelled C is used to perform the same function on a (spatial) sequence of inputs indicated as $x(1)$, $x(2)$, . . . , $x(i)$ and generate a (spatial) sequence of outputs indicated by $z(1)$, $z(2)$, . . . , $z(i)$. The same function might be performed by a single cell C if the inputs occurred as a (time) sequence and the outputs were generated as a (time) sequence. In such a realization the intercell message indicated by $y(i)$ in Figure 5.1(a) is remembered between inputs by a memory element (Figure 5.1(b)). This type of circuit is referred to as a *sequential circuit*. Whereas a combinational circuit maps inputs into outputs a sequential circuit maps (time) input sequences into (time) output

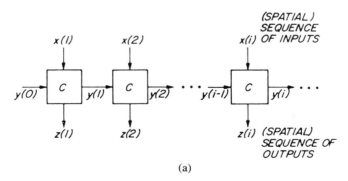

(a)

Figure 5.1   (a) An iterative array (b) The corresponding sequential circuit

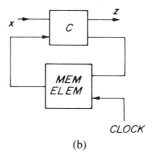

(b)

Figure 5.1 (continued)

sequences. The clock is used to synchronize events and the resulting circuit is called a synchronous sequential circuit with the clock defining successive inputs and outputs in the time sequences. Comparing the two circuits of Figure 5.1 we see that in the sequential circuit bit operations are performed sequentially rather than in parallel, and one module is used in "a time sharing mode" to generate all such bit operations, thus resulting in a significant reduction in hardware cost. In effect the spatial relationship between bits at different positions i and j of a linear cascade of modules is replaced by a time relationship affecting a single bit at two different instants of time i and j.

A function whose value depends on previous values of input variables as well as the present values is called a *sequential function*. Whereas a combinational function defines a mapping between inputs and outputs, a sequential function defines a mapping between input *sequences* and output *sequences*. Therefore a sequential function cannot be described by a truth table representation. To describe such functions we will make use of a mathematial model called a *sequential machine*. In this model the effect of all previous inputs on the output is represented by a *state* of the machine. If the set of possible input combinations* is denoted by I, the set of possible outputs by Z, and the set of possible states by Q the machine operates as follows: If initially in state $q_i \in Q$ the input $I_j \in I$ is applied, the output $z_k \in Z$ is generated and the machine goes to state $q_m \in Q$. Both z_k and q_m are uniquely determined from q_i and I_j. Thus the output of the machine at any time depends on the state and the input, and these also determine the next state. We shall be interested in sequential functions which can be described by sequential machines with a finite number of states (*finite state machines*). The operation of such a sequential machine can be described by a state table. The rows of the state table correspond to the states of the machine,† the columns correspond to inputs, and the entry in row q_i and column I_j represents the next state and output for the machine transition caused by applying input I_j to the

---

*The states of the machine will usually be labeled $q_1, q_2 \ldots$. No ambiguity arises if the states are labeled $A, B, C, \ldots$ or $1, 2, 3, \ldots$ as is frequently done in the literature. We will use each of these representations in the text.

†The expression input combination refers to the value of the set of binary input variables $\mathbf{x}_i$.

machine in state q_i. The next state of this transition is denoted by $N(q_i, I_j)$ and the output generated by the transition is denoted by $Z(q_i, I_j)$.

An example of such a state table is shown in Figure 5.2(a). This machine has four states (q_1, q_2, q_3, q_4), two possible inputs (0 and 1), and two possible outputs (0 and 1). The state table can be used to determine the output sequence generated for any input sequence and initial state.

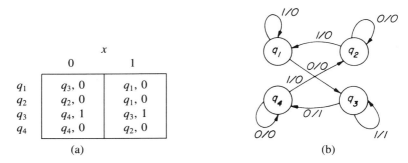

	x	
	0	1
q_1	q_3, 0	q_1, 0
q_2	q_2, 0	q_1, 0
q_3	q_4, 1	q_3, 1
q_4	q_4, 0	q_2, 0

(a)	(b)

Figure 5.2   (a) State table of a sequential machine (b) Corresponding state diagram

Thus if the input sequence 0101 is applied to initial state q_1 the output sequence 0110 is generated. This is determined in the following manner. The first input in the sequence, which is 0, is applied when the machine is in initial state q_1. From the state table entry in row q_1 and column 0, we observe that in response to this input a 0 output is generated and the machine goes to state q_3. In that state the second input 1 is applied. From row q_3 and column 1 we determine that this causes a 1 output and the machine remains in state q_3. The 3rd input 0 applied to this state generates a 1 output and the machine goes to state q_4. The 4th input, 1, applied to state q_4 generates a 0 input and the machine goes to state q_2. Thus if the input sequence 0101 is applied in initial state q_1, the output sequence 0110 is generated and the final state of the machine is q_2. Note that if the same input sequence is applied to initial state q_4, a different output sequence, 0000, is generated.

A sequential machine can also be represented in graph form (called a state diagram or state transition graph) in which there is a node corresponding to each state and a directed branch corresponding to each state transition (Figure 5.2(b)). The branch corresponding to a transition is labelled x_m/z_n where x_m is the input causing the transition and z_n is the output produced by the transition.

The state table actually represents similar information to that of the truth table for a cell in an iterative array. Consider the truth table for the parallel adder cell derived in Figure 4.8. In Figure 5.3(a) we have repeated this truth table and rearranged it into the form of a Karnaugh map. Figure 5.3(b) shows the state table for the analogous sequential adder. As we can see, the only difference is that the carry intercell signal C_i with value 0 or 1 in Figure 5.3(a) is replaced by a state with two possible values q_0 and q_1 corresponding to the carry remembered between successive inputs.

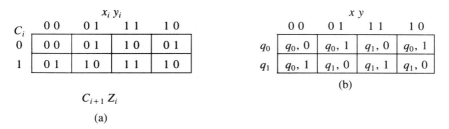

Figure 5.3 (a) Parallel adder truth table

C_i	$x_i\,y_i$ 0 0	0 1	1 1	1 0
0	0 0	0 1	1 0	0 1
1	0 1	1 0	1 1	1 0

$C_{i+1}\,Z_i$

(a)

	$x\,y$ 0 0	0 1	1 1	1 0
q_0	$q_0, 0$	$q_0, 1$	$q_1, 0$	$q_0, 1$
q_1	$q_0, 1$	$q_1, 0$	$q_1, 1$	$q_1, 0$

(b)

Figure 5.3 (a) Parallel adder truth table (b) Parallel adder sequential machine state table

A state table may also contain (*don't care*) unspecified entries. These represent conditions where the next state and/or the output need not be specified for a given transition from state q_i, input I_k, because the input I_k cannot (or is not permitted to) occur when the machine is in state q_i, or because the next state and/or the output are irrelevant or should be ignored when the input I_k occurs in state q_i. For example, in the table of Figure 5.4 assume that the sequential function is undefined for the input sequence $I_3\,I_2$ (i.e., this input sequence is prohibited). With initial state q_1, q_4, or q_5 the unspecified transitions in the table occur only for input sequences containing this prohibited subsequence. Thus, these transitions are don't cares.

	I_1	I_2	I_3
q_1	$q_1, 0$	$q_4, 0$	$q_2, 0$
q_2	$q_4, 1$	-	$q_3, 0$
q_3	$q_5, 1$	-	$q_3, 1$
q_4	$q_5, 1$	$q_4, 1$	$q_3, 1$
q_5	$q_1, 0$	$q_1, 0$	$q_3, 1$

Figure 5.4 Sequential machine with prohibited input sequence

This model of sequential machines in which the output depends on both the input and state is called the *Mealy machine model* [1]. In another model of sequential machines, called the *Moore machine model* [2], the output depends only on the state. In this model if an input I_j is applied to a state q_i the output $Z(q_i)$ which depends only on the initial state q_i is generated and the machine goes to a state $N\,(q_i, I_j)$ which depends on both q_i and I_j. The state table of a Moore machine has an output column with the entry $Z\,(q_i)$ in row q_i. The entry in input column I_j and row q_i is $N\,(q_i, I_j)$. An example of such a table is shown in Figure 5.5. The input sequence 011 applied to state q_1 generates the output sequence $011 = Z\,(q_1)\,Z\,(q_2)\,Z\,(q_4)$.

$$x$$

	0	1	z
q_1	q_2	q_3	0
q_2	q_1	q_4	1
q_3	q_2	q_2	0
q_4	q_1	q_4	1

Figure 5.5   Moore machine state table

Either of these two sequential machine models can be used to represent a sequential function [3]. For any Moore model machine M, there exists a Mealy model machine, M' which is equivalent to M in the following sense. For any input sequence **I** and initial state q of M, there is a state q' of M' such that M and M' generate the same output sequence in response to **I**, assuming corresponding initial states q and q'. Similarly for any Mealy model machine there exists a Moore model machine which is equivalent in the same sense.

For a given Moore model machine M an equivalent Mealy model machine M' can be generated by the following procedure.

Procedure 5.1

1. Assume the Moore model machine has the set of possible inputs I, the set of possible outputs Z, the set of states Q, and the next state transition function N (q_i, I_j) and output function Z (q_i). The corresponding Mealy machine has the same input, output, and state sets and the identical next state function N.
2. The output function Z' (q_i, I_j) of M' is defined as follows: If $Z(q_i) = Z_m$ then Z' $(q_i, I_j) = Z_m$ for all I_j.   ∎

For the Moore machine of Figure 5.5 the equivalent Mealy machine is described by the state table of Figure 5.6.

$$x$$

	0	1
q_1	$q_2, 0$	$q_3, 0$
q_2	$q_1, 1$	$q_4, 1$
q_3	$q_2, 0$	$q_2, 0$
q_4	$q_1, 1$	$q_4, 1$

Figure 5.6   An equivalent Mealy machine

For both the Mealy and Moore models, inputs and outputs can be assumed to occur at quantized instants of time, the initial state occurring at time $t = 0$ and the i-th input occurring at time $t = (i - 1)$ and causing a state transition at time $t = i$. Under this interpretation there is one difference between the operation of the Moore and Mealy model machines. This difference is seen by comparing the machines of Figure 5.5 and Figure 5.6. If the input $x = 0$ is applied to the machine of Figure 5.5 in initial state q_1 at time $t = 0$, the output Z $(q_1) = 0$

is produced at time $t = 0$, the state changes to q_2 at $t = 1$ and the output at $t = 1$ becomes $Z(q_2) = 1$. The corresponding operation of the machine of Figure 5.6 results in the outputs 0 at time $t = 1$ and state q_2 is reached at time $t = 1$, and the second output produced at time $t = 2$ will be 1. Thus the outputs of the Mealy machine occur one time period after the corresponding outputs of the Moore machine.

For a given Mealy machine M, it is also possible to define a Moore machine which is equivalent in the sense previously explained. In general the Moore machine will require a larger number of states. Since there are no substantial differences between the two models in terms of either theory or synthesis we will restrict ourselves to the Mealy model.

Physical realizations of sequential machines are called *sequential circuits*. A model of a sequential circuit is shown in Figure 5.1(b). The circuit C is combinational logic which generates the output $\mathbf{z}$ and the appropriate next state excitations as functions of the inputs $\mathbf{x}$ and the state $\mathbf{y}$. Before we can derive sequential circuits we must first consider a device we have not yet discussed called a *memory element*.

5.2   MEMORY ELEMENTS, DELAYS, AND CLOCKS

To represent the state of a sequential machine, memory elements are required. These devices generally have two stable conditions which can be represented as 0 or 1 states. Such memory elements are called *bistable multivibrators* or *flip-flops* (FF) and can store a single bit of information.

An SR (Set-Reset) flip-flop can be realized by the circuit of Figure 5.7(a) consisting of two cross-coupled NOR gates G_1 and G_2 (or by cross-coupled NAND gates). It has two inputs S and R, to gates G_1 and G_2 respectively. The outputs of these gates shall be denoted as y_1 and y_2 respectively. We wish this circuit to operate in such a manner that the two stable configurations are $y_1 = 1$, $y_2 = 0$ and $y_1 = 0$, $y_2 = 1$. For the input $S = R = 1$ the outputs y_2 and y_1 are both 0. Hence this input is always prohibited. If $S = 1$ and $R = 0$, the output of G_1, y_1, becomes 0 independent of the value of y_2. After y_1 becomes 0 the output of gate G_2 becomes 1 (since y_1 is an input to G_2). The memory

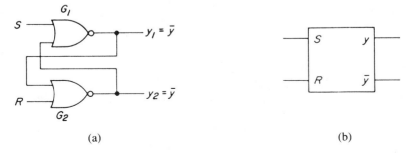

        (a)   (b)

Figure 5.7   (a) Realization (b) Representation (c) State table (d) Transition table for an SR flip-flop

y	\multicolumn{4}{c}{SR}
	00	01	11	10
0	0	0	-	1
1	1	0	-	1

$$Y = S + \bar{R}y$$

(c)

Present State	Desired Next State	Required Excitations S	R
0	0	0	-
0	1	1	0
1	0	0	1
1	1	-	0

(d)

Figure 5.7 (continued)

element remains in this configuration $y_1 = 0$, $y_2 = 1$, until the inputs change. If the inputs are $S = 0$ and $R = 1$ the output of gate G_2 becomes 0 which causes the output of gate G_1 to become 1. This configuration $y_1 = 1$, $y_2 = 0$, is also stable. For the inputs $S = 1$, $R = 0$ or $S = 0$, $R = 1$ the stable configuration reached does not depend on the state of the memory element when the inputs are applied. However if $S = R = 0$ the stable configuration reached does depend on this initial state. Suppose the flip-flop is stable with $y_1 = 1$, $y_2 = 0$ when the inputs $S = R = 0$ are applied. Since $y_1 = 1$ the output of gate G_2 remains 0. Since both inputs to G_1 are 0, the output y_1 remains 1. Hence the flip-flop remains in the same stable state $y_1 = 1$, $y_2 = 0$. Similarly for the initial state $y_1 = 0$, $y_2 = 1$, and $S = R = 0$, the final stable state would remain $y_1 = 0$, $y_2 = 1$.

If the SR flip-flop operates in this manner $y_2 = \bar{y}_1$. Thus the state of the flip-flop can be represented by a single binary variable y. Since the input $S = 1$ results in $y = 1$, the flip-flop will be said to be *set* if it is in state $y = 1$. Similarly in state $y = 0$ the flip-flop is said to be *reset*. An SR flip-flop is represented as shown in Figure 5.7(b).

The behavior of the SR flip-flop can be summarized as follows: it becomes set $(y = 1)$ if $S = 1$, $R = 0$ and it becomes reset $(y = 0)$ if $S = 0$, $R = 1$. If $S = R = 0$ the flip-flop remains stable in its present state. The input condition $S = R = 1$ is prohibited. This information can be represented by the state table of Figure 5.7(c) where the states are represented as 0 and 1 rather than q_0 and q_1. The flip-flop will be set if $S = 1$ or if $R = 0$ and $y = 1$. If we represent by Y the condition under which the flip-flop becomes (or remains) set, $Y = S + \bar{R}y$. This is called the *characteristic equation* of the flip-flop.

The information contained in the state table can be represented in another form called the *transition table* which is very useful for synthesis of sequential circuits. This table specifies the required input *excitations* for every possible combination of present state of the flip-flop and desired next state of the flip-flop. The SR-flip-flop transition table is shown in Figure 5.7(d). The first row of this table is interpreted in the following manner. If the flip-flop is to remain stable at $y = 0$, S must be 0 but R may be 0 or 1 and hence is unspecified.

In practice flip-flops are frequently enabled by a clock signal as shown in Figure 5.8(a). Clocked flip-flops can only change state when the clock input has the value 1. A clocked SR flip-flop is represented in Figure 5.8(b). We shall now consider the reasons which necessitate the use of a clock signal.

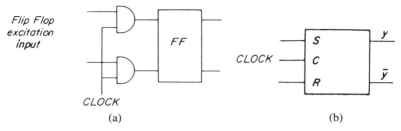

Figure 5.8 Clocked flip-flop

In practice there is a delay between signal changes on the inputs of a gate and the consequent changes on the gate output. Until now we have ignored the effect of gate delays on the behavior of circuits constructed from gates, since this effect is inconsequential for combinational circuits. However the consequences for sequential circuits can be serious. Consider the combinational circuit of Figure 5.9(a). If gates G_1, G_2, G_3 have associated delays of magnitudes Δ_1, Δ_2, Δ_3 respectively, this circuit can be modelled as shown in Figure 5.9(b) where the gates G_1', G_2', G_3' are assumed to be idealized zero delay gates. Suppose that at time t_0 the inputs are $x_1 = x_2 = x_3 = 1$, and at time $t > t_0$, x_1 changes

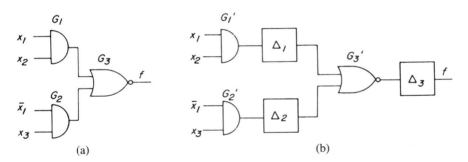

Figure 5.9 (a) A combinational circuit (b) Its gate delay model

to 0 while x_2 and x_3 remain at 1. Since $f(1,1,1) = f(0,1,1) = 0$ we would expect the output of the circuit to remain stable at 0. However the output of gate G_1 will change from 1 to 0 and the output of gate G_2 will change from 0 to 1. If $\Delta_1 < \Delta_2$ then the G_1 change will occur before the G_2 change. In the interval between the G_1 change and the G_2 change both inputs to G_3 are 0. Figure 5.10 illustrates the signals x_1, G_1, G_2, G_3 as functions of time. From this figure it is apparent that if $\Delta_1 < \Delta_2$, even by a very small amount ϵ, the circuit output will contain a 1-pulse of duration ϵ.

We thus see that due to delays a combinational circuit may produce a transient error. If the output of this circuit is an input to a flip-flop y, the erroneous transient 1-pulse may result in incorrectly setting or resetting y. The effect of this is a permanent or stable error rather than a transient error. In general a flip-flop will not respond to pulses of duration less than some minimum value called

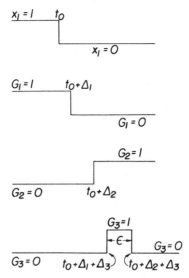

Figure 5.10   Signal timing diagram

the *trigger time*. Hence the pulse width must exceed the trigger time to produce such an error.

This problem can be eliminated by using a clock, which is assumed to be generated independently. The clock signal C can be used so that a flip-flop will only change state when $C = 1$ as shown in Figure 5.8. In this way transient flip-flop excitations can be *masked* so as not to affect the circuit operation. Sequential circuits which utilize clocks in this manner are called *synchronous* circuits. Sequential circuits can also be designed *asynchronously* without clocks [4]. We shall consider asynchronous sequential circuits in Chapter 6.

If the clock signal C has a period T, during which the clock pulse duration (width) (i.e., the time when $C = 1$) is T_p and $C = 0$ for time $T - T_p$, then T and T_p must be constrained in terms of the gate delays and the memory element trigger times to ensure proper circuit operation. Specifically $T - T_p$ must be sufficiently large to permit all flip-flop excitations to stabilize, (i.e., $C = 0$ during the period that flip-flop excitation inputs may be changing value). Similarly T_p must be larger than the trigger time of any flip-flop. The clock pulse width T_p also has an upper bound. Specifically if as in Figure 5.11 the outputs of a flip-flop y are inputs to a circuit E which generates the excitation inputs to some other FF y' (or to y itself) the clock pulse width T_p must be such that flip-flop y' (or y) does not respond to the change in y until the next clock period. Thus if the delay of the circuit E is ΔE, the delay of flip-flop y is Δy and the minimum trigger time of a flip-flop is Δs then $T_p < \Delta E + \Delta y + \Delta s$. Thus the maximum clock pulse width must be constrained.

Alternatively proper operation can be ensured by using a *master*-slave flip-flop, Figure 5.12, which consists of two flip-flops connected in cascade. The

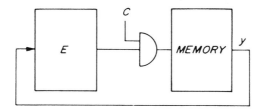

Figure 5.11   Circuit with clocked flip-flop excitation

first flip-flop can only change state if $C = 1$ while the second flip-flop changes to the same state as the first flip-flop when $C = 0$. If a master-slave flip-flop is utilized in a circuit such as that of Figure 5.11 the inputs to circuit E are taken from the outputs of the second flip-flop. Therefore these inputs cannot change when $C = 1$. When $C = 0$ these inputs may change which may then cause the outputs of E to change. However these changes cannot affect the state of the master-slave flip-flop until $C = 1$. Thus the maximum width of the clock pulse need not be restricted.

An alternative to a master-slave flip-flop configuration is an edge-triggered configuration. An edge-triggered flip-flop responds to input changes only on the leading edge of a clock pulse (i.e., when the clock goes from 0 to 1) or only on the falling edge of a clock pulse. Thus input changes do not affect the output except at the triggering edge and inputs must only be stable at that time. In contrast, in the master-slave configuration, inputs must remain stable throughout the period of the clock pulse. In general this longer period of required stability necessitates a slower clock.

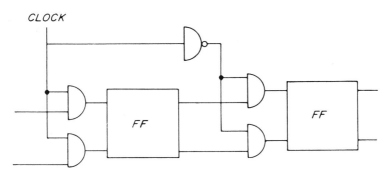

Figure 5.12   Master-slave flip-flop

A second type of memory element is the *JK flip flop*. This operates in a similar manner to the *SR* flip-flop, the input *J* being used to set the element and the input *K* to reset it. However the input condition $J = K = 1$ is permitted and results in the device changing state, i.e., if the present state is $y = 1$ the state becomes $y = 0$, and vice versa. The realization, representation and behavior of this element is shown in Figure 5.13. Note that if $J = K = 1$ only one of the inputs to the SR flip-flop will be 1. Specifically if $y = 1$, the R input is 1, the S input is 0 thus resetting the flip-flop, while if $\bar{y} = 1$, the S input is 1, the R input is 0 thus setting the flip-flop. Thus in either case the memory element changes state.

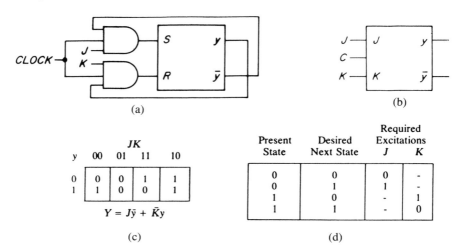

(a)   (b)

y	JK 00	01	11	10
0	0	0	1	1
1	1	0	0	1

$Y = J\bar{y} + \bar{K}y$

(c)

Present State	Desired Next State	Required Excitations J	K
0	0	0	-
0	1	1	-
1	0	-	1
1	1	-	0

(d)

Figure 5.13   (a) Realization (b)Representation (c) State table (d)Transition table of JK flip-flop

The T (*trigger*) flip-flop in Figure 5.14 operates like a JK flip-flop if the inputs J and K are constrained to always be equal. In this case these two inputs can be replaced by a single input T. If $T = 0$ the device remains in its present

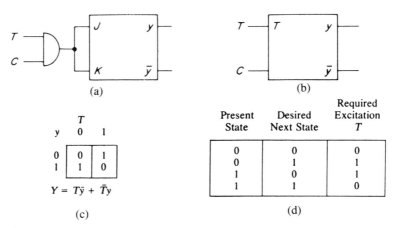

(a)   (b)

y	T 0	1
0	0	1
1	1	0

$Y = T\bar{y} + \bar{T}y$

(c)

Present State	Desired Next State	Required Excitation T
0	0	0
0	1	1
1	0	1
1	1	0

(d)

Figure 5.14   (a) Realization (b)Representation (c) State table (d)Transition table of T flip-flop

state, and if $T = 1$ the device changes state. Note that the two column state table corresponds to columns 00 and 11 of the table of Figure 5.13(c).

The D (*delay*) flip-flop, which is also called a *delay element*, behaves as an SR flip-flop if the inputs S and R are constrained to be complementary (i.e., $S = \bar{R}$), and replaced by a single input D. If $D = 1$ the device becomes set and if $D = 0$ the device becomes reset. Hence the state of a D flip-flop is always equal to the value of the previous excitation. The behavior of this element is as represented in Figure 5.15. Note that the two column state table corresponds to columns 01 and 10 of the table of Figure 5.7(c).

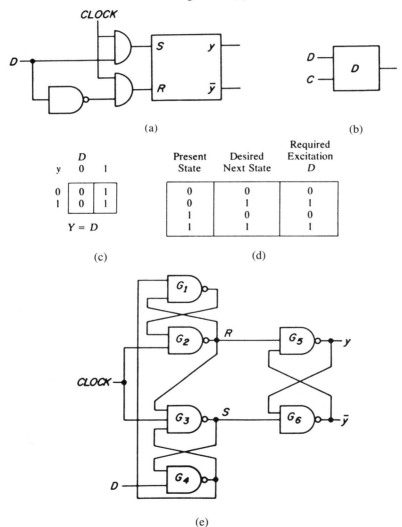

(a)

(b)

	D	
y	0	1
0	0	1
1	0	1

$Y = D$

(c)

Present State	Desired Next State	Required Excitation D
0	0	0
0	1	1
1	0	0
1	1	1

(d)

(e)

Figure 5.15 (a) Realization (b) Representation (c) State table (d) Transition table of D flip-flop (e) Positive edge-triggered D flip-flop

In practice gates have delay associated with them. That is, there is a non-zero elapsed time between an input change to a gate and the output change produced by the input change. The effect of this delay can be modeled by a *delay element of magnitude D*. If the input to the delay element is described by the Boolean time function $x(t)$, and the output by $y(t)$, then $y(t) = x(t - D)$ is the characteristic equation of a delay element of magnitude D. A D flip-flop operates in a similar manner to a delay element.

An edge-triggered D-flip-flop is shown in Figure 5.15(e). Its behavior is analyzed as follows. When the clock is 0, the values of R and S (the inputs to the (NAND) flip-flop generating the output) are both 1, causing the flip-flop to remain stable in its current state. If the clock becomes 1 with $D = 0$, then S becomes 0 driving y to 0. If the clock becomes 1 with $D = 1$ then G_4 goes to 0 driving G_1 to 1 and R becomes 0 thus driving y to 1. The D input must be maintained for a period of time T_1 before the clock trigger edge and T_2 after the clock trigger edge where T_1 is called the setup time and T_2 the hold time. The setup time is the delay associated with the gate pair G_4G_1 and the hold time is the delay associated with gate G_3.

In designing synchronous circuits, we shall assume that the clock has been properly designed or master-slave or edge-triggered FF's have been utilized to ensure proper operation.*

In addition to the CLOCK signal, flip-flops frequently have additional control signals CLEAR which reset the device and PRESET which set the device. These signals can be used to initialize the device since its normal excitation inputs may not be readily controllable when the circuit is an unknown initial state.

5.3 SEQUENTIAL CIRCUIT SYNTHESIS

5.3.1 State Table Derivation

The synthesis problem consists of designing a sequential circuit which performs the computation specified in some general description of a sequential function. This process consists of several distinct problems which can be represented by the block diagram of Figure 5.16.

There is no algorithmic procedure for the state table derivation step in the synthesis of sequential circuits. The major difficulty is in deciding what information must be remembered and how this information is to be represented as states of a sequential machine. Some types of computation can be formulated as either basically combinational or basically sequential processes. An example

---

*In the literature the term flip-flop is sometimes reserved for a master-slave device and the term *latch* is applied to the simple memory elements.

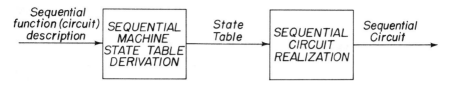

Figure 5.16 Sequential circuit synthesis—state table derivation

of such a computation is binary addition. In the previous chapter we showed how combinational circuit adders could be designed. Addition can also be formulated as a sequential process in the following manner. We assume that there are two binary inputs x and y. The sequence of x-inputs is interpreted as the binary representation of a single number $\mathbf{X}$, low order bits first. Similarly the sequence of y-inputs is interpreted as the binary representation of a number $\mathbf{Y}$. The binary output z, should generate a sequence equal to the binary representation of $\mathbf{X} + \mathbf{Y}$, low order bits being generated first. (The addition is effectively terminated by having the most significant bits of $\mathbf{X}$ and $\mathbf{Y}$ equal to 0.)

The essential information which must be remembered when performing the addition of the i-th bits of $\mathbf{X}$ and $\mathbf{Y}$ is the carry from the addition of bit $(i - 1)$ of $\mathbf{X}$ and $\mathbf{Y}$. Thus this sequential addition process can be represented by a sequential machine with two states, q_0 indicating a 0-carry and q_1 indicating a 1-carry. Since the initial carry is 0, the initial state of the machine is q_0. The state table of this sequential machine which is sometimes referred to as a *serial adder*, is shown in Figure 5.17. The entries of this table are determined in the following manner. A carry is generated (next state entry q_1) if the inputs x and y are both 1 or if there is a carry from the previous bit addition (present state

	xy			
	00	01	11	10
q_0	q_0, 0	q_0, 1	q_1, 0	q_0, 1
q_1	q_0, 1	q_1, 0	q_1, 1	q_0, 0

Figure 5.17 Serial adder

q_1) and $x = 0$, $y = 1$ or $x = 1$, $y = 0$. This determines all of the next state entries. The output is 1 if there is a carry from the previous bit addition (present state q_1) and the inputs are $x = y = 0$ or $x = y = 1$ or if there is no carry (present state q_0) and $x = 1$, $y = 0$ or $x = 0$, $y = 1$.

This sequential machine can be realized by a sequential circuit which is very similar to a single module of the combinational parallel adder of Figure 4.8(b). In general, performing a computation sequentially results in a time sharing of hardware and thus a more economical, but slower, circuit than the same computation performed combinationally.

Sequential circuits are also used for computations which cannot be realized by combinational circuits. The following example demonstrates the state table generation process for such sequential functions.

Example 5.1   We will derive a sequential circuit to act as a filter or smoothing device on an input x. The circuit will eliminate (filter out) input changes which persist for short periods of time (less than three clock periods). We assume that when the circuit is turned on its output will assume the value of the first input. After this the output will only change value if three consecutive inputs have the opposite value. Thus if the input signal is as shown in Figure 5.18(a), the output signal is as shown in Figure 5.18(b).

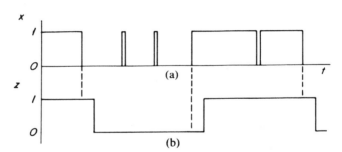

Figure 5.18   Input-output waveforms of a filter

	x		
	0	1	
q_0	q_1, 0	q_2, 1	initial state
q_1	q_1, 0	q_3, 0	stable 0 output − three 1's required to change
q_2	q_4, 1	q_2, 1	stable 1 output − three 0's required to change
q_3	q_1, 0	q_5, 0	stable 0 output − two 1's required to change
q_4	q_6, 1	q_2, 1	stable 1 output − two 0's required to change
q_5	q_1, 0	q_2, 1	stable 0 output − one 1 required to change
q_6	q_1, 0	q_2, 1	stable 1 output − one 0 required to change

(a)

Figure 5.19   (a) State table for filter (b) Reduced state table

	x	
	0	1
q_0	$q_1, 0$	$q_2, 1$
q_1	$q_1, 0$	$q_3, 0$
q_2	$q_4, 1$	$q_2, 1$
q_3	$q_1, 0$	$q_0, 0$
q_4	$q_0, 1$	$q_2, 1$

(b)

Figure 5.19   (continued)

The state table is derived in Figure 5.19(a). The initial state is labelled q_0. Let us consider the two input transitions defined from state q_0. If the input is 0, the output goes to a stable 0 which requires three consecutive 1 inputs to change. The state q_1 is used to remember this requirement and the transition is specified in row q_0, input 0 by q_1, 0. Similarly if the first input was 1 a stable 1 output would be produced which would not change unless three consecutive 0 inputs occurred. The state q_2 is used to remember this requirement and the transition is specified in row q_0, input 1 by q_2, 1.

We now consider the transitions in row q_1. If a 0 input occurs the output remains 0 and the requirement for the three consecutive 1 inputs to produce a 1 output remains unchanged. Thus the state remains q_1 and the transition is indicated by q_1, 0. If a 1 input occurs the output does not change since it is only the first of a required three consecutive 1 inputs. However the state must change to reflect the fact that only two additional consecutive 1 inputs are required to produce a 1 output, represented by state q_3. The transition is defined by q_3, 0. The transitions in row q_2 are defined in a similar manner to those in row q_1.

We now consider the transitions in row q_3. If a 0 input occurs the output remains 0 and the requirement for an output change reverts to three consecutive 1 inputs. Since state q_1 represents that condition, the transition is represented by q_1, 0. If a 1 input occurs the output stays at 0 since only two consecutive 1 inputs have occurred. However the requirement for change is now reduced to a single 1 input. A new state q_5 is used to remember this requirement and the transition in row q_3 column 1 is represented by q_5, 0.

In row q_5 a 0 input resets the requirement for change to three consecutive 1's and the transition is represented by q_1, 0. A 1 input completes the three consecutive 1 inputs and results in a 1 output. The output will remain 1 until three consecutive 0 inputs occur. The state q_2 has already been defined to remember this requirement so the transition is represented by q_2, 1.

The remaining entries in the state table are derived in an analogous manner.

■

In the state table of Figure 5.19(a) note that rows q_0, q_5 and q_6 are all identical. In fact the sequential machine of Figure 5.19(b) with five states also performs the function specified in Example 5.1. In the next section we will consider the problem of reducing the number of states in a sequential machine to the minimal number possible.

5.3.2   Reduction of State Tables

The first step in the design of a sequential circuit from a word description of the desired behavior of the circuit is the construction of a state table describing the operation of the circuit. Such a state table may contain more states than necessary. Since the complexity of a sequential circuit is often dependent on the number of states in the state table, it is desirable to reduce the number of states [5,6].

For a given state table M, we would like to obtain a state table M' which has fewer states than M, such that for *any input sequence*, M' produces the same output sequence as M, assuming appropriate initial states. For example, consider the two state tables shown in Figure 5.20. For the state table M, it is obvious that the output sequence generated will be the same for all input sequences if the initial state is D or E. Therefore, the output sequence for any input sequence will be unchanged if all next state entries E are changed to D. Furthermore, since E does not appear as a next state entry after this modification and the output sequences generated with initial state E are identical to those generated with initial state D for all input sequences, state E may be eliminated, resulting in the state table M'. Thus, the number of states in M can be reduced.

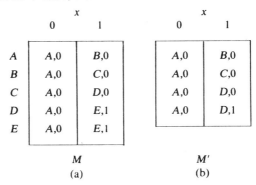

Figure 5.20   Two equivalent sequential machines

We shall first consider the case of completely specified machines, and then the much more difficult problem of incompletely specified machines.

If a state table M has several states which generate the same output sequences for any input sequences, then these states are equivalent and it is possible to define a reduced machine M' with fewer states having a single state corresponding to this set of states. The sets of equivalent states define a partition of the states of M. We will now develop a simple procedure for deriving this partition. Let us begin by considering those states which always produce identical outputs for input sequences of length 1. These correspond to rows of the state table which have the same outputs as each other in each of the input columns. For the table of Figure 5.21 states q_1, q_2, q_3, q_5, and q_6 all produce 0 outputs in column 0 and 1 outputs in column 1. State q_4 produces a different output than the others in column 0. Hence we can define the partition

$$\Pi_1 = \{q_1\ q_2\ q_3\ q_5\ q_6, q_4\}$$

which groups together states that produce identical outputs for all input sequences of length one.

| | x | |
	0	1
q_1	$q_3, 0$	$q_2, 1$
q_2	$q_3, 0$	$q_4, 1$
q_3	$q_5, 0$	$q_6, 1$
q_4	$q_5, 1$	$q_1, 1$
q_5	$q_1, 0$	$q_2, 1$
q_6	$q_5, 0$	$q_4, 1$

Figure 5.21 Non-minimal state table

Some of these states, however, may not produce the same output sequences for input sequences of length longer than one. Thus for input sequence 10 initial state q_1 produces the output sequence 10, whereas initial state q_2 produces the output sequence 11. Let us define Π_k to be the partition that groups together states producing the same output sequences as each other for all input sequences of length at most k. From this definition it is apparent that states which are not grouped in Π_i will also not be grouped in Π_{i+1}. We therefore can derive Π_{i+1} by considering the sets of states which are grouped in Π_i. Let us derive Π_2 for the machine of Figure 5.21. As previously explained states q_1 and q_2 do not produce the same outputs for input sequence 10. This can be readily determined by examining the next state entries of rows q_1 and q_2 in Figure 5.21. As we see in column 1 these entries are q_2 and q_4. From Π_1 we see that q_2 and q_4 do not produce the same outputs for all input sequences of length 1 since q_2 and q_4 are not grouped together in Π_1. Therefore, q_1 and q_2 do not produce the same output sequences for input sequences of length 2. This leads us to the following rule.

Rule 1

States q_i and q_j produce the same output sequences for all input sequences of length $\leqslant 2$ if and only if (1) they are in the same block of Π_1 (i.e., they produce the same output sequence for input sequences of length 1) and (2) in each input column I the next state entries $N(q_i, I)$ and $N(q_j, I)$ are in the same block of Π_1.

Applying this rule to the table of Figure 5.21 we derive

$$\Pi_2 = \{q_1\, q_3\, q_5,\, q_2\, q_6,\, q_4\}$$

Rule 1 can be generalized to enable Π_{k+1} to be derived from Π_k as follows.

Rule 1a

For a state table M states q_i and q_j are grouped in Π_{k+1} if and only if (1) q_i and q_j are grouped in Π_k and (2) in each input column I, the next state entries $N(q_i, I)$ and $N(q_j, I)$ are grouped in the same block of Π_k.

Applying this rule to the table of Figure 5.21 we see that $\Pi_3 = \Pi_2$. Consequently $\Pi_k = \Pi_2$ for all $k \geqslant 2$. The table of Figure 5.21 can thus be reduced to a three state machine as shown in Figure 5.22. State A corresponds to q_1, q_3 and q_5, state B to q_2 and q_6, and state C to q_4. The next state entries are derived from Figure 5.21 as follows. In column 0, rows q_1, q_3, and q_5 the outputs are all 0 and the next states are q_3, q_5, q_1 respectively, all corresponding to state A. Hence the entry in row A, column 0 is A, 0. In column 1 the outputs are 1 and the next states q_2, q_6, q_2 corresponding to B. The entry in row A, column 1 is thus B, 1. The remaining entries are similarly derived.

		x	
		0	1
(q_1, q_3, q_5)	A	A, 0	B, 1
(q_2, q_6)	B	A, 0	C, 1
(q_4)	C	A, 1	A, 1

Figure 5.22   Reduced state table

The following general procedure can thus be used to derive a minimal state sequential machine for the completely specified machine case.

Procedure 5.2   For a given completely specified machine M:

1. Derive Π_1 grouping all states having identical outputs to each other in all input columns.
2. From Π_i derive Π_{i+1}, using Rule 1(a).
3. Repeat until $\Pi_i = \Pi_{i+1}$.

4. Use Π_{i+1} to define the states of the reduced and minimal state machine M'. The transitions of M' are defined from the corresponding transitions of M.

■

Example 5.2.   Consider the sequential machine of Figure 5.23(a). The partition grouping states with identical outputs in both input columns is

$$\Pi_1 \;=\; \{q_1\, q_5\, q_8,\, q_2\, q_3,\, q_4\, q_6\, q_7\}$$

From this partition we derive

$$\Pi_2 \;=\; \{q_1\, q_5,\, q_8,\, q_2\, q_3,\, q_4\, q_7,\, q_6\}.$$

The state q_8 is not grouped with q_1 or q_5 since in column 0 the next state entry of q_8 is q_4, which is not in the same block of Π_1 as the next state entries of q_1 or q_5. Similarly q_6 is separated from q_4 and q_7 since their next state entries in column 1 are not in the same block of Π_1.

	x				x	
	0	1			0	1
q_1	q_8, 0	q_7, 1	$(q_1\, q_5)$	A	B, 0	E, 1
q_2	q_3, 0	q_5, 0	(q_8)	B	E, 0	F, 1
q_3	q_2, 0	q_8, 0	(q_2)	C	D, 0	A, 0
q_4	q_5, 1	q_8, 0	(q_3)	D	C, 0	B, 0
q_5	q_8, 0	q_4, 1	$(q_4\, q_7)$	E	A, 1	B, 0
q_6	q_5, 1	q_3, 0	(q_6)	F	A, 1	D, 0
q_7	q_1, 1	q_8, 0				
q_8	q_4, 0	q_6, 1				

(a)   (b)

Figure 5.23   (a) A non-minimal state table (b) The reduced state table

From Π_2 we derive the next partition

$$\Pi_3 \;=\; \{q_1\, q_5,\, q_8,\, q_2,\, q_3,\, q_4\, q_7,\, q_6\}.$$

The states q_2 and q_3 are separated since their next state entries in column 1 are not in the same block of Π_2.

From Π_3 we derive Π_4 which is identical thus terminating the iteration. The partition Π_3 is used to define the reduced machine of Figure 5.23(b). Each state corresponds to a block of Π_3. The next state entries are derived from the original table. Thus the next state entry $N\,(A,\, 1)$ corresponds to the next state entries $N\,(q_1,\, 1) = q_7$ and $N\,(q_5,\, 1) = q_4$. The states q_4 and q_7 correspond to state E. Each of the next state and output entries is derived in this manner.   ■

5.3.3   State Minimization in Incompletely Specified Machines

If the state table M is incompletely specified, it is sufficient to require that the reduced state table M' produce the same outputs as M whenever the latter is specified. A state q' of a state table M' *covers* a state q of table M if for *any input sequence* the output sequences of M' in initial state q' and M in initial state q are identical whenever the output of M is specified. Table M' *covers* table M if every state of M is covered by some state of M'. The state table reduction (or minimization) problem may be stated as follows. For a given table M, find a table M' which covers M such that for any other table M'' which covers M, the number of states in M' does not exceed the number of states in M'' [7].

For the tables in Figure 5.24, state A of M' covers states 1 and 2 of M and state B of M' covers states 2 and 3 of M. Therefore, table M' covers table M. Note that if M is started in state 1 with input sequence 100, the output sequence generated is 0--. Starting table M' in state A and applying the same input sequence generates the output sequence 001. The output generated by M' corresponding to the don't care entry in M is not always the same. Thus, if we were to form tables M_2 and M_3 by filling in the unspecified entry in M with 0 and 1, respectively (Figure 5.25), neither state A nor B of M' covers state 2 of M_2 or M_3 and hence M' would not cover M_2 or M_3.

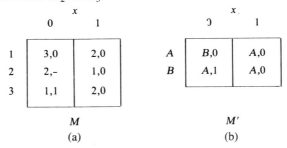

	x	
	0	1
1	3,0	2,0
2	2,-	1,0
3	1,1	2,0

M

(a)

	x	
	0	1
A	B,0	A,0
B	A,1	A,0

M'

(b)

Figure 5.24   An incompletely specified state table and a covering table

	x	
	0	1
1	3,0	2,0
2	2,0	1,0
3	1,1	2,0

M_2

(a)

	x	
	0	1
1	3,0	2,0
2	2,1	1,0
3	1,1	2,0

M_3

(b)

Figure 5.25   Two completely specified tables corresponding to the table of Figure 5.24(a)

5.3.3.1   Generation of Compatible Sets of States

If a table M can be covered by another table M' containing fewer states than M, then some state of M' must cover more than one state of M. If a set of states of M can be covered by the same state of some other table M', we will call this set a *compatible set* (or simply a *compatible*). Thus if M' covers M, each state of M' corresponds to a compatible set of states of M.

Thus the state minimization problem for an incompletely specified machine M can be considered to consist of the following two parts:

1. Find all compatible sets of states of M.
2. Select a set of compatibles which realize M.

As we shall see both of these problems are much more complex than for completely specified machines.

Two states q_i and q_j of a table M are compatible (denoted by $q_i \sim q_j$) if they never generate different specified outputs for any input sequence. Two states q_i and q_j are said to be *output compatible* if $Z(q_i, I_k) = Z(q_j, I_k)$ for all I_k for which both of them are specified. (Recall that $Z(q_i, I_k)$ is the output produced if the input I_k is applied when the circuit is in state q_i.) The following Lemma will enable us to derive a procedure for determining all incompatible state pairs.

Lemma 5.1   Two states q_i and q_j of a state table M are incompatible (i.e., not compatible) if and only if q_i and q_j are output incompatible or for some I_k, $N(q_i, I_k)$ and $N(q_j, I_k)$ are not compatible.

Proof   Necessity   Assume q_i and q_j are output compatible, and for all I_k, $N(q_i, I_k)$ and $N(q_j, I_k)$ are compatible. If q_i and q_j are incompatible, there exists an input sequence $\mathbf{I}$ for which they generate different output sequences. Let $\mathbf{I} = I_1 \mathbf{I}'$ (I_1 followed by $\mathbf{I}'$). Since q_i and q_j are output compatible, the input I_1 applied to q_i and q_j does not result in different outputs. Therefore, the input sequence $\mathbf{I}'$ applied to $N(q_i, I_1)$ and $N(q_j, I_1)$ must result in different outputs. This contradicts the assumption that $N(q_i, I_k)$ and $N(q_j, I_k)$ are compatible for all I_k.

Sufficiency   Exercise.   ∎

The following Lemma gives necessary and sufficient conditions for determining compatible sets of states from compatible pairs of states for incompletely specified state tables.

Lemma 5.2.   A set of states $Q = \{q_1, q_2, \ldots, q_n\}$ of a state table M is compatible if and only if for every pair of states $(q_i, q_j) \in Q$, $q_i \sim q_j$.

Proof   Exercise.   ∎

In general, a state table may have a great number of compatible sets of states. However, a particular class of compatibles will be of special interest. These are the compatibles which are not subsets of any other compatible set. We shall refer to these as *maximal compatibles* (MC's). The MC's of a table can be found by finding sets of states which satisfy Lemma 5.2.

The following procedure can be used to determine all incompatible pairs of states, and hence all compatible pairs of states.

Procedure 5.3

1. Form a set L consisting of all output incompatible pairs.
2. Add to L any pair of states (q_i, q_j) if for some input I_k the pair $(N\ q_i, I_k)$, $N\ (q_j, I_k))$ is in L (i.e., is a previously determined incompatible pair of states). The state pair (q_i, q_j) *implies* the state pair $(N\ (q_i, I_k), N\ (q_j, I_k))$.
3. Repeat Step 2 until no new pairs can be added to L. L contains all incompatible state pairs.   ■

Example 5.3   Using Procedure 5.3, the set of incompatible pairs of states for the table of Figure 5.26 is determined as follows:

	I_1	I_2	I_3
1	3,0	–	2,–
2	–	4,0	6,–
3	5,1	–	–,0
4	–	1,1	–
5	1,–	–	6,–
6	4,–	5,–	6,–

Figure 5.26   An incompletely specified machine

Output incompatible pairs: $\{(1,3), (2,4)\} = L = S_1$.
New pairs that imply S_1: $\{(1,5)\} = S_2$.
New pairs that imply S_2: $\{(3,5), (4,6)\} = S_3$.
New pairs that imply S_3: None
Set of incompatible pairs: $\{(1,3), (2,4), (1,5), (3,5), (4,6)\}$

All other pairs of states are compatible.   ■

The procedure for finding compatible and incompatible pairs of states for an n-state table can be tabularized using a *pair chart* such as that shown in Figure 5.27. Note that the chart contains a box for each pair of states $(q_i\ q_j)\ i \neq j$. If states q_i

and q_j are output incompatible, we place a cross ($\times$) in the box corresponding to (q_i, q_j). Otherwise, the box is filled with all pairs of states implied by (q_i, q_j). If (q_i, q_j) implies no state pairs, a check ($\sqrt{}$) is placed in that box. We now place $\times$'s in every box which contains a state pair (q_k, q_l) if the box corresponding to (q_k, q_l) has a $\times$. This is repeated until no more $\times$'s can be entered. All incompatible pairs now have $\times$'s in their respective boxes. For the table of Example 5.3, the pair chart is as shown in Figure 5.28.

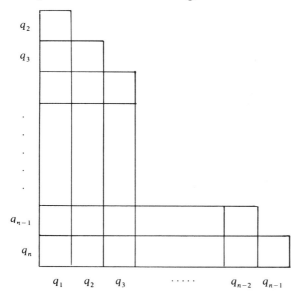

Figure 5.27   Typical pair chart

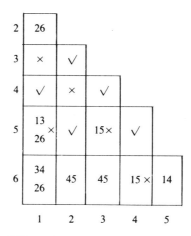

Figure 5.28   Pair chart for the table of Example 5.3

We now wish to determine compatible sets of states with more than two members. It is easy to show that the compatibility relationship does not have the transitivity property. That is, if state q_i is compatible to q_j (denoted by $q_i \sim q_j$) and $q_j \sim q_k$, it does not follow that $q_i \sim q_k$. This is exhibited by Table M of Figure 5.24. In this table, $1 \sim 2$ and $2 \sim 3$ but $1 \not\sim 3$ (indicating that 1 is not compatible with 3). Thus, we cannot find compatible sets by combining all states compatible to the same state.

Consider the state table and corresponding pair chart of Figure 5.29. We begin by grouping all five states and then decompose this set in accordance with the incompatible pairs listed in the pair chart. Thus column 1 of the chart indicates that $1 \not\sim 4$. We must therefore decompose the set of states by either eliminating 1 or 4 resulting in the two subsets 2345 or 1235 as shown in Figure 5.29(c).

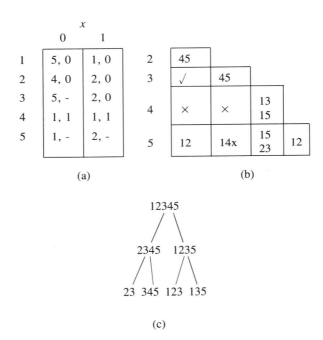

Figure 5.29 Pair chart for determination of maximal compatibles

From column 2 of the pair chart we see that $2 \not\sim 4$ and $2 \not\sim 5$. We therefore decompose the set 2345 by eliminating 2 or by eliminating both 4 and 5 as shown in Figure 5.29(c). The set 1235 is also decomposed into 123 and 135. Note that in this figure we generate the sets 23 and 123. Since $23 \subset 123$, then 23 is obviously not an MC and can be eliminated. The remaining columns of the pair chart indicate no additional incompatible pairs and hence the sets of states generated are compatible and need not be decomposed. It is easy to show that these sets are all of the MC's. For the table of Figure 5.29(a) the set of all

MC's is thus {123, 135, 345}. The procedure illustrated for this table can be formally stated as follows.

Procedure 5.4   We assume the state table has n states $q_i, q_2, \ldots, q_n$.

1. Initially let $L = \{q_i\, q_2 \ldots q_n\}$. Set $i = 1$.
2. Consider the leftmost column of the pair chart q_i, and let S_i be the set of all states which are incompatible with q_i (i.e., have X's in column q_i). Decompose each set in L which contains both q_i and some state in S_i into two subsets by eliminating q_i or by eliminating all elements in S_i.
3. Eliminate each set of L which is contained in some other set of L.
4. Increment i and repeat 2 and 3. Repeat until $i = n - 1$. The set L will then consist of all MC's.   ∎

Example 5.4   For the pair chart of Figure 5.28, the set of all MC's are derived using Procedure 5.4 as follows: Initially $L = \{123456\}$. From column 1 of the pair chart $S_1 = 35$ (i.e., $1 \not\sim 3$ and $1 \not\sim 5$). Therefore the set 123456 of L is decomposed into subsets 23456 (by eliminating 1) and 1246 (by eliminating both 3 and 5 which are contained in S_1). We then proceed to column 2 of the pair chart and find $S_2 = 4$. The set 23456 is decomposed into 3456 and 2356 and the set 1246 is decomposed into 126 and 146. The procedure continues by considering columns 3, 4, and 5 of the pair chart, as shown in Figure 5.30, resulting in the set of MC's $L = \{45, 34, 236, 256, 126, 14\}$. The circled sets are included as subsets of MC's and hence have been eliminated.   ∎

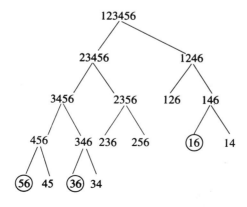

Figure 5.30   Derivation of maximal compatibles

Procedure 5.4 works by starting with all states together in one set and decomposing this set in all possible ways so as not to violate any incompatible pair of the pair chart. There exists a dual procedure that works by starting with the individual states and *composing* compatible sets by combining sets in accordance with the compatible pairs of the pair chart. In general Procedure 5.4 is computationally more efficient if the pair chart has relatively few incompatible pairs whereas the dual procedure is more efficient if the pair chart has relatively few compatible pairs.

For completely specified state tables the compatibility relation is transitive. Thus for completely specified state tables the compatibility relation is an equivalence relation,* which partitions the set of states into disjoint subsets. As we have seen previously in this case the procedure for finding MC's is greatly simplified.

We have thus developed a procedure for generating all MC's for a given state table M. Since for the reduced state table M', each row will correspond to a compatible set of states of M, each row of M' will correspond either to an MC or a subset of an MC of M. We must now consider the problem of choosing a minimal set of compatibles to define the reduced machine. As we have seen for completely specified machines the set of MC's defined a partition of the states of M and the set of all MC's defined the minimal state reduced machine. However for incompletely specified machines the problem is much more difficult.

5.3.3.2 Selecting a Minimal Set of Compatible Sets

If a table M is to be reduced to M', each row (state) of M' must correspond to a compatible set of states of M. It might seem plausible at first to select any minimal set of MC's which covers all states of M as the states of M'. However the problem is considerably more difficult than that. Consider the state table of Figure 5.31(a) whose MC's are computed in Figure 5.31(c). A minimal covering set of MC's is 12, 34. Suppose covering table M' has two states, A covering 1 and 2 of M and B covering 3 and 4 of M. We determine the next state entries of M' by examining the behavior of the corresponding states of M. Thus for input 0, the next state entries of 1 and 2 are 2 and 1 respectively, so the next state entry of A must cover 2 and 1, hence $N(A, 0) = A$. Similarly, the next state entries of 3 and 4 for input 0 are 2 and 1 respectively, so $N(B, 0) = A$ since A covers 1 and 2. For input 1 the next state entries of 1 and 2 are 3 and 1 respectively, so $N(A, 1)$ must be a state that covers both 3 and 1. However neither A nor B covers both 3 and 1 and hence M' cannot be specified so as to cover M.

Thus it is not sufficient to select as states of the covering table M' a minimal cover of states of M. If a row of M' corresponds to the compatible set C_i, then

---

*A relation R is an equivalence relation if it is *reflexive* (xRx for all x), *symmetric* (xRy if and only if yRx for all x, y), and *transitive* (if xRy and yRz, then xRz for all x, y, z).

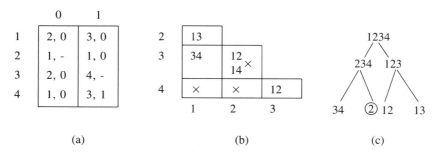

Figure 5.31 (a) State table (b) Pair chart (c) Derivation of maximal compatibles

the entry in the column I_j of M' must correspond to some compatible set C_m such that the next state entries in column I_j of all states in C_i must be contained in C_m.

Let C_i be a set of compatible states, and let $C_{ij} = \{q_k \mid q_k = N(q_m, I_j)$ for all $q_m \in C_i\}$. That is, C_{ij} is the set of next state entries of the states in C_i for input I_j. We say that the set C_{ij} is *implied* by the set C_i. A set of compatible sets $C = \{C_1, C_2, \ldots\}$ is *closed* if for every $C_i \in C$, all the implied sets C_{ij} are contained in some element of C for all I_j. *The set of compatible sets corresponding to the rows (states) of M' must be closed.* The problem of minimizing the number of states in a state table M reduces to the problem of finding a closed set C of compatible states, of minimal cardinality, which covers every state of M, i.e., a *minimal closed cover*. Note that the set of all MC's is *closed* but is not necessarily of minimal cardinality for a general state table.

For completely specified tables the problem of selecting a minimal closed cover is easily resolved. Since the MC's are disjoint for completely specified tables, the minimal cover consists of all MC's. Furthermore, the set of all MC's is always closed since *all* compatibility sets are contained in some MC.

Unfortunately selecting a minimal closed cover for incompletely specified tables is a much more difficult problem. For small tables one effective approach involves a branch and bound procedure. An initial solution is found (using heuristic approaches which will be demonstrated shortly). If this solution contains k states we then search for a solution with $k-1$ states, or prove that no such solution exists, using branching procedures and computation of lower bounds. For small tables this approach converges very rapidly. To ensure rapid determination of minimality it is desirable to have an easily computed lower bound. Obviously a lower bound on the number of sets in a minimal closed cover is the number of sets in a minimal cover. Although this lower bound cannot always be achieved it frequently can be used to significantly reduce the exhaustive branching required for verification of minimality.

The initial solution can be obtained with the use of an *implication graph* which represents the implications between MC's. The graph has a node for each MC

C_i and an edge from an MC to a node representing each compatibility set C_{ij} implied by C_i.*

Consider the table of Figure 5.26 whose MC's were derived in Example 5.4. The implication graph is shown in Figure 5.32. From this graph we see that all MC's which cover state 2 have edges to 45.

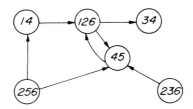

Figure 5.32   An implication graph

Therefore 45 is part of any closed cover. Since 45 has an edge to 126, that MC is also part of any closed cover. The edge from 126 to 34 implies that 34 is also part of any closed cover. We have now selected the three MC's 45, 126, 34, which is a closed set (no edges from any of these nodes to nodes not in the set) and is a cover (all six states are included in these three sets). Furthermore the smallest cover of the MC's must have at least three MC's since no set of two MC's covers all states. Thus these three MC's define a *minimal* closed cover which can be used to define a minimal reduced state table as shown in Figure 5.33. This table has one column for each column of the original table M and a row

	I_1	I_2	I_3
(126) A	$B, 0$	$C, 0$	$A, -$
(34) B	$C, 1$	$A, 1$	$-, 0$
(45) C	$A, -$	$A, 1$	$A, -$

Figure 5.33   Reduced state table

---

*It is possible that some C_{ij} is a subset of more than one MC. In this case a hyperarc (representing a logical OR) connects the node to all nodes containing C_{ij}.

(state) corresponding to each MC in the minimal closed cover. The entries in the table are determined as follows:

For a state corresponding to compatible set C_i and for input I_j the set of next state entries implied by C_i for input I_j is contained in some compatible set C_k within the selected cover (since the chosen cover is closed). Therefore the next state entry of row C_i, column I_j is defined to be C_k. Similarly the output associated with this transition can be defined to be the same as the specified outputs for the corresponding transitions in the original table.

In this example the initial solution obtained equaled the predicted lower bound. This is not always the case. Consider the table and implication graph of Figure 5.34. Since all three nodes are contained in a cycle, the only closed cover contains all three MC's. However this does not match the lower bound since 123, 345 is a cover of two sets. Although this cover is not closed (because of the edge from 345 to 135), if we consider subsets of MC's there are two other possible

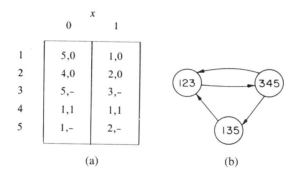

(a)   (b)

Figure 5.34 (a) A sequential machine (b) MC implication graph

two set covers {12, 345} and {123, 45}. The second one is closed and hence defines a minimal closed cover (Figure 5.35). This happened because the subset 45 did not have the same implications as the containing MC 345 and the covering of state 3 by 345 was superfluous since it was also covered by node 123. Thus we see that subsets of MC's must also be considered. In this example the search

	x	
	0	1
(123) A	B, 0	A, 0
(45) B	A, 1	A, 1

Figure 5.35 Reduced state table

for a minimal closed cover was simplified by the small number of MC's and by the fact that the lower bound could be achieved. More complex tables or cases, when the lower bound can not be achieved, may require more sophisticated branching techniques to ensure consideration and/or elimination of all possibilities as the following example illustrates.

Example 5.5   Consider the state table of Figure 5.36(a). The implication graph is shown in Figure 5.36(b). The lower bound in this case is three MC's for a cover. Since all five nodes of the implication graph are contained in a cycle the

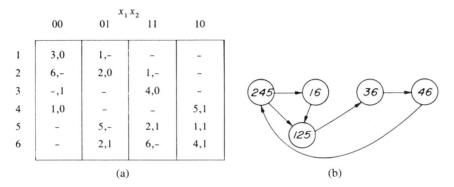

	00	01	11	10
1	3,0	1,-	–	–
2	6,-	2,0	1,-	–
3	-,1	–	4,0	–
4	1,0	–	–	5,1
5	–	5,-	2,1	1,1
6	–	2,1	6,-	4,1

(a)   (b)

Figure 5.36   (a) A sequential machine (b) MC implication graph

smallest closed cover determined from this graph has all five MC's. We now can search for a solution with four compatibility sets by considering subsets of MC's. Specifically we look for a subset which will have fewer implications (enabling the removal of an outgoing edge) but will satisfy all implications of incoming edges. Due to this second factor only the three state nodes 125 and 245 need be considered. Examining node 125 we see if we can select a subset which eliminates the edge to 36 and still satisfies the implication from 245. Subsets 15 and 25 accomplish the first objective but only subset 12 accomplishes the second objective. Applying the same general principles to node 245 we see the implication from 46 can be satisfied by subset 45 which also eliminates the edge to 16. In this way we obtain a closed cover with four sets (45, 125, 36, 46). However this still does not match the lower bound so we must prove that no solution exists with three sets. This can be shown using another branching technique. Since state 3 is only contained in one compatible set any closed cover will either have compatibility set 36 or else will have state 3 as an individual state. The only three set covers in which 3 is an individual state are (125, 46, 3), or (16, 245, 3), both of which are not closed, so this possibility is eliminated. If the closed cover contains set 36 by implication it must also contain 46 and 45 or 245. Thus at least four sets are required for a closed cover with element

36. We have thus proved (by exhaustive elimination) that the solution obtained previously is optimal. The reduced table is shown in Figure 5.37.

		x_1x_2			
		00	01	11	10
125	A	B, 0	A, 0	A, 1	A, 1
36	B	-, 1	A, 1	C, 0	C/D, 1
46	C	A, 0	A, 1	B/C, -	D, 1
45	D	A, 0	A/D, -	A, 1	A, 1

Figure 5.37   Reduced state table

Note that the compatible set implied by state B (corresponding to 36) and input 10 is state 4 which is contained in C or D. Thus the state entry of B for input 10 could be specified as C or D, which is denoted in the table of Figure 5.37 as C/D. Similarly, the next state entry for state D, input 01 is A/D.   ∎

The techniques presented in the preceding examples are adequate for small tables. For solution of larger tables an integer programming formulation can be used. This approach is based on defining the concept of *prime compatible sets* from which the minimal closed cover can be selected. Once the prime compatibles of a state table are determined, the next step is to obtain a minimal covering set of the prime compatibles. The problem can be formulated as a linear integer programming problem [8,9].

5.3.4   Sequential Circuit Realization

The problem of deriving a sequential circuit to realize a sequential machine specified by a state table is a well defined and relatively simple process. We assume that the type of memory elements to be used in the circuit has been specified. The first step in the sequential circuit derivation is called the *state (variable) assignment problem*. Since the memory elements are two-state devices, a binary variable y_i, called a *state variable*, is used to denote the state of each memory element. For a set of state variables if each variable is specified to be 0 or 1, a *state (variable) coding* is obtained. For a set of k state variables $y = (y_1, y_2, \ldots, y_k)$ there are 2^k different codings. The assignment of these codings to the states of a sequential machine is called a *state assignment*. A state assignment must assign at least one coding to each state and no coding can be assigned to more than one state. Thus an n-state machine requires at least $\lceil \log_2 n \rceil$ memory elements, where $\lceil x \rceil$ is the smallest integer $\geq x$, in order to obtain n distinct codings. A state assignment in which one coding is assigned to each state is called a *unicode assignment*.

If the next state of the flip-flop y_i is represented by Y_i, then since the next state depends on the present state which is represented by a coding of $\mathbf{y} = (y_1, \ldots, y_k)$, and the input which is represented by a coding of $\mathbf{x} = (x_1, \ldots, x_m)$ (the input variables) then $Y_i = f_i(\mathbf{x},\mathbf{y})$, $1 \leqq i \leqq k$. Similarily if the output variable set is $\mathbf{Z} = (z_1, z_2, \ldots, z_q)$ then $z_i = g_i(\mathbf{x},\mathbf{y})$, $1 \leqq i \leqq q$ for a Mealy machine and $z_i = g_i(\mathbf{y})$, $1 \leqq i \leqq q$ for a Moore machine.

A synchronous sequential circuit can be schematically represented as shown in Figure 5.38 [10]. The basic elements in a synchronous circuit are the clock to ensure proper operation, the memory elements to represent the state, and the

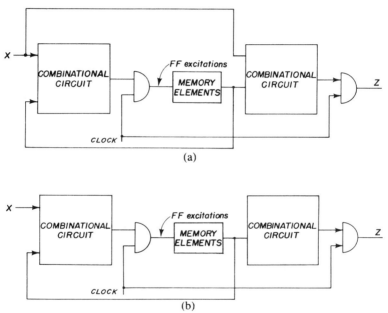

Figure 5.38   Schematic representation of synchronous sequential circuit (a) Mealy model (b) Moore model

combinational circuit to generate the flip-flop excitation inputs Y_E and the circuit outputs z_i. Once the state assignment has been specified, the derivation of this combinational logic will complete the sequential circuit design. To generate the flip-flop excitation logic it is necessary to determine the value of Y_E for every state transition. This problem can be divided into two parts, the determination of the next state vector Y for each transition, and the determination of the excitations Y_E from Y. The next values of the state variables, denoted by Y_i, can be obtained directly from the state table. It is convenient to represent Y_i on a Karnaugh map in the variables $\mathbf{y} = (y_1, \ldots, y_k)$ and $\mathbf{x} = (x_1, \ldots, x_n)$ (this simplifies the subsequent problem of deriving the logic for the combinational circuit). This map, which specifies the set of functions $Y = f_1(\mathbf{x},\mathbf{y})$, is called a *Y-map*. The transfer of information from the state table to the Y-map is simplified if each row of the Y-map represents a state variable coding and each column represents an input variable coding. The entry in a row of the Y-map corresponding to a coding for state q_i and input I_k of a sequential machine M, must correspond to the coding for $N\,(q_i,\,I_k)$. If $2^k > n$, some codings may not be assigned to any state. The entries in the Y-map for the corresponding rows are left unspecified. Since the outputs are also functions of the inputs $\mathbf{x}$ and the state variables $\mathbf{y}$, it is possible to use the same Karnaugh map to represent the functions $z_i = g_i\,(\mathbf{x},\mathbf{y})$. The resulting map is called a *Y-Z map*.

Example 5.6 Consider the sequential machine M of Figure 5.39(a). We shall derive a sequential circuit realization using T flip-flops as memory devices. The four state machine requires two state variables y_1, y_2, which are randomly assigned as shown in Figure 5.39(a). Using the state table and state variable assignment we will derive the necessary combinational logic functions to generate

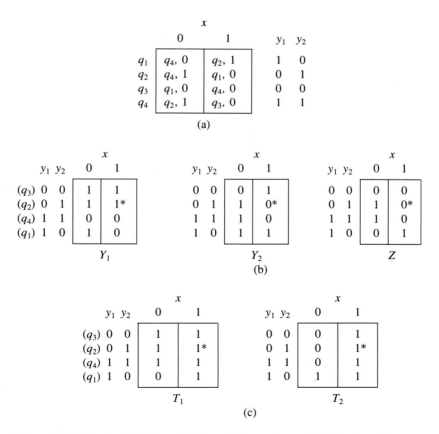

Figure 5.39 (a) A state table and state variable assignment (b)The Y and Z maps (c)The flip-flop excitation maps.

the output Z and the flip-flop excitations T_1 and T_2. The first step is to derive the Karnaugh maps shown in Figure 5.39(b). These maps plot the output Z and the flip-flop next values Y_1, Y_2 as functions of x, y_1, y_2. On each map each row corresponds to a state and each column to an input column of M. Note that the order of the rows in the Karnaugh map will not in general be the same as in the state table. This order is determined by the state assignment. The entries in the Karnaugh map are easily derived. For example let us consider row $y_1 = 0$, $y_2 = 1$ and column 1. This corresponds to state q_2 and input 1. From the state table the next state should be q_1, corresponding to $Y_1 = 1$, $Y_2 = 0$, and the output should be 0. These correspond to the entries indicated by asterisks in row $y_1 = 0$, $y_2 = 1$ and column 1 of the three Karnaugh maps. Using the T flip-flop excitation matrix of Figure 5.14, we can now derive the Karnaugh maps for the flip-flop excitations T_1 and T_2 shown in Figure 5.39(c). The entry in row $y_1 = 0$, $y_2 = 1$ and column 1 is derived as follows. From the Y-maps of Figure 5.39(b) we see that flip-flop y_1 must become set (i.e., $y_1 = 0$, $Y_1 = 1$). From the excitation map of the T flip-flop, this transition requires $T_1 = 1$. Similarly flip-flop y_2 must be reset (i.e., $y_2 = 1$, $Y_2 = 0$) which also requires $T_2 = 1$. The other entries of the maps of Figure 5.39(c) are derived in a similar manner. From the Karnaugh maps of T_1, T_2 and Z the following sum of products expressions are derived using the procedures presented in Chapter 3.

$$T_1 = x + \bar{y}_1 + y_2$$
$$T_2 = x + y_1 \bar{y}_2$$
$$z = \bar{x} y_2 + x y_1 \bar{y}_2$$

■

In Example 5.6 the Karnaugh maps used had four rows and two columns (rather than two rows and four columns) to make them similar to the state table and thus facilitate the representation of the state table transitions. With some experience it is possible to represent the transitions of several state variables on a single Karnaugh map as illustrated in the following example.

Example 5.7   For the state table and state assignment of Figure 5.40, the Y-Z map can be represented in the form of a Karnaugh map (Figure 5.41(a)) with eight rows, one for each of the state codings, and two columns for the inputs

	x			State Assignment		
	0	1		y_1	y_2	y_3
q_1	q_2, 0	q_3, 1	1	0	0	0
q_2	q_1, 0	q_2, 0	2	0	0	1
q_3	q_5, 1	q_3, 1	3	1	0	1
q_4	q_4, 1	q_5, 1	4	1	0	0
q_5	q_4, 0	q_1, 0	5	1	1	1

(a)   (b)

Figure 5.40   State table and state variable assignment

	y_1	y_2	y_3	x 0	1
(q_1)	0	0	0		
(q_2)	0	0	1		
	0	1	1		
	0	1	0		
	1	1	0		
(q_5)	1	1	1		
(q_3)	1	0	1		
(q_4)	1	0	0		

	y_1	y_2	y_3	x 0	1
(q_1)	0	0	0	0010	1011
(q_2)	0	0	1	0000	0010
	0	1	1	----	----
	0	1	0	----	----
	1	1	0	----	----
(q_5)	1	1	1	1000	0000
(q_3)	1	0	1	1111	1011
(q_4)	1	0	0	1001	1111

$$Y_1, Y_2, Y_3, Z$$

Figure 5.41 Y-Z matrix

$x = 0$, $x = 1$. The state to which each coding is assigned is indicated in parentheses on the left side of the Karnaugh map. The entries of the map can be determined from the corresponding state table transitions and state assignment. For instance the entry in row 100 (which is assigned to state q_4) and column 1 is the coding for the state $N (q_4, 1) = q_5$ which is 111, and the associated transition output $z = 1$. For those codings which are not assigned to any state (010,011,110) the entries are unspecified. The completed Y-Z map is shown in Figure 5.41(b). ∎

The Y- (and Y-Z) map specifies the next value for each state variable Y_i for each transition. The required flip-flop excitations for the corresponding transition (from y_i to Y_i) can be determined from the Y map and the transition table of the particular memory element type as specified in Figures 5.7, 5.13–5.15. The Karnaugh map specifying these excitations as functions of the variable sets **y** and **x** is called the *excitation map*.

For the different types of flip-flops described in the previous section the excitation inputs are determined from the value of Y_i and y_i for a given transition. For D flip-flops (delay elements) the excitation map is identical to the Y map, since $Y_i = D_i$. For T flip-flops, $T_i = 1$ for all transitions in which y_i changes value (i.e., the next value, Y_i, is not equal to the present value y_i) and $T_i = 0$ for all transitions in which $Y_i = y_i$. For SR flip-flops $S_i = 1$ and $R_i = 0$ for all transitions in which $y_i = 0$ and $Y_i = 1$, $S_i = 0$ and $R_i = 1$ for all transitions in which $y_i = 1$ and $Y_i = 0$. If $y_i = Y_i = 0$, then $S_i = 0$ and R_i is unspecified, and if $y_i = Y_i = 1$, S_i is unspecified and $R_i = 0$. For JK flip-flops if $y_i = 0$ and $Y_i = 1$, $J_i = 1$ and K_i is unspecified, if $y_i = Y_i = 0$, $J_i = 0$ and K_i is unspecified, if $y_i = 1$ and $Y_i = 0$, then J_i is unspecified and $K_i = 1$, and if $y_i = Y_i = 1$, then J_i is unspecified and $K_i = 0$.

The Y-map of Figure 5.41(b) is transformed into the excitation map of Figure 5.42 assuming T flip-flops.* The entry in row 111 and column 0 of the Y-map has

---

*In this map all three excitation functions have been specified on a single Karnaugh map. Since this map will be used to derive minimal two level realizations of the functions, it may be more convenient for inexperienced designers to represent each function on a separate Karnaugh map.

next state coding 100. For this transition, the value of state variable y_1 stays fixed at 1 ($y_1 = Y_1 = 1$), therefore T_1 must be 0. Similarly $y_2 = 1$ and $Y_2 = 0$ implies $T_2 = 1$, and $y_3 = 1$ and $Y_3 = 0$ implies $T_3 = 1$. The corresponding entry (row 111, column 0) of the map of Figure 5.42 specifies these excitations.

			x	
y_1	y_2	y_3	0	1
0	0	0	001	101
0	0	1	001	000
0	1	1	- - -	- - -
0	1	0	- - -	- - -
1	1	0	- - -	- - -
1	1	1	011	111
1	0	1	010	000
1	0	0	000	011

$$T_1, T_2, T_3$$

Figure 5.42 T flip-flop excitation matrix

The other entries are derived in a similar manner. We derive minimal sum of products expressions for each of the excitations considered individually, resulting in

$$T_1 = x \bar{y}_1 \bar{y}_3 + x y_2$$
$$T_2 = y_2 + \bar{x} y_1 y_3 + x y_1 \bar{y}_3$$
$$T_3 = y_2 + x \bar{y}_3 + \bar{x} \bar{y}_1.$$

If sharing is permitted T_1, T_2, and T_3 can be considered as a multi-output function to derive minimal cost solutions for the set of excitation functions.

The output function z does not depend on the type of memory elements being used. This function can be determined from the Y-Z-map of Figure 5.41(b) as

$$z = y_1 \bar{y}_2 + x \bar{y}_3.$$

The excitation maps for SR flip-flops and JK flip-flops corresponding to the Y-map of Figure 5.41(b) are shown in Figures 5.43 and 5.44 respectively with minimal sum of products expressions for each of the excitations.

If delay elements or D-flip-flops are used the excitation map is identical to the Y-map of Figure 5.41(b) and the excitation equations are:

$$D_1 = \bar{x} y_1 + y_1 \bar{y}_2 + x\bar{y}_3$$
$$D_2 = \bar{x} y_1 \bar{y}_2 y_3 + x y_1 \bar{y}_3$$
$$D_3 = \bar{y}_1 \bar{y}_3 + x \bar{y}_2 + y_1 \bar{y}_2 y_3$$

Note that the more complex JK flip-flop has much simpler excitation functions than the T and D flip-flops.

y_1	y_2	y_3	x 0	1
0	0	0	001	101
0	0	1	000	00-
0	1	1	- - -	- - -
0	1	0	- - -	- - -
1	1	0	- - -	- - -
1	1	1	-00	000
1	0	1	-1-	-0-
1	0	0	-00	-11

$$S_1, S_2, S_3$$

$$S_1 = x\bar{y}_3$$
$$S_2 = xy_1\bar{y}_3 + \bar{x}y_1\bar{y}_2y_3$$
$$S_3 = \bar{y}_1\bar{y}_3 + x\bar{y}_2$$

(a)

y_1	y_2	y_3	x 0	1
0	0	0	- -0	0-0
0	0	1	- -1	- -0
0	1	1	- - -	- - -
0	1	0	- - -	- - -
1	1	0	- - -	- - -
1	1	1	011	111
1	0	1	000	0-0
1	0	0	0- -	000

$$R_1, R_2, R_3$$

$$R_1 = xy_2$$
$$R_2 = y_2$$
$$R_3 = y_2 + \bar{x}\bar{y}_1y_3$$

(b)

Figure 5.43 *SR* flip-flop excitation matrix

y_1	y_2	y_3	x 0	1
0	0	0	001	101
0	0	1	00-	00-
0	1	1	- - -	- - -
0	1	0	- - -	- - -
1	1	0	- - -	- - -
1	1	1	- - -	- - -
1	0	1	-1-	-0-
1	0	0	-00	-11

$$J_1, J_2, J_3$$

$$J_1 = x\bar{y}_3$$
$$J_2 = xy_1\bar{y}_3 + \bar{x}y_1y_3$$
$$J_3 = x + \bar{y}_1$$

(a)

y_1	y_2	y_3	x 0	1
0	0	0	- - -	- - -
0	0	1	- -1	- -0
0	1	1	- - -	- - -
0	1	0	- - -	- - -
1	1	0	- - -	- - -
1	1	1	011	111
1	0	1	0-0	0-0
1	0	0	0- -	0- -

$$K_1, K_2, K_3$$

$$K_1 = xy_2$$
$$K_2 = 1$$
$$K_3 = y_2 + \bar{x}\bar{y}_1$$

(b)

Figure 5.44 *JK* flip-flop excitation matrix

With some experience it becomes relatively easy to derive the flip-flop excitation maps directly from the state table and state assignment, without going through the intermediate step of generating the Y-maps.

In the previous examples the state assignment was randomly selected. As we shall now see, there are many possibilities for this assignment, and the choice may have a significant impact on the complexity of the resulting sequential circuit.

5.3.4.1   *State Assignment*

A valid state assignment for a state table M must associate a unique coding in the state variables $y_1, y_2, \ldots, y_k$ with each state of M. Using S_0 binary state variables, the total number of codings available is 2^{S_0}. Hence if M has n states, S_0 must be such that $2^{S_0} \geqq n$. This condition can be rewritten as $S_0 \geqq \lceil \log_2 n \rceil$ where $\lceil x \rceil$ is the smallest integer $\geqq x$. The following table specifies the number of state variables required for various values of n. Using S_0 state variables the

Number of States	Number of State Variables Required
2	1
$3 \leqq n \leqq 4$	2
$5 \leqq n \leqq 8$	3
$9 \leqq n \leqq 16$	4
.	.
.	.
.	.
$2^{i-1} + 1 \leqq n \leqq 2^i$	i

encoding of n states can be done in many ways [11]. The total number of unicode state assignments is

$$\binom{2^{S_0}}{n} n! = 2^{S_0}!/(2^{S_0} - n)! \quad \text{where } i! = \prod_{j=1}^{i} j$$

which corresponds to selecting n of the 2^{S_0} codes in all ways and assigning them to the n states in all possible ways. However some of these state assignments are effectively identical in that they lead to identical circuit realizations. For example consider the state assignments of Figure 5.45. State Assignment 2 can be derived from State Assignment 1 by interchanging the variables ($y_2' = y_1$, $y_1' = y_2$). Of course this does not alter the logical complexity of the circuit. Similarly each variable of Assignment 3 corresponds to the complement of a

State Assignment 1			State Assignment 2			State Assignment 3		
State	y_1	y_2	State	y_1'	y_2'	State	y_1''	y_2''
q_1	0	0	q_1	0	0	q_1	1	1
q_2	0	1	q_2	1	0	q_2	1	0
q_3	1	0	q_3	0	1	q_3	0	1
q_4	1	1	q_4	1	1	q_4	0	0

Figure 5.45   Three 4-state assignments

variable of State Assignment 1 ($y_1'' = \bar{y}_1$, $y_2'' = \bar{y}_2$). Assuming the excitation function for each variable is realized as a separate minimal two level circuit, the complexity will not be altered by complementing a variable. Under these assumptions two State Assignments A and B are equivalent if each variable of A is identical to, or the complement of, a variable of B. (If we assume that the excitation functions will be considered as a set, and a shared logic two level realization derived, then Assignments A and B are equivalent if all variables of A are identical to variables of B or all variables of A are the complements of variables of B).

For a unicode assignment with S_0 state variables there are $S_0!$ permutations of the variables and 2^{S_0} ways of complementing the set of S_0 variables. Thus it can be shown [11] that the number of intrinsically different state assignments is

$$\frac{2^{S_0}!/(2^{S_0} - n)!}{S_0! 2^{S_0}} = \frac{(2^{S_0} - 1)!}{S_0!(2^{S_0} - n)!}$$

The table of Figure 5.46 shows the number of state assignments for different values of n.

n	S_0	Number of State Assignments
4	2	3
5	3	140
8	3	840
9	4	$>10^6$

Figure 5.46   Number of state assignments

In general different state assignments will lead to logic realizations which may vary considerably in complexity [12,13]. Furthermore the determination of the state assignment which leads to the most economical realization will be influenced by the type of memory elements being utilized. Thus for the state table of Figure 5.47, and the State Assignments A and B, if T flip-flops are used as memory elements, Assignment A leads to the excitation functions

	x		State Assignment A		State Assignment B	
	0	1	y_1	y_2	y_1'	y_2'
q_1	q_3	q_2	0	0	0	0
q_2	q_4	q_1	0	1	1	1
q_3	q_1	q_3	1	0	1	0
q_4	q_2	q_3	1	1	0	1

Figure 5.47   A state table and two state assignments

$$T_1 = \bar{x}$$
$$T_2 = x(\bar{y}_1 + y_2)$$

while Assignment B leads to the excitation functions

$$T_{1'} = \bar{x} + \bar{y}_1' + y_2'$$
$$T_{2'} = x(\bar{y}_1' + y_2')$$

Therefore Assignment A leads to the more economical logic realization. However if D-flip-flops are used as memory elements the respective excitation functions are

$$D_1 = \bar{x}\,\bar{y}_1 + x\,y_1$$
$$D_2 = \bar{x}\,y_2 + x\,\bar{y}_1\,\bar{y}_2$$
$$D_{1'} = \bar{y}_1' + x\,\bar{y}_2'$$
$$D_{2'} = \bar{x}\,y_2' + x\,\bar{y}_1'\,\bar{y}_2'$$

and Assignment B leads to the more economical realization.

For tables of four or fewer states there are only three different (non-equivalent) state assignments, so all assignments can be evaluated before selecting one. However for five states there are 140 different state assignments and this number rises rapidly to more than one million for 9-state tables. It is thus apparent that exhaustive evaluation is not a feasible solution to the problem of deriving a state assignment which leads to the simplest excitation logic. This *state assignment problem* is very difficult and no completely effective solution procedure has been discovered. An algebra of partitions and set systems has been developed which can be effectively utilized to find good state assignments for relatively small tables [14,15]. As with combinational circuits the importance of the component minimization problems has been reduced by the advent of MSI and LSI.

We shall now consider some MSI components commonly used in sequential circuits.

5.3.5 MSI Sequential Components

As with combinational components, some sequential components occur with great frequency and can be considered as basic modules. Typically these involve a set of bits which constitute a word. The flip-flops used to store this word form a *register* and the element performs similar or identical logical operations on each bit of the word.

5.3.5.1 *Registers*

A (k-bit) register is a set of (k) flip-flops which is used to store a (k-bit) word. The flip-flops are ordered and usually controlled by common signals including a Clock, Clear, and Set which allow all bits to be cleared, set, or store independent inputs simultaneously. To avoid the necessity of clock signal restrictions, master-slave flip-flops are usually employed. Figure 5.48 shows a 3-bit register composed of *SR* flip-flops.

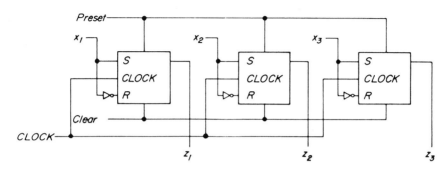

Figure 5.48 A 3-bit register

5.3.5.2 *Shift Registers*

Frequently in digital circuits it is desired to shift the contents of a register either left or right. In Chapter 2 we saw that multiplication of a binary number by 2^k could be accomplished by shifting the number to the left (assuming the leftmost bit is the most significant bit) k positions and shifting in 0's in the least significant position. A *unidirectional* shift register can shift in only one direction while a *bidirectional* shift register can shift in both directions. The simplest type of shift register consists of a linear array of K master-slave flip-flops each one of which is connected to its right (or left) neighbor. All flip-flops are controlled by a common CLOCK. A single input x is used to enter data in the leftmost flip-flop and a single output Z is available from the rightmost flip-flop. The shift register may be set to any state by a sequence of k successive inputs and shifts. This is referred to as *serial input*. Such a shift register is shown in Figure 5.49. More sophisticated shift registers may have the ability to shift in both directions, have parallel input and output capability, and be able to be preset or cleared. An appropriate set of control signals is required to specify the desired behavior at any instant of time. A variant of shifting is *rotation* in which the contents of the flip-flops are shifted to the right and the contents of the rightmost cell are moved

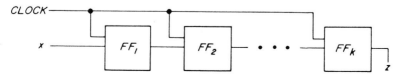

Figure 5.49 A shift register

into the leftmost cell (right rotation), or the shifting is to the left with the leftmost cell contents moved into the rightmost cell (left rotation). Rotation can be easily implemented by connecting the serial output signal to the serial input signal. A general shift register is represented in Figure 5.50. The control signals C_1 and C_2 determine one of four possible types of functional behavior for the element, parallel load (the values of the register flip-flops are determined from the inputs $A_1, \ldots, A_n$), shift left (with the value of Q_n set to the value of A_{n+1}) shift right (with the value of q_1 set to the value A_0), or clear (reset the register).

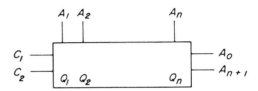

Figure 5.50   A general shift register

5.3.5.3   Counters

A counter is another common type of sequential circuit which in effect counts modulo k input pulses (or input changes) on some input by cycling through a sequence of states $q_0, q_1, \ldots, q_{k-1}$ in order. Such a circuit can be described by the canonical k-state sequential machine shown in Figure 5.51.

	x	
	0	1
q_0	q_0	q_1
q_1	q_1	q_2
q_2	q_2	q_3
$\vdots$	$\vdots$	$\vdots$
q_{k-2}	q_{k-2}	q_{2-1}
q_{k-1}	q_{k-1}	q_0

Figure 5.51   State table for a modulo k counter

For the special case where $k = 2^p$ a particularly simple realization of this device can be obtained by associating the k-bit binary coding corresponding to i with state q_i. Using T flip-flops's (of a master-slave variety) as memory elements, and a state assignment of this type, a modulo 2^k counter consists of k flip-flops with excitations defined by

$$T_i = x \cdot \prod_{j=1}^{i-1} y_j \text{ for } 1 < i \leq k$$

$$T_1 = x$$

Thus this state assignment leads to the modular realization of Figure 5.52 which can be rearranged as a modified shift register as shown in Figure 5.52(b). (Similar realizations with other types of flip-flops can be obtained.) This type of counter

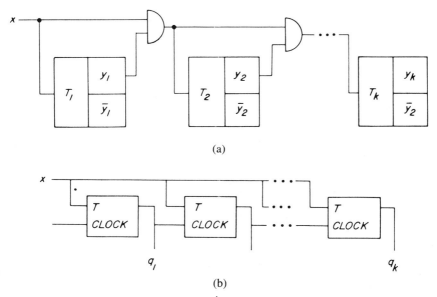

(a)

(b)

Figure 5.52 (a) Realization of a modulo k counter (b) Modified shift register realization

is called a *ripple* counter because of the manner in which the output of each flip-flop ripples to successive flip-flops. Ripple counters have the advantage of modularity (i.e., bigger counters can be constructed by adding identical modules to the linear array) but are *asynchronous* in nature since the operating speed is proportional to k, the number of flip-flops. By realizing the excitation logic for each flip-flop as a single AND gate (instead of a chain of AND gates), the operational speed becomes independent of k (and hence the counter is called *synchronous*), but it is no longer modular in the aforementioned sense of having identical modules.

More complex counting devices frequently have several different modes of operation including the ability to count up or down and to be initialized by a parallel load or clear. A general counter of this type is represented in Figure 5.53. The value of the control signals C_1 and C_2 determine one of four possible types of functional behavior, INCREMENT, DECREMENT, Parallel Load (the reg-

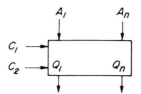

Figure 5.53   A general counter

ister is set to the value of the inputs $A_1, \ldots, A_n$), and Hold (the contents of the register are unchanged).

A slight modification of the basic circuit is required if $k \neq 2^p$. This basically involves clearing all flip-flops in the counter when the state is q_{k-1}. The circuit of Figure 5.54 illustrates the design of a *decade* (i.e., modulo 10) counter, where E is an enable signal.

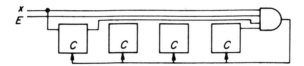

Figure 5.54   A decade counter realization

5.3.5.4   Buses

A *bus B* is essentially a set of connections used to transmit related bits of data which constitute a word from a source S to a destination D. If B can only transmit data from S to D it is called *unidirectional*, if it can also transmit data from D to S it is called *bidirectional*. Figure 5.55 illustrates a system with four registers and a bidirectional bus between each pair of registers. Buses generally do not

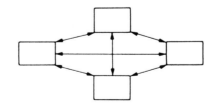

Figure 5.55   A system with dedicated buses

perform logical functions, but may contain logic elements which enable the transmission of data to be affected by control signals. Buses also require circuits for signal amplification. They may also have the capability of temporarily storing information in registers associated with the bus.

The buses of Figure 5.55 can only be used to transmit data between two specific registers. Such buses are said to be *dedicated*. Dedicated buses have the advantage of enabling data to be transmitted simultaneously between several pairs of registers. However $n(n-1)/2$ buses are required to connect n registers in all possible ways using dedicated buses. An alternative solution is the use of shared buses which can be used by a set of possible source registers and a set of possible destination registers. The use of shared buses is illustrated in Figure 5.56. Data cannot be simultaneously transmitted between different pairs of registers which share a bus. Access to the bus is effected through a switching circuit (such as a multiplexor) under the supervision of a control unit (which we shall consider in Chapter 7).

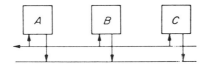

Figure 5.56   A system with shared buses

Complex digital systems (e.g., digital multipliers) can be designed from basic building blocks including registers, counters, sequential circuits which act as controllers, and modular combinational logic circuits. We shall consider such design procedures in Chapter 7.

5.4   LIMITATION OF FINITE STATE MACHINES

There exist computations which cannot be performed by finite state machines. These are computations which may require an arbitrarily large amount of memory. Consider the design of a machine whose input is a sequence of 0's and 1's. Starting in an initial state q_0 at time t_0 we want the output z at time $t \geqq t_0$ to be 1 if the number of 0-inputs from t_0 to t is equal to the number of 1-inputs from t_0 to t, and z should be 0 if the number of 0-inputs is not equal to the number of 1-inputs from t_0 to t. It is impossible to design a finite state sequential machine which can perform this computation. Informally this is because such a machine must remember at each instant of time t, the difference between the number of 0- and 1-inputs from t_0 to t. But this quantity may be arbitrarily large and hence such a machine must have a potentially unlimited amount of memory. Formally suppose machine M has k states and M performs the computation specified. If we apply the input sequence $I = \underbrace{00\ldots0}_{r \text{ times}}\ \underbrace{11\ldots1}_{r \text{ times}}$ to M in initial state q_0 the last output should be 1. Let us denote the state after the i-th input as q_i. Suppose $r > k$. Then q_r must be the same as q_j for some $j < r$ since the machine has k

$< r$ states and hence must enter a state cycle in which it cycles through a set of states periodically when given $r > k$ consecutive 0-inputs. Furthermore the input sequence $11. . .1$ applied to state q_r of M results in a 1-output. Therefore

$$\text{the input sequence } \mathbf{I}' = \underbrace{00. . .0}_{j \text{ times}} \quad \underbrace{\overset{r \text{ times}}{11. . .1}}_{r > j \text{ times}} \text{ applied to } M \text{ in initial state } q_0$$

results in the last output equal to 1. But this is incorrect since at that time the number of 0-inputs and 1-inputs are unequal. Hence M does not perform the desired computation.

   A different type of mathematical machine, called a *Turing machine*, has been formulated that is capable of performing this computation and also others which cannot be performed by finite state machines [16,17]. A Turing machine has a control unit with a finite number of states. The inputs to the machine are written on an arbitrarily long tape and the control can read from the tape and write on the tape and move in both directions on the tape. The operation of the Turing machine is as follows: Let the machine be initially in some state q_0 and read some input symbol x_i. On reading the input symbol, the control unit overwrites x_i with some symbol x_j, changes state to q_j and moves either to the right or left of the symbol just processed. Since the control unit has a finite number of states, a Turing machine can be described by a table similar to the state table. For every combination of input symbol (on the tape) and internal state of the control unit, the table specifies the next state, the symbol to be written on the tape and the direction of shift.

   Turing machines are used primarily for the study of computability and other aspects of the theory of computation. Such machines only represent theoretical models of computation.

REFERENCES

1. Mealy, G.H., "A Method for Synthesizing Sequential Circuits," *Bell System Technical Journal*, vol. 34, pp. 1045–1079, September, 1955.
2. Moore, E.F., "Gedanken-experiments on Sequential Machines," pp. 129–153, *Automata Studies*, Annals of Mathematical Studies, no. 34, Princeton University.
3. Cadden, W.J., "Equivalent Sequential Circuits," *IRE Transactions on Circuit Theory*, vol. CT-6, March, 1959.
4. Unger, S.H., *Asynchronous Sequential Switching Circuits*, John Wiley, New York, 1969.
5. Ginsburg, S., "A Synthesis Technique for Minimal State Sequential Machines," *IRE Trans. Electron. Computers*, vol. EC-8, no. 1, pp. 13–24, March, 1959.
6. Ginsburg, S., "On the Reduction of Superfluous States in a Sequential Machine," *J. Assoc. Computing Machinery*, vol. 6, pp. 259–282, April, 1959.
7. Paull, M.C., and S.H. Unger, "Minimizing the Number of States in Incompletely Specified Sequential Switching Functions," *IRE Trans. Electron. Computers*, vol. EC-8, pp. 356–366, September, 1959.
8. Grasselli, A., and F. Luccio, "A method for minimizing the number of internal states in incompletely specified sequential networks," *IEEE Trans. on Electronic Computers*, vol. EC-14, pp. 350–359, June, 1965.

9. Grasselli, A., and F. Luccio, "A Method for Combined Row-Column Reduction of Flow Tables," *IEEE Conf. Record 1966 Seventh Symposium Switching and Automata Theory*, pp. 136–147, October, 1966.

10. Huffman, D.A., "The Synthesis of Sequential Switching Circuits," *J. Franklin Institute*, vol. 257, pp. 161–190, Mach, 1954, pp. 275–303, April, 1954.

11. McCluskey, E.J., and S.H. Unger, "A Note on the Number of Internal Variable Assignments for Sequential Switching Circuits," *IRE Trans. on Electronic Computers*, vol. EC-8, pp. 439–440, December, 1959.

12. Armstrong, D.B., "A Programmed Algorithm for Assigning Internal Codes to Sequential Machines," *IRE Trans. Electronic Computers*, vol. EC-11, pp. 466–472, August, 1962.

13. Dolotta, T.A., and E.J. McCluskey, "The Coding of Internal States of Sequential Circuits," *IEEE Trans. on Electronic Computers*, vol. EC-13, pp. 549–562, October, 1964.

14. Hartmanis, J., "On the State Assignment Problem for Sequential Machines I," *IRE Trans. Electronic Computers*, vol. EC-10, pp. 157–165, June, 1961.

15. Hartmanis, J., and R.E. Stearns, *Algebraic Structure Theory of Sequential Machines*, Prentice-Hall Inc., Englewood Cliffs, N.J., 1966.

16. Hopcroft, J.E., and J.D. Ullman, *Formal Languages and Their Relation to Automata*, Addison-Wesley, Reading, Mass., 1969.

17. Turing, A.M., "On Computable Numbers with an Application to the Entscheidungs-problem," *Proc. London Math. Soc.*, vol. 42, pp. 230–236, 1936.

PROBLEMS

5.1 The circuit shown below is proposed for a new type of flip-flops. Derive its transition table and evaluate its usefulness compared with *D*, *RS*, *JK* flip-flops.

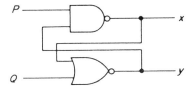

Figure 5.57 Problem 5.1

5.2 a) Derive a state table for the circuit of Figure 5.58. Assume all flip-flops are clocked.

   b) Derive a circuit from the state table of (a) using the same state assignment but using *SR* flip-flops as memory elements.

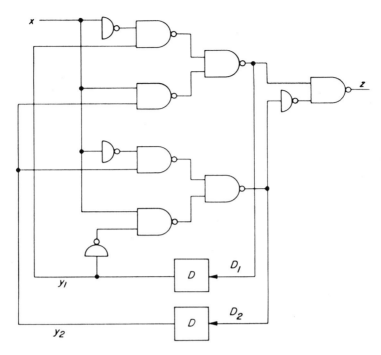

Figure 5.58   Problem 5.2

5.3   A sequential circuit for the state table of Figure 5.59 is to be constructed using D flip-flops as memory elements and one of the two state assignments shown. Which assignment is more economical in terms of hardware requirements? Assume two level sum of products logic.

	x		State Assign. #1		State Assign. #2	
	0	1	y_1	y_2	y_1	y_2
q_1	q_3, 0	q_2, 1	0	0	0	0
q_2	q_4, 1	q_1, 0	0	1	0	1
q_3	q_1, 0	q_4, 1	1	0	1	1
q_4	q_2, 1	q_3, 0	1	1	1	0

Figure 5.59   Problem 5.3

5.4   a) Derive a state table for the circuit of Figure 5.60. Assume all flip-flops are clocked.

   b) Give a word description of the sequential function realized by this circuit.

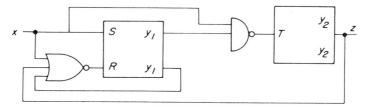

Figure 5.60   Problem 5.6

5.5   Derive a state table for the circuit of Figure 5.61.

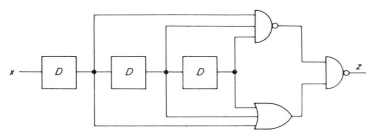

Figure 5.61   Problem 5.4

5.6   Analyze (i.e., derive a state table for) the synchronous sequential circuit of Figure 5.62.

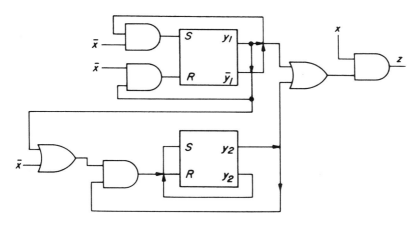

Figure 5.62   Problem 5.5

5.7 Reduce the following state table to a minimum state equivalent table.

	x	
	0	1
q_1	$q_3, 0$	$q_2, 1$
q_2	$q_3, 1$	$q_1, 1$
q_3	$q_5, 0$	$q_2, 1$
q_4	$q_6, 0$	$q_1, 0$
q_5	$q_1, 0$	$q_7, 1$
q_6	$q_4, 1$	$q_3, 1$
q_7	$q_5, 1$	$q_3, 1$

Figure 5.63   Problem 5.7

5.8 Derive a state table to operate as follows: there is one input x and one output z. The initial state ($t = 0$) is q_0. Let $U(t) = $ the number of 1-inputs to the circuit from $t = 0$ to t and $V(t) = $ the number of 0-inputs from $t = 0$ to t. The output at time t, should be 1 if and only if $V(t) - U(t) = 3k$ for k an integer, i.e., $V(t) - U(t) = \ldots -9, -6, -3, 0, 3, 6, 9, \ldots$. Reduce the table.

5.9 Using T flip-flops as memory devices design a sequential circuit to realize the following state table, using the state assignment shown to the right of the table. The combinational logic realizing the flip-flop excitation should be minimal two level sum of products.

	x		y_1	y_2
	0	1		
q_1	q_3	q_1	0	0
q_2	q_2	q_3	0	1
q_3	q_4	q_2	1	1
q_4	q_2	q_1	1	0

Figure 5.64   Problem 5.9

5.10 Design a circuit to operate as a counter with two control inputs C_1 and C_2. C_1 determines the modulus of the count and C_2 determines the increment. If $C_1 = 0$ the counter counts modulo 3 and if $C_1 = 1$ the counter counts modulo 4. If $C_2 = 0$ the counter increments by 1 at each count and if $C_2 = 1$ the counter decrements by 1 at each count.

5.11 Construct the state diagram for a machine with one input, x, one output, z, and $z = 1$ if the previous four inputs and the present input constitute a sequence of five symbols with exactly two 1's, three 0's and the first two symbols in the sequence are 00.

5.12 Derive a state table for the following circuit.

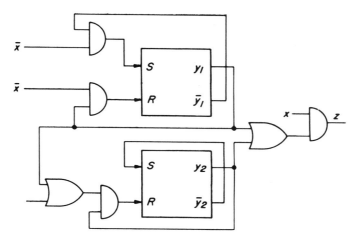

Figure 5.65 Problem 5.12

5.13 Construct a state table for a synchronous sequential machine having two inputs x_1 and x_2 and two outputs z_1 and z_2. The input data to x_1, x_2 consists of two n-bit numbers, n_1, n_2, which are input serially, bit by bit, most significant bit first. The output sequences should be serial bit by bit representations of $z_1 = \max(n_1, n_2)$, and $z_2 = \min(n_1, n_2)$.

5.14 Consider the sequential circuit of Figure 5.66. Obtain an equivalent circuit which requires less than half the number of gates.

5.15 Derive a state table for a sequential circuit which has one input x, and one output z. The initial state is q_0 and the first two outputs should be 0. After that, the output at time t is 1 if and only if the inputs at time t, $t-1$, $t-2$ contain exactly two 1-inputs and one 0-input. Reduce the table.

5.16 Reduce the state table of Figure 5.67 to an equivalent minimum state version.

5.17 a) Design a sequential circuit to operate as a constant multiplier as follows. The machine has one input x and one output z. If the input is interpreted as a serial representation of the number **x** (low order bits first) the

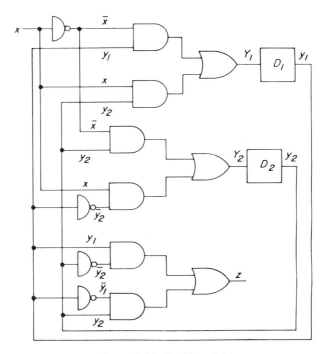

Figure 5.66   Problem 5.14

	x	
	0	1
q_1	q_5, 0	q_2, 1
q_2	q_6, 0	q_4, 0
q_3	q_5, 0	q_2, 1
q_4	q_6, 0	q_2, 0
q_5	q_3, 0	q_6, 1
q_6	q_2, 0	q_3, 0

Figure 5.67   Problem 5.16

output sequence should represent the number $2 \cdot x$ (low order bits first).

b) Same as above but output represents $3 \cdot x$.

5.18 Construct the state diagram for a machine with one input, x, one output z, and $z = 1$ if the previous four inputs and the present input constitute a sequence of five symbols with exactly three 1's, two 0's, and the first two symbols in the sequence are 11.

5.19 Design a sequential network using JK flip-flops with two control signal inputs x_1, x_2, which operates as specified below and counts modulo 8.

x_1x_2	Operation
0 0	No change of state
0 1	Acts as counter, increments by 2
1 1	Acts as counter, increments by 1
1 0	Acts as counter, decrements by 1

5.20 For each of the following functions specify a finite state table to realize that function if possible, or prove it is impossible.

a) The output of the machine is 1 if and only if at least two of the previous three inputs were zero.

b) The output of the machine at time t is 1 if and only if for the input sequence up to and including t, the number of odd length 1 sequences is even.

c) The output of the machine at time t is 1 if and only if for the input sequence up to and including t, the length of the longest 0 sequence is even.

5.21 Use *JK* flip-flops as memory elements and design a modulo 8 counter which counts in *Gray Code* as shown below.

Decimal Number	Gray Code Number		
0	0	0	0
1	0	0	1
2	0	1	1
3	0	1	0
4	1	1	0
5	1	1	1
6	1	0	1
7	1	0	0

5.22 For the following state table, derive three different state assignments and determine the best one assuming *JK* flip-flops as memory elements.

	x	
	0	1
q_1	$q_2, 0$	$q_1, 1$
q_2	$q_4, 0$	$q_3, 0$
q_3	$q_2, 0$	$q_3, 1$
q_4	$q_5, 1$	$q_5, 1$
q_5	$q_1, 0$	$q_2, 0$

Figure 5.68 Problem 5.22

5.23) For the pair chart of Figure 5.69 find all maximal compatibles.

	1	2	3	4	5	6
2						
3						
4	×	×	×			
5			×			
6						
7	×					×

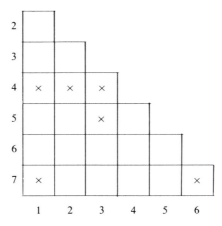

Figure 5.69 Problem 5.23

5.24 For the incompletely specified sequential machine in Figure 5.70 find a minimal state covering table.

	x_1x_2 = 00	01	11	10
q_1	–,–	–,–	q_5,1	–,–
q_2	–,–	q_5,1	q_4,–	–,–
q_3	q_3,0	q_2,1	–,–	q_1,0
q_4	q_3,0	q_1,1	q_4,0	–,1
q_5	q_4,0	–,–	q_3,–	q_4,0

Figure 5.70 Problem 5.24

5.25 Find minimal state tables equivalent to each of the following fully specified tables:

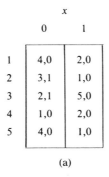

	x = 0	1
1	4,0	2,0
2	3,1	1,0
3	2,1	5,0
4	1,0	2,0
5	4,0	1,0

(a)

Figure 5.71 Problem 5.25

$x_1 x_2$

	00	01	11	10
1	2,0	3,0	2,1	1,0
2	5,0	3,0	2,1	4,1
3	1,0	2,0	3,1	4,1
4	3,1	4,0	1,1	2,0
5	3,0	3,0	3,1	5,0

(b)

x

	0	1
1	8,0	7,1
2	3,0	5,0
3	2,0	1,0
4	5,1	8,0
5	8,0	4,1
6	5,1	3,0
7	1,1	8,0
8	4,0	6,1

(c)

Figure 5.71 (continued)

5.26 For the following state table find all maximal compatibles.

$x_1 x_2$

	00	01	11	10
1	—	5,1	1,-	3,1
2	—	2,-	5,1	6,1
3	6,0	—	—	2,1
4	-,1	—	3,0	—
5	1,-	5,0	6,-	—
6	4,0	6,-	—	—

Figure 5.72 Problem 5.26

5.27 Find minimal covering tables for each of the following partially specified tables.

$x_1 x_2$

	00	01	11	10
1	5,0	4,-	4,-	—
2	4,1	3,0	—	1,-
3	1,-	3,1	—	—
4	2,-	—	3,-	5,-
5	2,-	5,-	3,-	1,-

(a)

x

	0	1
1	-,0	4,-
2	1,1	5,1
3	-,0	4,-
4	3,1	2,1
5	5,-	1,-

(b)

Figure 5.73 Problem 5.27

$$x$$

	0	1
1	3,-	—
2	—	6,0
3	4,1	5,-
4	6,1	—
5	5,-	1,-
6	4,1	7,1
7	2,0	3,0

(c)

Figure 5.73 (continued)

5.28 For the table of Figure 5.74 determine all possible values of A and B which make the table irreducible.

	I_1	I_2	I_3	I_4
1	A,0	-,0	2,0	-,-
2	B,1	3,-	-,-	4,-
3	2,-	-,-	1,0	-,-
4	4,-	5,1	1,0	-,-
5	1,-	1,-	-,-	-,-

Figure 5.74 Problem 5.28

Chapter 6

ASYNCHRONOUS
SEQUENTIAL CIRCUITS

6.1   INTRODUCTION

Sequential circuits may be classified as synchronous or asynchronous. In the former, circuit inputs are allowed to change only during periods when the clock pulses essentially disable the circuit and prevent it from changing states. These clock pulses also mask the effects of delays associated with gates and lines. Hence gates and lines can be assumed to have zero delay and the outputs and states of the circuits are of interest only at fixed instants of time.

The aforementioned restrictions simplify the analysis and synthesis of synchronous circuits considerably. However, under certain conditions, the restrictions required for synchronous operation are not satisfied. For example, consider two synchronous circuits A and B operating under the control of independent clocks. Suppose we wish to design the circuits so that an interrupt signal generated by the circuit A will cause B to stop operation. Upon receiving this interrupt, B should not lose any information about its internal state prior to the occurrence of the interrupt signal. Clearly, we cannot assume any correlation between the arrival of the interrupt signal and the clock pulses of B. The circuit that processes the interrupt signal should be designed without taking advantage of any clock pulses.

Circuits which are designed to operate without synchronizing clock pulses are called asynchronous circuits. Such circuits are used in applications in which inputs occur at random times. They are also used as interfaces to control interactions between two synchronous circuits operating at different speeds such as a digital computer and a peripheral unit. In addition it is sometimes possible to design asynchronous circuits which are faster than synchronous circuits that perform the same function.

Analysis and synthesis techniques used for asynchronous circuits may sometimes be applicable to synchronous circuits. For synchronous circuits with clock pulse widths comparable to gate delays, it may be necessary to analyze them as asynchronous circuits in order to resolve some timing problems. In fact, synchronous circuits may be considered to be a special case of asynchronous circuits with certain constraints on input changes, which lead to simpler analysis and synthesis procedures. Methods of analyzing asynchronous circuits are also useful in analyzing some faults in synchronous circuits since a fault in a synchronous circuit may have the same effect as the clock assuming a constant value of one or zero, thereby causing it to operate as an asynchronous circuit.

Figure 6.1 shows the models of synchronous and asynchronous sequential circuits. The only apparent difference between these models is that the memory elements are clocked for the synchronous and unclocked for the asynchronous case. In the synchronous case each transition corresponds to the following sequence of events.

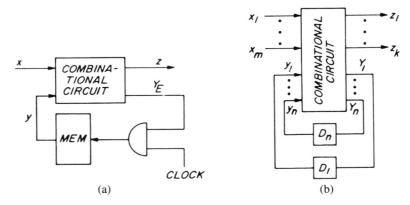

(a)   (b)

Figure 6.1   (a) Model of synchronous sequential circuit (b) Model of
asynchronous sequential circuit

1. An input (x) change occurs while the clock is off. This change causes the circuit C to become unstable but does not cause any changes in the outputs of memory elements due to the absence of the clock pulse.

2. After C stabilizes in response to the input change the clock goes on (becomes 1) and the memory elements and outputs may change value. The change in value of the memory elements may cause C to again change value. These subsequent changes do not further affect the outputs or memory elements since it is assumed that the clock pulse is sufficiently narrow that it is no longer on.

Thus each input leads to exactly one state transition and one output.

A synchronous circuit is modeled by a synchronous sequential machine whose behavior can be represented by a state table as shown in Figure 6.2(a). The four input columns shown represent possible inputs and the transitions indicated occur when the clock pulse comes on. The status when the clock pulse is off may be

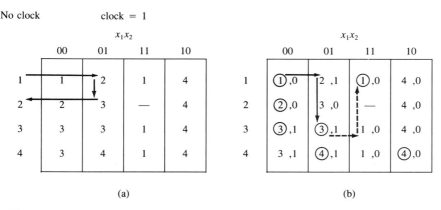

Figure 6.2 (a) State transition within a synchronous machine state table (b) State transition within an asynchronous flow table

thought of as being represented by the leftmost column of states as shown. A transition from state 1 to state 2 occurs as shown by the arrows, in the state table.

The behavior of an asynchronous circuit differs in that there is no clock pulse which can be turned off to cause the circuit to stabilize. Thus an input change in an asynchronous circuit may precipitate a *sequence* of changes of state and output as follows.

1. An input (x) change occurs which causes C to become unstable. This results in the generation of output and flip-flop excitation signals which may cause a change in the value of some memory elements. This change may produce subsequent changes in the memory elements, thus producing a sequence of state and output changes.
2. Eventually the memory elements stabilize in a condition for which the excitation signals do not lead to further changes.*

We shall refer to the mathematical model of an asynchronous sequential circuit as an *asynchronous* sequential machine. A convenient means of representing an asynchronous sequential machine is a *flow table*. As in the state table of a synchronous machine, the flow table has a row corresponding to each internal state, and a column corresponding to each input combination (also called *input state*). A combination of an input state and an internal state is called a *total state*. For every total state, the flow table specifies the next internal state and the output.

---

*Alternatively it is possible that an oscillation may occur. However we shall be primarily interested in the design of circuits which do not have such oscillations.

We denote the next state and the output for the total state (q_1, I_j) by $N(q_i, I_j)$ and $Z(q_i, I_j)$ respectively. If $N(q_i, I_j) = q_i$, q_i is said to be a *stable state* under the input I_j and is circled in the flow table, as shown in Figure 6.2(b). All other states are unstable.

Unlike synchronous circuits which are generally assumed to operate with pulse inputs, asynchronous sequential circuits are usually assumed to operate with level inputs (although this assumption is not necessary). Since there are no clock pulses, state transitions are caused by input changes. If a transition from stable configuration (q_i, I_m) caused by changing I_m to I_n results in state q_j and (q_j, I_n) is not stable, the state changes again to $N(q_j, I_n)$ and continues to change within column I_n until a stable configuration is reached. The interval between successive input changes is assumed to be sufficient for the circuit to complete its response to the previous input change and reach a stable state. This mode of operation is called *fundamental mode* [1].

Another common assumption is that only one input variable is allowed to change at a time, since inputs which change together cannot be presumed to change exactly simultaneously, due to delays in circuit gates. We shall show later in this chapter how this assumption can be relaxed.

In the machine specified by the flow table of Figure 6.2(b) if the circuit is initially stable in state 1 with inputs 00, a change to input 01 will cause a sequence of two transitions ultimately leading to state 3, as shown by the solid directed lines in the flow table. If this input is followed by input 11, the machine will reach the stable state 1, as shown by the dotted lines. Note that in the transition from state 1 to state 3 the output first changes from 0 to 1, then goes back to 0 and then back to 1. We thus see that asynchronous flow tables can represent output pulse sequences as well as stable behavior.

6.2   CLASSIFICATION OF ASYNCHRONOUS FLOW TABLES

Asynchronous flow tables are commonly classified according to the maximum number of state changes and output changes produced by a single input change. Three different cases can be defined with respect to the number of state changes.

1. *Normal mode*   In any transition the state changes at most once before stabilizing.
2. *Non-normal fundamental mode*   There exists at least one transition in which the state changes more than once before stabilizing but no transition in which a state oscillation may occur.
3. *Non-fundamental mode*   There exists at least one transition which leads to a state oscillation and never stabilizes.

The table of Figure 6.2(b) is non-normal fundamental mode since the transition from stable configuration (1,00) produced by changing x_2 to 1, results in the state sequence 1, 2, 3 before stabilization occurs. The machine represented by the flow table M_2 of Figure 6.3 will produce single-output changes for input transitions between I_0 and I_1. However, if the input I_3 is applied when the machine is stable in the total state $(2, I_1)$ or $(4, I_1)$, the machine will not reach a stable state but will cycle through states 2, 3, and 4. The number of output changes produced and the final state reached will depend on the duration of the input I_3. Fundamental mode operation is impossible in this case. Flow tables such as M_2 where fundamental mode operation is impossible are called *nonfundamental mode flow tables*. They are characterized by the presence of state cycles in one or more columns.

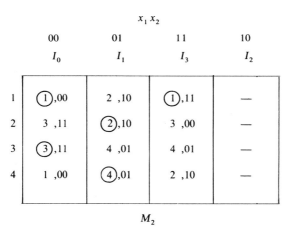

$$M_2$$

Figure 6.3   A non-fundamental mode flow table

Flow tables may also be characterized by the number of times the output may change value in a transition. Two cases are defined.

1. *Single Output Change (SOC) flow tables*   In any transition the output value changes at most once.
2. *Multiple Output Change (MOC) flow tables*   In some transition the output value may change more than once. Thus a single input change may produce a sequence of output changes.

Normal mode tables may be either SOC or MOC. Both tables of Figure 6.4 are normal mode. The table of Figure 6.4(a) is SOC while that of Figure 6.4(b) is MOC since the transition from 1 to 2 results in the output sequence $0 \rightarrow 1 \rightarrow 0$.

It is possible to define non-normal fundamental mode tables or non-fundamental mode tables which are SOC. However in these cases the sequence of state transitions defined is superfluous.

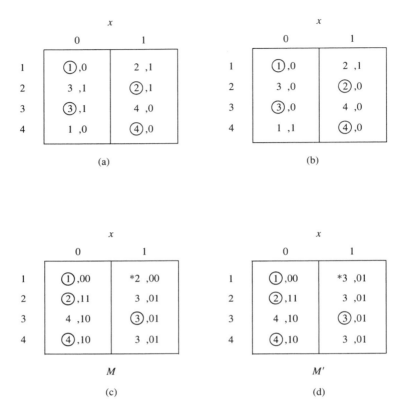

Figure 6.4 (a) An SOC flow table (b) An MOC flow table (c) An SOC non-normal mode table (d) An equivalent normal mode table

Figures 6.4(c) and (d) show two SOC tables that differ in only one entry (indicated by an asterisk). In the flow table M, an input change $0 \to 1$ with the circuit initially in state 1 causes a transition to state 2 and then to state 3. The output changes from 00 to 01 when the machine reaches state 2. In the flow table M', the transition from state 1 due to the input change $0 \to 1$ is directly to state 3. The output changes to 01 as soon as the input changes. The only difference between the external behavior of the two tables is the duration of certain outputs. Flow tables M and M' may be considered to be equivalent if the duration of outputs is of no consequence, since they produce the same output sequence for all input sequences.

For the most part we shall restrict ourselves to considering only normal mode SOC tables, which behave similarly to synchronous machines, each transition producing a single state and output change. We shall now consider the problem of asynchronous circuit synthesis beginning as before with the derivation of the flow table model.

6.3   FLOW TABLE SPECIFICATION

The first step in the design of an asynchronous sequential circuit is the construction of a flow table describing the circuit behavior from a word description of the function to be realized. In doing this, it is often relatively easy to first construct a *primitive flow table* which has exactly one stable state in each row.

Example 6.1   Consider an asynchronous counter with two binary inputs x_1, x_2. The input $x_1 = x_2 = 0$ is a reset input which clears the counter to an initial state producing the output 00. Only a single input variable is allowed to change in a transition. The count is to be incremented by one when the input x_1, $x_2 = 01$ is received and incremented by two when the input x_1, $x_2 = 10$ is received, the count being modulo 4. The input x_1, $x_2 = 11$ does not produce any change in the count. The outputs z_1, z_2 represent the current count.

Figure 6.5 is a primitive* flow table for the asynchronous counter described above. For each row q_1 of the table, next state entries are specified for input states that may follow the input state containing the stable state in row q_i. The reset state, 1, is stable in column 00. This input may be followed by 01 which results in a next state entry of 2 and a count of 1 (z_1, $z_2 = 01$) or by 10, resulting in a next state entry 3 and a count of 2 (z_1, $z_2 = 10$). The entry in row 1, column 11 is unspecified. The stable state 2 in column 01 may be followed by the inputs 00 or 11, resulting in a reset to state 1 or a transition to state 4 with no change in count respectively. The remaining entries are similarly specified. Outputs are specified only for stable states, assuming that the outputs may change at any time during a transition.   ∎

A flow table generated from a word description of a sequential function, such as the primitive flow table of Example 6.1, usually contains more internal states than necessary to realize the specified function. For more economical realizations, it may be desirable to reduce the number of states in a flow table. A primitive flow table is particularly useful in deriving an equivalent table with the minimum number of states.

6.4   FLOW TABLE REDUCTION

The methods of state table reduction discussed in Chapter 5 are also applicable to asynchronous flow tables with only minor modifications. The single-input

---

*In a primitive flow table, there is at most one stable entry in each row.

$$x_1 x_2$$

	00	01	11	10
1	①,00	2	—	3
2	1	②,01	4	—
3	1	—	5	③,10
4	—	6	④,01	7
5	—	8	⑤,10	9
6	1	⑥,10	5	—
7	1	—	10	⑦,11
8	1	⑧,11	10	—
9	1	—	11	⑨,00
10	—	13	⑩,11	12
11	—	2	⑪,00	3
12	1	—	4	⑫,01
13	1	⑬,00	11	—

Figure 6.5   Primitive flow table for Example 6.1

change restriction often makes it possible to reduce some flow tables that are not otherwise reducible. This restriction can be easily modelled by unspecified entries in a primitive flow table. However, if a flow table has two or more stable states in a row, the single input change constraint cannot be accurately modelled by unspecified entries, since a particular input may be permitted from one of the columns with a stable state within the row but not from another. Therefore, the reduced version of a primitive table may require fewer states than that of the corresponding non-primitive table if only single input charges are permitted. Consider the flow table of Figure 6.6(a) and the corresponding primitive table of Figure 6.6(b), assuming single input variable changes. The table of (a) is not reducible while the primitive table of (b) can be reduced to the 3-state table of Figure 6.6(c). Of course any normal mode SOC table can be expanded to a primitive flow table as an initial step in the state minimization procedure.

   With fundamental mode operation, input changes occur only when the circuit is in a stable state. Furthermore, the exact times at which output changes occur and the duration of output signals are usually not of interest, provided they are

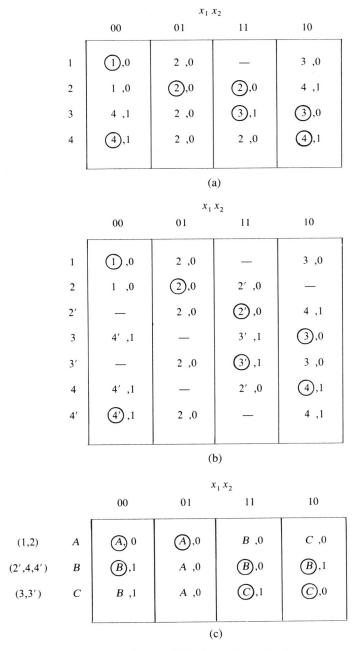

Figure 6.6 Flow table reduction

within certain bounds. Instead, we are interested only in the output sequences generated by input sequences. These facts sometimes enable additional types of state mergers for non-normal mode tables which are not possible in the synchronous case.

In a fundamental mode SOC flow table, the output associated with an unstable state must be the same as the output associated with the stable state at the beginning or the end of the transition. If we assign the same output to these unstable states as to that of the final stable state, the only effect of this change will be in the timing of the output changes. If we are not concerned with this effect, the flow table so obtained may be considered to be equivalent to the original table. Also, if a state is unstable in a particular column, its next state and output can be made the same as the stable state in that column that will be ultimately reached from the unstable state. That is, if q_i is unstable in column I_k, and q_j is the stable state that will be reached from q_i, we make $N(q_i, I_k) = q_j$ and $Z(q_i, I_k) = Z(q_j, I_k)$. This procedure, which we shall refer to as *normalization*, converts a fundamental mode SOC table into a normal mode flow table.

Lemma 6.1   If a pair of states q_i and q_j of an SOC flow table M are compatible, then q_i and q_j are compatible in the normal mode flow table M' obtained by normalizing M.

Proof   Exercise.   ∎

Normalizing an SOC table does not destroy any compatible pairs but may make some new pairs compatible. The state table reduction method discussed in Chapter 5 can be applied to the normal mode flow table so obtained. It follows from Lemma 6.1 that the flow table obtained by minimizing the number of states in the normalized flow table will not exceed the number of states obtained by reducing the original table.

Example 6.2   The flow table shown in Figure 6.7(a) has no compatible pair of states. Since this table has only single-output changes, it can be converted to the normal mode flow table of Figure 6.7(b) by changing the entries indicated by asterisks. Now (1,3) and (2,4) are compatible pairs which form a closed set and may be merged to obtain the reduced table of Figure 6.7(c). This reduction would have been impossible had the original table represented a synchronous machine.   ∎

The state minimization problem for MOC flow tables is somewhat more complex and will not be considered here.

Having completed the problem of flow table specification, we now proceed to considering asynchronous circuit synthesis, deriving a circuit to realize the flow table generated.

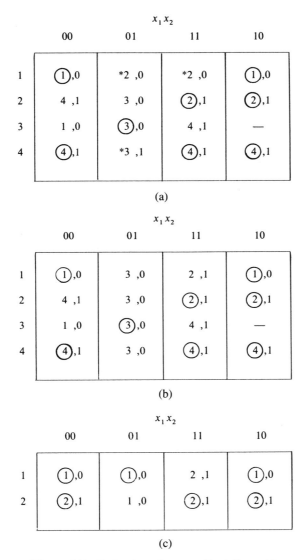

Figure 6.7 Reduction of a normalized flow table

6.5 SYNTHESIS OF ASYNCHRONOUS CIRCUITS

In Chapter 5 we referred to a basic problem created by the absence of clock pulses, namely *hazards*, and illustrated it with the circuit of Figure 5.9. It is helpful to examine a Karnaugh map of the function, as shown in Figure 6.8(a)* to analyze the source and possible solution for hazards. The

---

*For expositional simplicity we examine the Karnaugh map of the function's complement, $\bar{f}$.

transition which caused the problem is represented by an arrow on the map. As we see the hazard is caused by the change of a single x variable (x_1) which causes a transition between two adjacent 1-points which are covered by different cubes. If we add additional logic to the realization by including a third cube which covers both of the adjacent points (Figure 6.8(b)) the hazard will be eliminated.* Thus as we shall see later (Section 6.7), hazards produced by single input variable changes are relatively easy to eliminate.

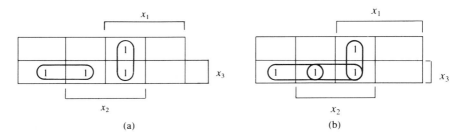

(a)   (b)

Figure 6.8   (a) Karnaugh map showing transition with hazard
(b) Karnaugh map showing prevention of hazard

A related problem is caused by the concurrent† change of two (or more) variables, as illustrated by the Karnaugh map of Figure 6.9. The transition from point a to point d involves a change in value of variables x_1 and x_3. Because of the lack of a synchronous clock these variables will not be perceived as changing

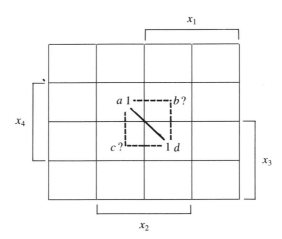

Figure 6.9   Karnaugh map showing transition with two variables changing value

---

*This will be discussed in much more detail later in this chapter.
†The term *concurrent* is used for signals that change at about the same time but not in exact synchronism.

in synchronism. This is referred to as a *race* condition. If x_1 is perceived as changing first the transition from a to d will in effect be made through intermediate point b, while if x_3 is perceived as changing first the transition passes through intermediate point c. If both points b and c are 1-points, a single cube $x_2 x_4$ covering all four points a, b, c, d can be used to eliminate any possible transient. In this case the race is called *non-critical*. However if either b or c or both are 0-points this cannot be done. In this case a transient may be generated and the race is called *critical*. We now translate these problems into restrictions on the circuit.

Figure 6.1(b) shows a general model of asynchronous sequential circuits [2] which we shall use for most of our discussions in this chapter. This is the same model as for synchronous circuits except for the absence of a clock. In synchronous circuits clocked D-flip-flops can be modelled as delay elements* of identical magnitude.

We shall assume unclocked D-flip-flops as asynchronous circuit memory elements. These also correspond to delay elements but cannot be assumed to be of identical magnitude. However we do assume that the magnitude of these *inserted* delay elements significantly exceeds the magnitude of the random stray delay associated with the circuit logic.

The internal state of the circuit is represented by the state variables y_i and the next state values of the state variables are denoted by Y_i, $i = 1, 2, \ldots , n$. The variables $x_1, \ldots , x_m$ and $z_1, \ldots , z_k$ represent the inputs and outputs respectively of the circuit.

The sequence of events corresponding to a state transition subjects the combinational excitation logic C to a sequence of two excitations (for a normal mode realization) as follows:

1. An input (x) change occurs.
2. The change produces a state variable (y) change.

As we observed before C can be designed to be well behaved if it is only subjected to single variable changes. By assuming only one x variable can change in any transition we accomplish this restriction for the first of these two excitations. (We will see later in Section 6.9 how this restriction can be eliminated.) The second excitation requires us to restrict the state assignment so that only one state variable is required to change value in any transition. We next consider this state assignment problem.

---

*A delay element is a device with one input x and one output z where the output at time t has the same value as the input at time $t-D$ (i.e., $z(t)=x(t-D)$, and D is called the magnitude of the delay element).

6.5.1 State Assignment

The first step in designing an asynchronous sequential circuit that realizes a given flow table is to represent the internal states by combinations of values of binary state variables. This is called the asynchronous state assignment problem and differs from its synchronous counterpart in several respects.

For a synchronous machine, $\lceil \log_2 n \rceil = S_0$ state variables are necessary and sufficient for representing n states, and the assignment can be made arbitrarily without affecting the proper operation, as long as no coding is assigned to more than one state, although the structural complexity of the realization will usually depend on the assignment. For an asynchronous flow table additional constraints must be satisfied in order to avoid critical races and hence S_0 state variables may not be sufficient.

In order to make the critical race concept more concrete, we consider the flow table,* state assignment A, and realization shown in Figure 6.10. Let the circuit be stable in state 2 (represented by $y_1 = 0$, $y_2 = 1$) and input $x = 1$. For the transition when x changes value from 1 to 0, G_2 will begin to change to 1 and both Y_1 and Y_2 will begin to change value. If y_2 changes to 0 before y_1 changes to 1, G_2 will change to 0 and the variable y_1 may oscillate, or even stabilize at $y_1 = 0$ instead of $y_1 = 1$ if the delay associated with G_4 is sufficiently large. Similar problems occur if y_1 changes value first. In effect the circuit may pass through state 1, represented by $y_1 = y_2 = 0$, if y_2 changes first, or state 4, represented by $y_1 = y_2 = 1$, if y_1 changes first. However, both of these states lead to state 1 in column 0 of the flow table rather than the correct next state 3, which will be reached if y_1 and y_2 change simultaneously. Thus, the final state reached will depend on the relative magnitudes of stray delays in the circuit. In practice, the stable state may be indeterminate or the circuit may oscillate due to similar problems. This difficulty does not occur in synchronous circuits because the clock prevents the state variable values from being used to generate excitations until they become stable, thus effectively ensuring that they appear to change simultaneously.

When two or more variables change during a transition, a *race* is said to occur among the changing variables. In the flow table of Figure 6.10, the state variables y_1 and y_2 of assignment A are involved in a race in the transition from state 2 to state 3 and also the transition from state 4 to state 1. If the final state reached may depend on the order of changes, as in this case, the race is said to be *critical*. Otherwise it is called a *noncritical race*.

In assignment B for the same flow table, all transitions are between states that differ in exactly one state variable (adjacent states). This assignment is *race-free* and is therefore suitable for the asynchronous flow table. A race-free assignment is sufficient but not necessary for proper operation, as we shall see later.

---

*Note that output entries have been omitted from the flow table. In the rest of this chapter, output entries will be omitted from flow tables whenever we are interested only in their state behavior. We shall assume that such flow tables are reduced.

x			Assignment A		Assignment B	
	0	1	y_1	y_2	y_1	y_2
1	①	2	0	0	0	0
2	3	②	0	1	0	1
3	③	4	1	0	1	1
4	1	④	1	1	1	0

(a)

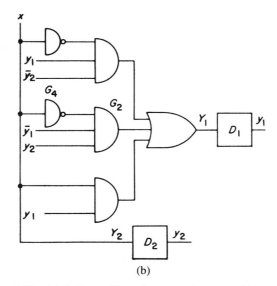

(b)

Figure 6.10   (a) A flow table and state assignments (b) Realization

The combination of state variable values used to represent a state is called the *coding* of the state. The assignments considered so far used only one coding per state and are called *unicode assignments*.

We now consider the following problem: Is it possible for any flow table to derive a unicode assignment in which each transition only requires a single state variable to change? Unfortunately, the answer is No!

Consider the flow table of Figure 6.11(a). The undirected graph of Figure 6.11(b) has nodes corresponding to the states of the flow table. It has an edge between two nodes if and only if there is a direct transition between the two states. This graph, which we shall call the *adjacency graph* of the flow table, shows states

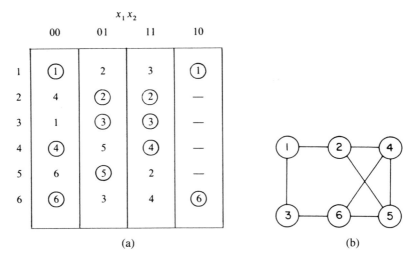

Figure 6.11   (a) A flow table (b) Its transition graph

whose codings should be adjacent. From the adjacency graph, we see that the codings of states 2, 4, and 5 must be adjacent to one another as must the codings of states 4, 5, and 6, in order to be able to make all state transitions by changing only one state variable. However, it is impossible to have three binary codings such that each pair of these codings differs in exactly 1 bit. Suppose states q_i, q_j, and q_k have codings C_i, C_j, C_k respectively. If C_i and C_j differ only in variable y_1, and C_j and C_k differ only in variable y_2, then C_i and C_k will differ in both y_1 and y_2. It follows that there exists no unicode state assignment for the flow table of Figure 6.11(a) such that all transitions are between adjacent states.

Different methods could be used to resolve the difficulty encountered in the above example. One method is to permit transitions between nonadjacent states. When two or more variables are required to change during a transition, these variables may change simultaneously if there are no critical races, or they may change in some prescribed order. Another method involves the use of more than one coding per state. Transitions will be accomplished by a *sequence* of single state variable changes, thus in effect implementing a non-normal mode realization of a normal mode flow table.

6.5.1.1   Connected Row Set Assignments

One method of obtaining an assignment such that any transition can be made by a sequence of single variable changes is to assign a set of codings R_i to each row (state) q_i of the flow table. The set of codings (points) assigned to a row of the flow table is called a *row set*. If any member in a row set can be reached from any other member in the same set by a sequence of single variable changes without passing through any point that is not in the set, the set of codings is called a *connected row set*. Two connected row sets R_i and R_j are said to be *intermeshed* if there is some coding in R_i that is adjacent to some coding in R_j. In order to use a connected row set assignment for a flow table, the row sets assigned to states between which there are transitions must be intermeshed. Let R_i and R_j be intermeshed connected row sets assigned to states q_i and q_j respectively. A transition from q_i to q_j is made by first making a sequence of transitions within R_i until a point adjacent to some point in R_j is reached, and then making the transition to the point in R_j. The intermeshed nature of R_i and R_j guarantees that this can always be done.

Example 6.3 A connected row set assignment for the flow table of Figure 6.11 is shown in the Karnaugh map and table of Figure 6.12. The arrows indicate how two transitions are made. If the circuit is stable in state 5, represented by the coding 100 in Figure 6.12(a), and the input changes to 00, the first step of

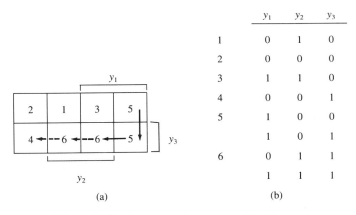

Figure 6.12 A connected row set state assignment

the transition will be to 101 (another coding for state 5) by changing y_3. Then y_2 will change to 1 to reach state 6 represented by 111. Now if the input changes to 10 and then 11, state 4 represented by 001 is reached via 011, which is in the row set assigned to state 6. This transition is shown by the dotted arrows in Figure 6.12. ∎

With the assignment shown in Figure 6.12, any state transition in the flow table of Figure 6.11 can be made in at most two steps. The maximum number of steps required for any state transition using a particular state assignment is referred to as the *transition time* of the assignment. Thus, the assignment of

Figure 6.12 has a transition time of 2. The transition time of the state assignment used affects the minimum period between input changes and the speed of operation of the sequential circuit (assuming fundamental mode operation).

The external source generating the x variable inputs cannot generate a new input until the circuit has stabilized. Since the external source does not know, in general, which transition is being made must assume a worst case, and therefore must *never* generate changes in a time span shorter than the transition time of the circuit it feeds.

We now consider the problem of finding a connected row set state assignment using the minimum number of state variables. The general procedure is as follows.

Procedure 6.1

1. Derive and list the required adjacencies for each state of the table. A state q_i must be adjacent to q_j if there is a transition from q_i to q_j or from q_j to q_i. Initially attempt to find a state assignment with $k = S_0 = \lceil \log_2 n \rceil$ state variables.
2. Find a k variable state assignment which satisfies all adjacency requirements, or prove by exhaustive elimination that none exists. If none exists increment k by 1 and repeat (2).   ∎

Step 2 of this procedure may require a significant amount of work. A useful heuristic is to first consider the states which have the greatest number of required adjacencies. The quantity $2^{S_0} - n$ is the number of excess codings after each state is assigned one coding. Frequently if this quantity is small it is difficult to find an S_0 variable connected row set assignment. However by increasing the number of variables by one, the number of available codes doubles and a connected row set assignment can often be easily generated. The following example illustrates the application of Procedure 6.1 to three different flow tables.

Example 6.4

a) We first consider the flow table of Figure 6.11(a). The required adjacencies for this table are as follows:

State	Required Adjacencies
1	2, 3
2	1, 4, 5
3	1, 6
4	2, 5, 6
5	2, 4, 6
6	3, 4, 5

States 2, 4, 5, 6 all have three required adjacencies so we arbitrarily choose one of these states, say 2, to begin and arbitrarily assign coding 000 in a three variable map to 2. The three adjacent codings are arbitrarily assigned to states 1, 4, 5 which must be adjacent to 2 (Figure 6.13(a)). This satisfies all transitions to and from state 2.

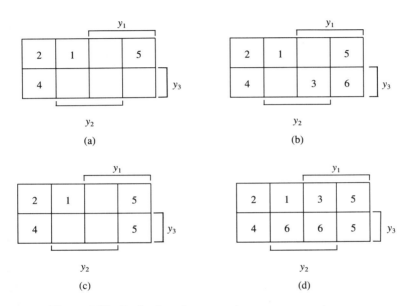

Figure 6.13 Derivation of connected row set state assignment

We next consider state 6, which now has the most unsatisfied transitions. Since 6 must be adjacent to both 4 and 5 we assign coding 100 to state 6, and assign coding 111 to 3, to fulfill all the required adjacencies of 6 (Figure 6.13(b)). The remaining adjacency requirements are between 1 and 3, and 4 and 5. However it is impossible to assign connected row sets to 4 and 5 to make them adjacent. We see that we made a mistake in assigning coding 101 to state 6 because that was a natural coding for a row set to connect 4 and 5. So we back up and assign that coding to state 5 (Figure 6.13(c)). The three adjacencies for state 6 can then be satisfied by assigning row set (011, 111) to state 6 and coding 110 to state 3 (Figure 6.13(d)), thus completing a minimum variable state assignment satisfying all required adjacencies.

b) Figure 6.14(a),(b) show a flow table and the adjacencies to be satisfied by the different row sets. Since there are six states, at least three variables are necessary in any state assignment. First, we assign an arbitrary coding, say

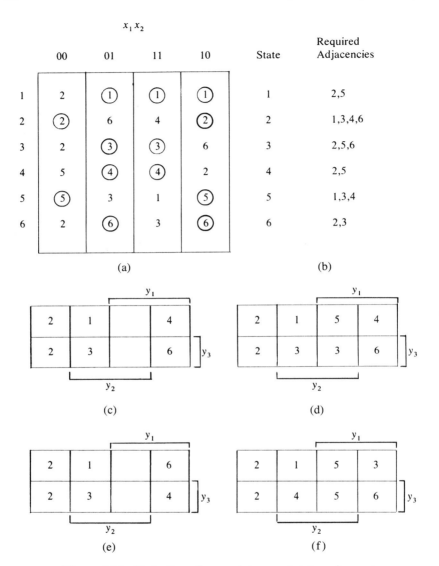

Figure 6.14 Derivation of connected row set state assignment

000, to state 2, which has the largest number of adjacencies. Any point in a k-cube has only k points adjacent to it. Since four adjacencies are needed for state 2, a single 3-variable coding is not sufficient for state 2. If we assign a second coding adjacent to the first coding, then the two codings together will have four adjacent points which can be assigned to states 1, 3, 4, and 6. One possible assignment for state 2 and its four adjacent states is shown in Figure 6.14(c). Now, state 5 has to be adjacent to states 1, 3, and 4, requiring the assignment of the coding 110 to this state and the coding 111 to 3. Thus a connected row set has been formed for state 3. Examining the flow table, we note that all required adjacencies have been satisfied. The complete state assignment is shown in Figure 6.14(d). Since the assignment required only three state variables, it is an assignment with the minimum number of variables. The search process does not always function so smoothly. Figure 6.14(e) shows another assignment for state 2 and its four adjacent states. Since state 5 has to be adjacent to states 1, 3, and 4, both the unused codings have to be assigned to state 5. However, the requirement that state 3 be adjacent to states 2 and 6 cannot be satisfied, and we are unable to obtain a connected row set assignment with three variables. Another valid connected row set assignment is shown in Figure 6.14(f).

c) Figure 6.15 shows a 7-state flow table and its adjacency constraints. We start with $S_0 = \lceil \log_2 7 \rceil = 3$ state variables. Since states 1 and 2 both have four required adjacencies they each require two codings, because on a three variable map each coding is only adjacent to three other codings. However, 1 and 2 cannot each have two codings since we have seven states and only eight codings. We therefore look for a solution on a four variable map, which is quite easily found (Figure 6.15(c)). ■

	$x_1 x_2$				State	Required Adjacencies
	00	01	11	10		
1	①	2	3	①	1	2,3,4,6
2	3	②	②	4	2	1,3,4,5
3	③	7	③	③	3	1,2,7
4	1	④	④	④	4	1,2,6
5	⑤	⑤	2	7	5	2,7
6	—	4	⑥	1	6	1,4,7
7	5	⑦	6	⑦	7	3,5,6

(a)   (b)

Figure 6.15 (a) A flow table with required adjacencies (b) A connected row set state assignment

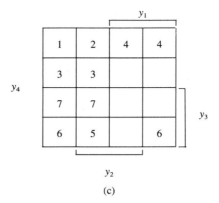

(c)

Figure 6.15   (continued)

It is sometimes possible to modify the flow table so as to reduce the number of adjacency constraints to be satisfied and possibly the number of state variables required in a connected row state assignment.

Consider the flow table of Figure 6.16(a) and the associated set of required adjacencies. It is easily seen that a connected row set assignment requires three

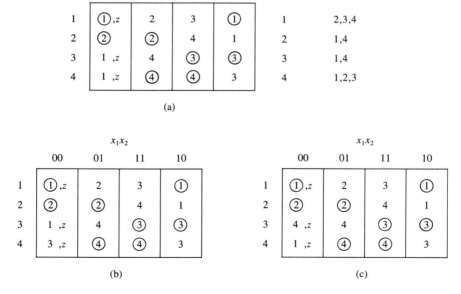

Figure 6.16   (a) A flow table (b)List of required adjacencies (c) A modified equivalent table (d) Another modified equivalent table

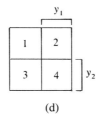

(d)

Figure 6.16   (continued)

state variables. Now consider column 00 of the flow table which has two transitions to the same stable state, $4 \rightarrow 1$ and $3 \rightarrow 1$. Assuming the three outputs labelled z are all identical, it is possible to modify the transitions in this column to a non-normal mode but output equivalent table as shown in Figure 6.16(b) and (c). In the table of Figure 6.16(b) the transition $4 \rightarrow 1$ was replaced by $4 \rightarrow 3 \rightarrow 1$. In the table of Figure 6.16(c) the transition $3 \rightarrow 1$ was replaced by $3 \rightarrow 4 \rightarrow 1$. In the table of Figure 6.16(b) it is no longer required that states 1 and 4 be adjacent and the state assignment of Figure 6.16(d) satisfies all required adjacencies for this table.

This type of table modification is only applicable to normal mode SOC tables which have two different transitions to the same stable state in the same input column (i.e., $N(q_i, I_j) = N(q_k, I_j) = q_m$, where q_m is not q_i or q_k. If we modify the table by making $N(q_i, I_j) = q_k$, leaving $N(q_k, I_j) = q_m$, there will be no change in the behavior of the machine, except that the transition $q_i \rightarrow q_m$ in the column I_j is replaced by $q_i \rightarrow q_k \rightarrow q_m$. Alternatively, we could make $N(q_k, I_j) = q_i$ leaving $N(q_i, I_j) = q_m$. This modification is the opposite of normalization discussed in Section 6.4 and may result in a state assignment requiring fewer variables.

Note that this technique cannot be applied to the table of Figure 6.16(a) since that table has no column with two different transitions to the same stable state.

6.5.1.2   *Universal Connected Row Set State Assignments*

For any given number n of states, a state assignment that is valid for *any* n-state flow table is called a *universal state assignment*. Such assignments can be constructed using systematic procedures, but frequently require more state variables than an assignment for a specific flow table with the same number of states. However, they provide useful upper bounds on the number of variables required for a flow table with a given number of states.

We shall first consider a class of universal assignments which require $2S_0 - 1$ state variables for an n-state table [3], where $S_0 = \lceil \log_2 n \rceil$. The universal assignment for four states is shown in Figure 6.17. In order to show that this is indeed a universal assignment, we have to verify that the codings for each state are connected and that the row sets assigned to any pair of states are intermeshed. This is readily verified from Figure 6.17(a) since the two codings for each state

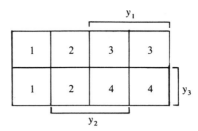

Figure 6.17   Universal connected row set state assignment for four states

differ only in one variable and for any pair i, j of states, there is a coding for state i that differs from a coding of state j in only one variable.

The above universal assignment can be generalized to obtain assignments for larger numbers of states. Consider the Karnaugh map of Figure 6.18. The variables y_1, y_2, and y_3 divide the map into octants as shown. The map is constructed so that variables with odd-numbered subscripts, y_1, y_3, y_5, define columns and those with even-numbered subscripts, y_2, y_4, define rows. The codings assigned to any state consist of a column in one octant and a row in an adjacent octant (defined by changing the value of y_2 for half of the states and the value of y_3 for the other half). Therefore, the codings of every state form a connected set. Furthermore, for every pair of states q_i and q_j, there exist codings of the two states in adjacent octants, and since rows in an octant are connected to all columns in every adjacent octant (and vice versa), there exist codings for states q_i and q_j which differ in exactly one variable. Therefore, the assignment of Figure 6.18 is a universal 8-state connected row set assignment.

The pattern of Figure 6.18 can be used for generating universal assignments for any number of states equal to an integral power of 2.

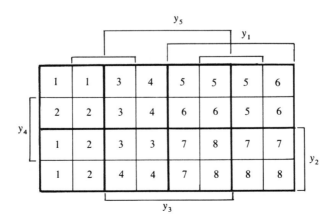

Figure 6.18   Universal 8-state connected row set assignment

We have seen that three variables are used in a 4-state assignment. In order to double the number of states, we have to double the number of rows and columns. This can be accomplished by adding two variables. The number of variables required for a universal n-state assignment using this construction is therefore $2S_0 - 1$.

If noncritical races are permitted and utilized, at most four transition times are required for making any state transition when a $(2S_0 - 1)$ universal assignment is used for any n-state table, independent of n. In the worst case, the transitions involved will be (1) a transition within any column (row) in an octant, defined by variables y_1, y_2, y_3 (possibly involving a noncritical race), (2) changing an octant variable (y_1, y_2, or y_3) to reach an adjacent octant, (3) a transition within a row (column) in the new octant (possibly involving a noncritical race again), and finally (4) a transition to a coding of the destination state by changing an octant variable. Another universal state assignment having $2S_0$ state variables but requiring only two transition times has also been derived by Huffman [3]. (See Problem 6.15.)

In connected row set state assignments each used coding is assigned exclusively to a single row set. We shall now consider a class of assignments in which some codings are in effect *shared* by two or more different states.

6.5.1.3   Shared Row Assignments

In connected row set assignments, transitions between different pairs of states are made using disjoint paths (intermediate states). However, if two different state transitions occur under different inputs, these transitions need not be made disjoint and may share one or more intermediate states. Such assignments, which are called *shared row assignments*, frequently require fewer state variables than connected row set assignments.

A *connected path* between two points a and b is an ordered sequence of points beginning at a and ending at b, such that all consecutive pairs of points are adjacent. A valid shared row state assignment for a normal mode flow table must satisfy the following two conditions: (1) the point (or points) representing every state must be distinct from those representing all other states, and (2) there must be a connected path associated with every transition, disjoint from the paths associated with all other transitions *in the same column* of the flow table, except when they have the same final state.

Consider the flow table of Figure 6.15 which is repeated in Figure 6.19. From the required set of adjacencies we see that both states 1 and 2 require a second coding (on a three variable map). However there is one spare coding. Let us consider sharing this coding between states 1 and 2. As shown in the state assignment in Figure 6.19(c), the spare coding 001 is adjacent to both states 1 and 2. In Figure 6.20 we see how this spare coding is used to define connected paths for transitions for each of the four input columns. Note that in column 00 the extra coding is used to define a connected path for the transition $4 \rightarrow 1$, and hence in effect acts as part of a row set for state 1. In column 10 it is used for

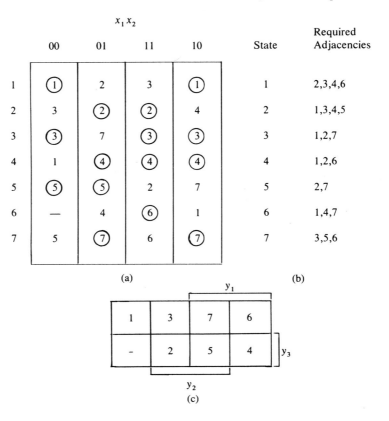

(a)   (b)

(c)

Figure 6.19   Derivation of shared row state assignment

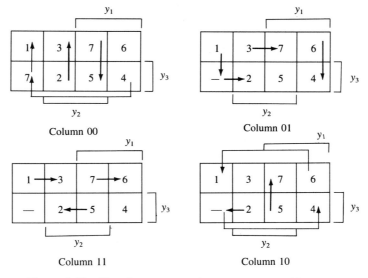

Figure 6.20   Shared row state assignment state transitions

the transition $2 \rightarrow 4$ and hence acts as part of the row set for state 2. Thus the coding is shared, depending upon the value of the input, between states 1 and 2.

As in the case of a connected row set assignment, the procedure for deriving a shared row set assignment is exhaustive in nature. The adjacency constraints used for the former are also useful for the latter.

Although there are no known universal shared row assignments for tables of arbitrary size, Saucier [4] has obtained such assignments with one coding per state for 8- and 12-state normal mode flow tables. These assignments requiring four and five variables respectively are shown in Figure 6.21. Both assignments were obtained and proved to be minimal by an exhaustive search algorithm using a computer. Figure 6.21(c) shows the defined connected paths for a table with an input column defining the transitions $1 \rightarrow 7$, $2 \rightarrow 4$, $6 \rightarrow 8$, $3 \rightarrow 5$.

The state assignments discussed so far require a sequence of state variable changes for a state transition. This may not be desirable from the point of view of the speed of operation of the circuit because input changes cannot be permitted to occur until the entire sequence of state variable changes is completed. As-

$y_1 y_2$

$y_3 y_4$	00	01	11	10
00	1	2		
01			3	4
11	5	6		
10			7	8

(a)

$y_1 y_2 y_3$

$y_4 y_5$	000	010	110	100	101	111	011	001
00	1	2			9	10		
01			3	4				
11	5	6						
10			7	8			11	12

(b)

Figure 6.21 Universal shared row state assignments (a) 8-state assignment (b) 12-state assignment (c) Multistep transitions defined on state assignment

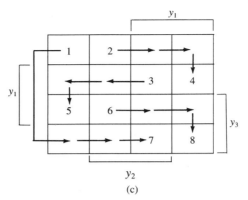

Figure 6.21   (continued)

signments in which all variables that must change during a transition are allowed to change simultaneously are called *single transition time (STT) assignments.*

6.5.1.4   Single Transition Time Assignments

One method of completing all transitions in a single transition time is to assign adjacent points to states between which transitions are to be made. As was pointed out earlier, this is impossible in general using a unicode assignment (although it may be possible for some specific flow tables). However, it is possible to assign a set of codings to each state of any flow table, such that for any two states q_i and q_j, *every* coding assigned to q_i is adjacent to *some* coding assigned to q_j. Unlike the connected row set assignment discussed earlier, the points assigned to any state need not form a connected set since transitions are not made between points in the same row set. Such assignments are sometimes called *one-shot assignments.*

Consider the state assignment of Figure 6.22, which assigns two codings to each of four states. Both of the codings for each of the four states are adjacent to some coding assigned to each of the other three states. From the map, it is clear that if each state of any 4-state flow table is assigned the two corresponding codings shown, then all transitions can be made by changing exactly one variable. Thus, it is a universal single transition time state assignment for any 4-state table.

	$y_1\, y_2$			
y_3	00	01	11	10
0	1	3	4	2
1	4	2	1	3

Figure 6.22   Universal 4-state one-shot assignment (Hamming code)

Using concepts related to Hamming error correcting codes this type assignment can be generalized to n state tables where $n = 2^{S_0}$, requiring $n-1$ state variables. Since transitions should be permitted between all pairs of states and only one variable is allowed to change during any transition, such an assignment will require at least $n-1$ variables. Thus, if $n = 2^k$, the Hamming code assignment is a universal assignment with the minimum number of variables, in which all transitions are made with single variable changes.

Because of the large number of state variables required this type of state assignment is only of theoretical interest and will not be considered further here.

The number of variables required for an STT assignment can be reduced considerably by allowing more than one variable to change simultaneously, but without critical races. We shall now consider STT assignments with a single coding per state, usually referred to as *unicode* assignments. Such assignments were first proposed by Liu [5] and further developed by Tracey [6]. For an STT assignment, if several variables change during a transition the precise order of change cannot be prespecified. It is useful to define the *transition subcube*, $T(q_i, q_j)$, associated with states q_i and q_j as the set of all points that may be passed through during a transition between q_i and q_j (including q_i and q_j), assuming that the variables that change during a transition may do so in any arbitrary order. The transition subcube $T(q_i, q_j)$ consists of all points which are identical to q_i and q_j in the variables in which q_i and q_j agree. For example, if q_i and q_j are assigned $y_1\, y_2\, y_3\, y_4 = 0110$ and 1100 respectively, the circuit may pass through 0100 or 1110. The transition subcube $T(q_i, q_j)$ contains the four points 0100, 0110, 1100, and 1110 and is denoted by $T(q_i, q_j) = -1-0$ or $T(q_i, q_j) = y_2\, \bar{y}_4$ indicating that y_1 and y_3 may assume any value during the transition.

The intersection of $T(q_i, q_j)$ and $T(q_m, q_n)$, denoted by $T(q_i, q_j) \cap T(q_m, q_n)$, consists of those points contained in both subcubes. If in a column I_k of a flow table there are transitions from q_i to q_j and from q_m to q_n, where $q_n \neq q_j$, there is a critical race (assuming all variables change simultaneously) unless $T(q_i, q_j) \cap T(q_m, q_n) = \phi$ (i.e., there are no points contained in both subcubes). (This requirement is comparable to the disjoint path requirement for multi-step shared row state assignments.) In order that $T(q_i, q_j) \cap T(q_m, q_n) = \phi$, there must be some variable y_p which takes the value 0 for both q_i and q_j and the value 1 for q_m and q_n or vice versa. (Exercise.)

Liu [5] has developed a simple procedure for obtaining a state assignment with this property. The method consists of assigning a set of state variables associated with each column of the flow table so as to distinguish the stable states in that column from one another, each such stable state having a unique coding in the associated variables. Unstable states in the column are assigned the same values as the stable states reached from them. This procedure is only applicable to normal mode flow tables.

Procedure 6.2 (Liu's unicode STT assignment.) Let the normal mode flow table have m columns, $I_1, I_2, \ldots, I_m$ and let the column I_j have α_j stable states,

$1 \leq j \leq m$. For every column I_j, define $\lceil \log_2 \alpha_j \rceil$ variables $y_{j1}, y_{j2}, \ldots, y_{j\alpha_j}$ so that

(a) each stable state in column I_j has a unique coding in these variables;
(b) if $N(q_i, I_j) = q_k \neq q_i$, then the states q_i and q_k have the same coding in these variables.   ∎

Example 6.5   Consider the flow table shown in Figure 6.23. The column 00 has two stable states, 2 and 5, which are distinguished by y_1. States 1, 3, and 6, all of which lead to state 2 in the column 00, and state 2 itself are assigned $y_1 = 0$. States 4 and 5 are assigned $y_1 = 1$, since state 4 leads to the stable state 5 in the column 00. Similarly, the variables y_2 and y_3 are used to distinguish between the four stable states in column 01. The unstable states 2 and 5 are assigned the same values for the variables y_2 and y_3 as the states 6 and 3 respectively. Column 11 has three states and requires two state variables. How-

	00	01	11	10		y_1	y_2	y_3	y_4	y_5
1	2	①	①	–		0	0	0	0	0
2	②	6	4	②		0	1	1	1	–
3	2	③	③	–		0	0	1	0	1
4	5	④	④	–		1	1	0	1	–
5	⑤	3	1	⑤		1	0	1	0	0
6	2	⑥	3	–		0	1	1	0	1

$x_1 x_2$

Figure 6.23   Liu-type assignment for a flow table—Example 6.4

ever, it is possible to distinguish between them even if one variable is partially unspecified. Since $y_4 = 0$ for states 1 and 3, $y_4 = 1$ will distinguish state 4 from them and y_5 may be unspecified for state 4. We will shortly demonstrate how such unspecified entries may be useful in reducing the number of state variables required. Column 10 necessitates a variable to distinguish stable states 2 and 5. The previously defined variable y_1 or y_3 can be used for this purpose.   ∎

Lemma 6.2   Procedure 6.2 generates an STT state assignment without critical races.

Proof   Consider a transition from q_i to q_j in column I_k. By the construction of the state assignment, all the variables y_{ki} defined for column I_k remain constant during this transition, and the transition subcube $T(q_i, q_j)$ is specified in these variables. For any other transition (within I_k) from q_m to q_n, $q_n \neq q_j$, this set of variables distinguishes q_m and q_n from q_i and q_j. Therefore $T(q_i, q_j) \cap T(q_m, q_n) = \phi$, and no point outside $T(q_i, q_j)$ can be reached during the transition from q_i to q_j. Hence, no state $q_n \neq q_j$ can be reached during the transition, and there is no critical race in the transition. Two states will have the same coding only if the flow table can be reduced.   ∎

For columns with more than two stable states there is some flexibility in assigning codes. This flexibility can sometimes be used to make assignments in which some state variables can be eliminated.

Example 6.6   Consider the flow table of Figure 6.24(a). The assignment table of Figure 6.24(b) is obtained by using Procedure 6.2. State variables y_1 and y_2 are defined by column 00, y_3 and y_4 by column 01, and y_5 and y_6 by column

	$x_1 x_2$					y_1	y_2	y_3	y_4	y_5	y_6
	00	01	11	10							
1	4	①	2	-		0	1	0	0	0	0
2	3	②	②	-		0	0	0	1	0	0
3	③	③	5	-		0	0	1	0	0	1
4	④	④	6	-		0	1	1	1	1	-
5	⑤	3	⑤	-		1	0	1	0	0	1
6	⑥	1	⑥	-		1	1	0	0	1	-

(a)   (b)

	y_1	y_2	y_3	y_4	y_5
1	0	1	0	0	0
2	0	0	0	1	0
3	0	0	1	0	0
4	0	1	1	1	1
5	1	0	1	0	0
6	1	1	0	0	1

(c)

Figure 6.24   Reduction of state variables in Liu-type assignment—Example 6.5

11. The variable y_6 is identical to y_3 for all states for which y_6 is specified. Therefore y_6 can be removed and the resulting set of five variables of Figure 6.24(c) is still a valid STT assignment.   ∎

However this approach is not optimal. Consider the table of Figure 6.25. Procedure 6.2 generates the four variable assignment of Figure 6.25(b), where y_1 corresponds to column 00, y_2 to column 01, y_3 to column 11 and y_4 to column 10. Since y_1 and y_2 are identical, one of these may be eliminated resulting in the three variable assignment of Figure 6.25(c). However, if we list required adjacencies for this table we derive the two variable assignment of Figure 6.25(d) which is a unicode STT assignment since each transition only requires the change of a single state variable. Hence Liu's procedure obviously does not lead to a minimal variable unicode STT assignment.

| | $x_1\,x_2$ | | | | y_1 | y_2 | y_3 | y_4 | y_1 | y_3 | y_4 | y_a | y_b |
	00	01	11	10									
1	①	2	①	3	0	0	0	0	0	0	0	0	0
2	1	②	1	②	0	0	0	1	0	0	1	0	1
3	③	4	1	③	1	1	0	0	1	0	0	1	0
4	3	④	④	2	1	1	1	1	1	1	1	1	1
	(a)				(b)				(c)			(d)	

Figure 6.25   A flow table with several STT state assignments.

Another type of unicode STT assignment which frequently requires fewer variables than the Liu assignment discussed above has been developed by Tracey [6]. However, the Liu assignment is useful in certain special types of realizations [7]. Tracey's method always generates a minimal variable unicode STT assignment.

Instead of distinguishing between all states in a column, Tracey's method considers all pairs of transitions in each column. Let us define a *partial dichotomy* (or simply *dichotomy*) of the states of a machine as a disjoint 2-block partition of a subset of the set of states. We can then associate a dichotomy with any pair of transitions in a column of a flow table. The dichotomy associated with the transitions $q_i \rightarrow q_j$ and $q_k \rightarrow q_m$ is $(q_i, q_j; q_k, q_m)$. A state variable is said to *cover* a dichotomy if that variable is 0 for all states in one block and 1 for all states in the other block. For example, a variable y_p covers a dichotomy $(q_i, q_j; q_k, q_m)$ if $y_p(q_i) = y_p(q_j) = 0$ and $y_p(q_k) = y_p(q_m) = 1$, or vice versa, where $y_p(q_n)$ denotes the value of the state variable y_p associated with state q_n.

If a column has a stable state q_j and a transition $q_k \rightarrow q_m$, we can associate a degenerate dichotomy $(q_j; q_k, q_m)$ with the stable state and the transition. Similarly, a dichotomy $(q_j; q_m)$ can be associated with a pair of stable states in a column. The following Lemma, due to Tracey [6], gives necessary and sufficient conditions for a unicode single transition time assignment for any normal mode flow table.

Lemma 6.3   A state assignment for a normal mode flow table is a unicode STT assignment if and only if for every pair of transitions $q_i \rightarrow q_j$ and $q_k \rightarrow q_m$, $q_j \neq q_m$, appearing in the same column of the table, the dichotomy $(q_i, q_j; q_k, q_m)$ is covered by some y-variable. The dichotomies should also include the degenerate (2-state and 3-state) dichotomies that may be required in each column.

Proof   Sufficiency From the definition of the covering of a dichtomy by a state variable, it follows that the variable covering the dichotomy $(q_i, q_j; q_k, q_m)$ will be 0 during the transition $q_i \rightarrow q_j$, and 1 during the transition $q_k \rightarrow q_m$ or vice versa. The transition subcubes $T(q_i, q_j)$ and $T(q_k, q_m)$ are therefore disjoint and there can be no critical races involving these two transitions. If for every stable state q_j, and every transition $q_k \rightarrow q_m$ in the same column, the degenerate dichotomy $(q_j; q_k, q_m)$ is covered by some y-variable, then $q_j \notin T(q_k, q_m)$ and the state q_j cannot be reached during the $q_k \rightarrow q_m$ transition, independent of the order of change of the variables. Covering of the dichotomies of the type $(q_j; q_m)$ guarantees that stable states in any column are always distinguished.

Necessity   If a column contains transitions $q_i \rightarrow q_j$ and $q_k \rightarrow q_m$ and the dichotomy $(q_i, q_j; q_k, q_m)$ is not covered by any variable, the transition subcubes $T(q_i, q_j)$ and $T(q_k, q_m)$ will not be disjoint. Since there will be one or more points contained in both transition subcubes, the next states for these transient states cannot be uniquely specified so as to eliminate critical races if state variables are permitted to change simultaneously during the transition. Similarly, if the dichotomy $(q_j; q_k, q_m)$ is not covered by any variable, the transition subcube $T(q_k, q_m)$ will contain the state q_j, and the stable state q_j may be reached during the transition from q_k to q_m. The covering of the dichotomy $(q_i; q_j)$ is necessary to ensure that the states q_i and q_j can be distinguished.   ∎

Let us now reconsider the table of Figure 6.25 which is repeated in Figure 6.26(a). The state assignment of Figure 6.26(b) is defined using Tracey's procedure, where the dichotomy of column 00 defines y_1, the dichotomy of column 01 defines y_2, the two dichotomies of column 11 define y_3 and y_4, and the dichotomy of column 10 defines variable y_5. However this state assignment can be simplified. Since y_1 and y_2 are identical one of them, say y_2, can be eliminated. Since y_3 and y_1 are identical except for the unspecified entry in state 3 of y_3, y_3 can be eliminated. Similarly y_4 is identical to y_5 except for the unspecified entry in state 2 of y_4 so y_4 can be eliminated. The resulting assignment, shown in Figure 6.26(c), is identical to the minimal assignment of Figure 6.25(d). Note that Liu's procedure would define a single variable for column 11, which could not be eliminated. This variable could be viewed as a combined y_3 and y_4. Thus

	$x_1 x_2$ 00	01	11	10		y_1	y_2	y_3	y_4	y_5		y_1	y_5
1	①	2	①	3		0	0	0	0	0		0	0
2	1	②	1	②		0	0	0	-	1		0	1
3	③	4	1	③		1	1	-	0	0		1	0
4	3	④	④	2		1	1	1	1	1		1	1
		(a)						(b)				(c)	

Figure 6.26   A flow table and minimal STT assignment

Liu's method in effect defines localized variable minimization on a column but does not achieve global minimization.

The problem of obtaining a unicode STT assignment with the minimum number of state variables can be solved for small flow tables using methods similar to those used for the sequential machine state reduction problem. The concept of maximal compatibles used for the latter is also useful for deriving minimal variable STT assignments.

This procedure is complicated somewhat by the fact that each dichotomy is actually an unordered set of two state pairs for which there are two corresponding ordered state pairs, either one of which it is sufficient to cover. We shall not cover this subject in greater detail. Suffice it to say that the procedure for generating maximal compatibles can be generalized to form a covering table whose solution generates a minimal variable unicode STT assignment.

If more than one coding is assigned to some or all states of a flow table, it may be possible to obtain STT assignments with fewer variables than a unicode STT assignment. Although such *multicode STT assignments* may require fewer variables than unicode assignments, general methods for constructing them and bounds on the number of state variables required are not known at present [8].

We have now developed several different techniques for deriving valid state assignments for asynchronous flow tables. The remaining step to complete synthesis is designing the combinational excitation logic circuit.

6.5.2   Specification of the Y-Map

As with synchronous circuits, once the state assignment has been specified, the logic circuit can be realized with the use of Y-maps and/or flip-flop excitation maps. However, there are several important differences between the asynchronous and synchronous cases. In the synchronous circuit Y-map specification, those entries corresponding to codes which were not assigned to any state could be left unspecified, since the actual circuit could never reach such a configuration. For asynchronous circuits using shared row state assignments or STT assign-

ments, unassigned codes may be entered during transitions. The entries of the
Y-map in this case must be specified so that the transition is properly completed.
The entries which must be specified and how they must be specified depend on
the type of assignment used. All possible intermediate codes for any transition
must be specified. In addition, the entries corresponding to a code for a state q_i
in column I_k will not always be equal to $N(q_i, I_k)$. If this is part of a multistep
transition, the entry may correspond to an intermediate state in the transition.
The following examples demonstrate the construction of Y-maps for shared row
and unicode STT assignments.

Example 6.7   Consider the flow table for each input column and the shared
row assignment of Figure 6.27(a). The transitions are made as shown in
Figure 6.27(b) and the Y-map of Figure 6.27(c) is obtained. The transition from
state 5 to state 6 in column 00 as shown in Figure 6.27(b) is a multistep transition
$011 \rightarrow 111 \rightarrow 101$. Therefore, the next state entry for 011 in column 00 is
specified as 111, and the next state entry of the unassigned code 111 is specified
as 101 in column 00 [Figure 6.27(c)]. Similarly, the transition from state 4 to
state 5 in column 01 is specified as $110 \rightarrow 111 \rightarrow 011$, and the state 6 to state
4 transition in column 11 as $101 \rightarrow 111 \rightarrow 110$. All other transitions are between
adjacent states. In general, in shared row as well as connected row set assignments, each transition is accomplished by a sequence of single variable changes,
and the Y-map is defined accordingly.   ■

Example 6.8   Consider the flow table of Figure 6.28(a) and the 3-variable
unicode STT assignment shown to the right of the flow table. The associated Y-

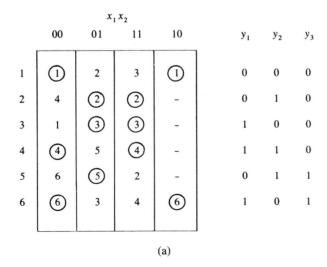

(a)

Figure 6.27 Y-map specification for a shared row state assignment—Example 6.6

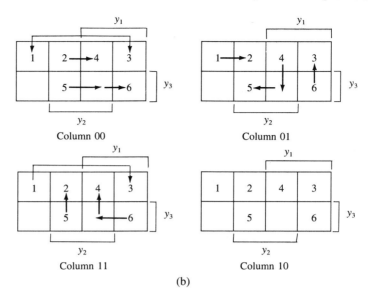

(b)

	y_1	y_2	y_3	$x_1 x_2$ 00	01	11	10
(1)	0	0	0	000	010	100	000
	0	0	1	—	—	—	—
(5)	0	1	1	111	011	010	—
(2)	0	1	0	110	010	010	—
(4)	1	1	0	110	111	110	—
	1	1	1	101	011	110	—
(6)	1	0	1	101	100	111	101
(3)	1	0	0	000	100	100	—

(c)

Figure 6.27   (continued)

map is shown in Figure 6.28(b). If a coding is assigned to state q_i, and $N(q_i, I_k)$ $= q_j$, the next state entry of this coding in column I_k is the coding assigned to state q_j. All variables which must change value are permitted to be excited simultaneously. Since these variables may change in any order, all points in the transition subcube $T(q_i, q_j)$ in column I_k must be specified with the coding for state q_j. Thus since the transition subcube associated with the transition from

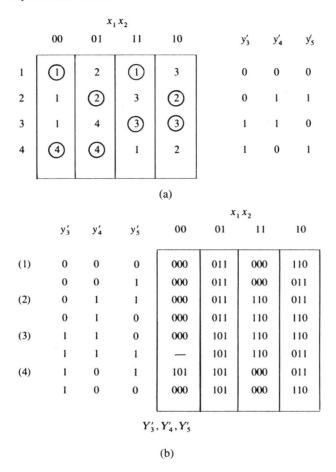

Figure 6.28 *Y*-matrix specification for a unicode STT assignment—Example 6.7

state 3 to state 1 in column 00 of the table of Figure 6.28(a) is --0, the four codings 000, 100, 010, and 110 in the *Y*-map, all have entries 000 corresponding to state 1. ∎

The outputs of the sequential circuit were ignored in the previous examples. In a normal mode flow table, if $N(q_i, I_k) = q_j$, then $Z(q_i, I_k) = Z(q_j, I_k)$. In order to keep the output constant during the $q_i \rightarrow q_j$ transition, all points that may be entered during the transition must be assigned the output $Z(q_i, I_k)$. If a multistep transition is used as in connected row set or shared row assignments, all codings in the transition are assigned this output in column I_k. In a unicode STT assignment, all points in the transition subcube $T(q_i, q_j)$ are assigned this output in column I_k.

6.6   DELAYS AND HAZARDS

So far we have only concerned ourselves with the problem of ensuring that the inputs to the combinational logic which generates the memory excitation functions (in the mode of Figure 6.1) are restricted in such a way that the next state and output can be unambiguously determined in any transition, and hence with idealized combinational excitation logic, the circuit will function properly. We have done this by assuming that only one input variable changes at any time, and by restricting the state assignment so that any transition is accomplished by the change of a single state variable, a sequence of single state variable changes, or, in the case of an STT assignment, the state variables which do not change value in the transition and the input variables unambiguously determine the desired next state and output. However the combinational excitation logic is not ideal, and care must be exercised in its design to ensure proper operation.

Any physical switching circuit has delays associated with gates and interconnecting lines. While these delays were not important in synchronous circuits because of the clock pulse, their effects on the operation of asynchronous circuits are significant. The delays associated with gates and lines are usually called *stray delays* to distinguish them from delays that may be *inserted* in the circuit to ensure proper operation. The stray delay in a line may represent the time taken for a signal to propagate along the line. A gate may operate only when its inputs are above some threshold value. Since a signal cannot change instantaneously, the effect of the rate of change of signal value and the threshold for switching can be most conveniently represented by a suitable delay at the gate input. Similarly, the switching time associated with the gate may be represented by a delay at the gate output. Although the exact values of the stray delays in a circuit are usually unknown because of the variation in the properties of the components used, the range of values is known. We shall assume that the values of stray delays range from 0 to some known upper bound much less than the magnitude of delay elements which can be inserted in feedback loops and used as memory elements. Stray delays are assumed to be lumped at the inputs and outputs of gates and in connecting lines.

Two types of delays are of interest. A *pure delay* of magnitude D produces an output $f(t-D)$ in response to an input $f(t)$. That is, the output is merely delayed by a fixed amount D, and the output and input waveforms are identical. An *inertial delay* of magnitude D delays an input change by D if it persists for at least time D. Input changes of duration less than D are not transmitted through the inertial delay. Thus, inertial delays can be used to represent the property of some physical devices that require the inputs to persist for a certain length of time before the device responds to it. For example, a pulse of short duration at the input of a flip-flop may have no effect on its state. Figure 6.29 illustrates the difference between pure and inertial delays. Stray delays may be assumed to have both pure and inertial components.

A circuit is said to contain a *hazard* if there exists some possible combination of values of stray delays which will produce a spurious pulse or cause the circuit

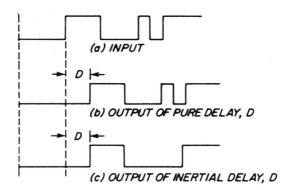

Figure 6.29   Behavior of pure and inertial delays (a) Input   (b) Output of pure delay
                 D (c) Output of inertial delay, D

to enter an incorrect stable state, for some input change. Note that a hazard represents only a possibility of malfunction. A specific circuit may not malfunction even though a hazard exists, because the relative magnitudes of actual stray delays may ensure proper operation, and hence the hazard represents the worst case.

The possibility of the occurrence of spurious pulses on the outputs of a purely combinational circuit for certain input changes is called a *hazard*. Hazards are usually divided into two classes—*static* and *dynamic*. A static hazard is said to be present when the output of a circuit is required to remain constant during a transition, but for some distribution of stray delays, the output may contain one or more pulses (i.e., the output changes an even number of times). Static hazards are classified as *0- and 1-hazards*, depending on whether the output is specified to be 0 or 1 during the transition. A dynamic hazard may produce a sequence of three (or a greater odd number) output changes when a single change is required.

The study of hazards is important both from a synthesis and analysis point of view. Specifically we have the following two problems:

1. Synthesis of hazard free excitation functions.
2. Analysis of arbitrary circuits to determine the existence of any hazards.

We first consider the problem of synthesis, restricting ourselves to sum-of-product realizations. As we have previously seen static-1 hazards can occur in such circuits if there are two adjacent 1-points which are not covered by a common product term.* However static 0-hazards and dynamic hazards do not ordinarily occur as we prove in the following Lemma.

Lemma 6.4   Let C be a two-level sum-of-products circuit which realizes a combinational function f. Let I_1 and I_2 be two input states which differ only in

---

*The circuit of Figure 5.9 is actually a 2-level sum-of-products complemented.

the value of one variable x_k, and consider the transition between I_1 and I_2. For this transition

a) C has a static 0-hazard if and only if $f(I_1) = f(I_2) = 0$ and there is an AND gate having both x_k and $\bar{x}_k$ as inputs, and the remaining inputs to this gate are 1 for both of the input states I_1 and I_2.

b) C has a static 1-hazard if and only if $f(I_1) = f(I_2) = 1$ and there is no product term (AND gate) that is 1 for both I_1 and I_2.

c) C has a dynamic hazard if and only if $f(I_1) \neq f(I_2)$ and C has an AND gate with both x_k and $\bar{x}_k$ as inputs and the remaining inputs to this gate are 1 for both I_1 and I_2.

Proof (of part (a)).   *Sufficiency:* Consider the transition $I_1 \rightarrow I_2$, and without loss of generality, let $x_k = 0$ in I_1. When the input state is I_1, the outputs of all AND gates will be 0. Consider the gate satisfying the conditions of the lemma. Let the stray delays be such that the $0 \rightarrow 1$ change in x_k reaches the AND gate before the $1 \rightarrow 0$ change in $\bar{x}_k$. Thus, all the inputs to the AND gate may be 1 for a long enough period to produce a spurious 1 output, resulting in the sequence $0 \rightarrow 1 \rightarrow 0$ at the output of the circuit.

Necessity: Since the OR gate itself cannot produce a 1 output if all its inputs are 0, one of the AND gates must produce the $0 \rightarrow 1 \rightarrow 0$ transient if a static hazard exists. An AND gate can produce such an output sequence only if at least one input undergoes a $0 \rightarrow 1$ change and at least one input undergoes a $1 \rightarrow 0$ change, while the remaining inputs stay fixed at 1. Since x_k is the only input variable that changes during the input transition, the inputs that change can only be x_k and $\bar{x}_k$ and the remaining inputs to that gate must be 1.   ∎

The proofs of parts (b) and (c) of the Lemma are similarly straightforward and are left as an exercise.

It follows from Lemma 6.4 that a 2-level sum-of-products realization will contain static hazards for transitions during which the output is required to remain at 0 only if it contains terms with both a variable and its complement. Such terms are clearly unnecessary and may be discarded without changing the function realized, and at the same time eliminating this class of static hazards. Dynamic hazards are also eliminated in this way. Finally static 1-hazards can be eliminated if each pair of adjacent 1-points is covered by a common product term.

Example 6.9   Consider the circuit of Figure 6.30(a) and the transition from the input state 111 to 011. When the input state is 111, $a = 1$ and $b = 0$. When the input x_1 changes to 0, a changes from 1 to 0, while b changes from 0 to 1. If the $0 \rightarrow 1$ change on b reaches the OR gate after the $1 \rightarrow 0$ change on a has reached it (due to a larger stray delay in the path to b than in the path to a), then both the inputs to the OR gate may be 0 long enough to produce a 0 output. This hazard can be removed by adding an AND gate realizing $x_2 x_3$ to the realization. The term $x_2 x_3$ will be 1 for both the input states 111 and 011 (Figure 6.30(b)).

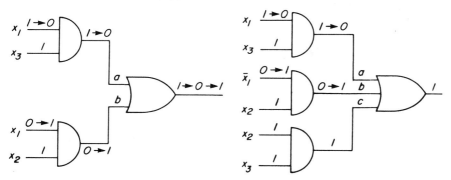

Figure 6.30 Combinational circuit with a static hazard—Example 6.7

Another method of eliminating the transient during the $111 \rightarrow 011$ transition is to delay the $1 \rightarrow 0$ change on a (possibly by inserting a delay element) so that the $0 \rightarrow 1$ change on b reaches the OR gate first. However, this will produce a transient during the transition from 011 to 111. ∎

From Lemma 6.4 it follows that a 2-level sum-of-products realization of a function f will have no static 0-hazards and will only have static 1-hazards for single input variable changes if there exist two adjacent 1-points of f which are not covered by a common product term. Such a hazard can be eliminated by adding a product term which covers both of these 1-points to the realization. It can be shown that all static logic hazards in a sum-of-products realization of f can be eliminated by including every prime implicant of the function in the realization and excluding terms containing a variable and its complement [9]. For single input variable changes the inclusion of *all* prime implicants is sufficient but not necessary to have each pair of adjacent 1-points covered by a common product term and hence eliminate all static hazards (See Problem 6.9).

We can thus realize hazard-free sum-of-products circuits. The principle of duality can be used to derive similar results for product-of-sums circuits.

6.7 TYING IT ALL TOGETHER—A COMPLETE SYNTHESIS EXAMPLE

So far we have discussed different problems related to synthesis. The following example demonstrates the complete synthesis of an asynchronous sequential circuit from a flow table, including some of the alternative design options which may be available during the design.

Example 6.10 The flow table of Figure 6.31 has transitions between every pair of states. Therefore, a connected row set or shared row state assignment will require more than two variables, since every state must be adjacent to three other states. However it is possible to obtain 3-variable STT assignments so we will only consider these. The Hamming assignment (Figure 6.22) is such an assign-

$$x_1 x_2$$

	00	01	11	10
1	①,0	2 ,1	①,1	3 ,1
2	1 ,0	②,1	3 ,0	②,0
3	1 ,0	4 ,1	③,0	③,1
4	④,1	④,1	1 ,1	2 ,0

Figure 6.31   Flow table for Example 6.8

ment. A unicode STT assignment must cover the dichotomies (12, 4), (13, 4), (12, 34), (14, 23), and (13, 24). The 3-variable assignment of Figure 6.32(a) covers all of these dichotomies.

	y_1	y_2	y_3			y_1	y_2	y_3	00	01	11	10
1	0	0	0	(1)		0	0	0	000,0	011,1	000,1	110,1
2	0	1	1			0	0	1	000,0	011,1	000,1	011,0
3	1	1	0	(2)		0	1	1	000,0	011,1	110,0	011,0
4	1	0	1			0	1	0	000,0	011,1	110,0	110,1
		(a)		(3)		1	1	0	000,0	101,1	110,0	110,1
						1	1	1	—	101,1	110,0	011,0
				(4)		1	0	1	101,1	101,1	000,1	011,0
						1	0	0	000,0	101,1	000,1	110,1

$$x_1 x_2$$

(b)

Figure 6.32   (a) A unicode STT state assignment (b) Y, z-map

We shall only consider the generation of the excitation logic for the unicode STT assignment. The Y, z-map of Figure 6.32(b) is obtained by assigning to every point in a transition subcube the same next state and output as the final stable state.

To ensure proper operation the circuit should contain no static hazards. If each Y_i is realized in the sum-of-products form, it is sufficient to verify that for any transition $(q_i, I_j) \rightarrow (q_m, I_k)$ in which Y_i is to remain constant at 1 the points (q_i, I_j) and (q_i, I_k) are covered by a single term of Y_i and all points in the transition subcube $T(q_i, q_m)$ in column I_k must be covered by a single term of Y_i. This assumes that delay elements are inserted in all feedback loops.

Thus the transition $(3, 11) \rightarrow (4, 01)$ requires the terms $x_2 y_1 y_2$ and $\bar{x}_1 x_2 y_1$ in Y_1. From the Y, z-map, we obtain the following hazard free expressions for the next state and output functions:

$$Y_1 = \bar{x}_1 y_1 y_3 + \bar{x}_1 x_2 y_1 + x_1 x_2 y_2 + x_1 \bar{x}_2 \bar{y}_3$$
$$+ x_1 y_2 \bar{y}_3 + x_2 y_1 y_2$$
$$Y_2 = \bar{x}_1 x_2 \bar{y}_1 + x_1 y_2 + x_1 \bar{x}_2 + x_2 \bar{y}_1 y_2$$
$$Y_3 = \bar{x}_1 y_1 y_3 + \bar{x}_1 x_2 + x_1 \bar{x}_2 y_3 + \bar{x}_2 y_1 y_3$$
$$z = \bar{x}_1 y_1 y_3 + \bar{x}_1 x_2 + x_2 \bar{y}_2 + x_1 \bar{x}_2 \bar{y}_3 + x_1 \bar{y}_2 \bar{y}_3 \quad \blacksquare$$

6.8 ANALYSIS OF HAZARDS

6.8.1 Combinational Hazards

In addition to being able to synthesize hazard-free circuits, it is also important to be able to analyze circuits for hazards.

We have restricted our discussions so far to hazards in 2-level sum-of-products realizations. The following Lemma provides a method of determining whether any combinational circuit contains static hazards, by transforming it into a 2-level sum-of-products form. It can be proven by showing that each type of transformation used does not add or remove static hazards [10].

Lemma 6.5 If the Boolean expression representing a combinational circuit is transformed into a sum-of-products expression using only the associative and distributive laws and DeMorgan's Law (which can always be done), the resulting expression will have the same static hazards as the original circuit. $\quad \blacksquare$

From Lemmas 6.4 and 6.5 it follows that a combinational circuit has static hazards if and only if the corresponding sum-of-products expression E derived by use of the associative and distributive laws and DeMorgan's Law, has a product term P containing both x and $\bar{x}$ for one variable only, and if all other literals in P are set to 1, $E = x \bar{x}$ or if for some possible transition between 1-points I_1 and I_2, no product term of E covers both I_1 and I_2. However Lemma 6.5 is not valid for dynamic hazards. (See Problem 6.14.) Let E be a Boolean expression corresponding to a multiple level combinational circuit. From Lemma 6.5 it can be shown that if by assigning constants to some set of variables the resulting expression becomes $x + x \bar{x}$ or $x(x + \bar{x})$, then the original circuit has a dynamic hazard for the transition caused by changing x while the other variables remain constant at the appropriate values which cause E to assume the appropriate form.

Example 6.11 Consider the circuit of Figure 6.33 and the corresponding Boolean expression

$$E(x_1, x_2, x_3, x_4) = \bar{x}_1 (\bar{x}_2 + \bar{x}_3) + (x_1 + \bar{x}_2)(x_2 + x_3 x_4)$$

Note that this expression has not been simplified. We can determine the existence of static or dynamic hazards by attempting to reduce E to an expression of the form $x_i \bar{x}_i$, $x_i + \bar{x}_i$, $x_i + x_i \bar{x}_i$ or $(x_i + \bar{x}_i) x_i$ for each of the four variables. We first

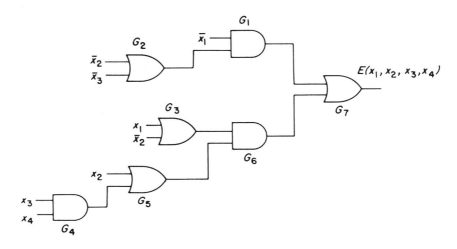

Figure 6.33   A combinational circuit

attempt to assign values to x_2, x_3, and x_4 so as to reduce E to an expression in x_1 of the proper form. In order that the variable x_1 in the term $(x_1 + \bar{x}_2)$ not be eliminated we must assign $\bar{x}_2 = 0$ which implies $x_2 = 1$. E then reduces to

$$E(x_1, 1, x_3, x_4) = \bar{x}_1 (\bar{x}_3) + x_1.$$

By assigning $\bar{x}_3 = 1$ which implies $x_3 = 0$ we obtain $E(x_1, 1, 0, x_4) = x_1 + \bar{x}_1$. Thus the transition brought about by changing x_1 when $x_2 = 1$, $x_3 = 0$ and $x_4 = 0$ or 1 defines a static 1-hazard. Similarly since $E(0, x_2, 1, 0) = \bar{x}_2 + \bar{x}_2 x_2$, the transition brought about by changing x_2 with $x_1 = 0$, $x_3 = 1$, $x_4 = 0$ is a dynamic hazard. It is easily confirmed that changes in x_3 or x_4 alone do not define hazardous transitions.   ■

The equation approach just presented can be used to determine whether any hazards exist but it requires the complete unsimplified Boolean expression and hence may be limited in practice to relatively small circuits. A somewhat different simulation based approach can be used to determine whether a specific transition involves a static hazard. This approach only requires a circuit description instead of the more complex unsimplified Boolean expression. A three-valued algebra is used with signal values 0, $\frac{1}{2}$ 1. The value $\frac{1}{2}$, is used to represent signals that are changing value. For a transition $I_1 \rightarrow I_2$, the output of the circuit for input

$I_1, f(I_1)$ is first computed. Then *all* changing inputs are set to $\frac{1}{2}$ and the output of the circuit is recomputed where the output of an AND is equal to the minimum value of any of its inputs, the output of an OR is the maximum value of any of its inputs, and the output of a NAND (NOR) is $1 - \min$ (inputs) $(1 - \max$ (inputs)). This is referred to as the *halves pass*. Finally $f(I_2)$ is computed. A static hazard exists for this transition if and only if $f(I_1) = f(I_2)$ and the halves pass output is $\frac{1}{2}$. If $f(I_1) \neq f(I_2)$ the halves pass value will always be $\frac{1}{2}$, whether or not there is a dynamic hazard. Hence this method is not capable of detecting dynamic hazards.

Example 6.12   For the circuit of Figure 6.33, consider the transition $I_1 \rightarrow I_2$ where $I_1 = (0, 1, 0, 0)$ and $I_2 = (1, 1, 0, 0)$. In Example 6.11 we saw that this transition defined a static 1-hazard. Using the three-valued algebra we first compute $Z(I_1) = Z(0, 1, 0, 0) = 1$. For the halves pass we must compute $Z(\frac{1}{2}, 1, 0, 0)$. The outputs of gates G_2, G_4, and G_5 are unchanged at values 1, 0, and 1 respectively. The output of gate G_3 is max $(\frac{1}{2}, 0) = \frac{1}{2}$ and the output of G_1 is min $(\frac{1}{2}, 1) = \frac{1}{2}$. Since G_6 has inputs from G_3 and G_5 its output is min $(\frac{1}{2}, 1) = \frac{1}{2}$ and the output of G_7 is max $(\frac{1}{2}, \frac{1}{2}) = \frac{1}{2}$. Since $Z(I_2) = Z(1, 1, 0, 0) = 1$, the static 1-hazard for this transition is confirmed.

Applying the same technique to the two transitions $I_3 = (0, 0, 1, 0) \rightarrow I_4 = (0, 1, 1, 0)$ and $I_5 = (1, 0, 1, 1) \rightarrow I_6 = (1, 0, 1, 0)$ leads to the output sequence $1 \rightarrow \frac{1}{2} \rightarrow 0$ in both cases. Since the $I_3 \rightarrow I_4$ transition defines a dynamic hazard whereas the $I_5 \rightarrow I_6$ transition does not, we see that this procedure cannot be used to predict dynamic hazards.   ∎

Instead of requiring three different signal evaluation passes, as the 3-valued algebra does, it is possible to use a single pass with a more complex 8-valued algebra.

This algebra (similar to a 9-valued algebra proposed by Fantauzzi [11]) can be used for detecting static and dynamic hazards in combinational circuits. The 8 possible values of a signal are 0, 1, $+$ indicating a $0 \rightarrow 1$ transition, $-$ indicating a $1 \rightarrow 0$ transition, $S0$ indicating a static 0-hazard, $S1$ for a static 1-hazard, $D+$ indicating a dynamic hazard in a $0 \rightarrow 1$ transition and $D-$ for a dynamic hazard in a $1 \rightarrow 0$ transition. Only one computation is required in place of the three passes for the ternary algebra. For two input AND- and OR-gates and inverters, the outputs can be computed from the tables of Figure 6.34. Thus the output of an AND gate with inputs $+$ and $-$ is $S0$. The principles of associativity and commutativity can be shown to be valid for this algebra.

In addition to the eight values used here, Fantauzzi [11] uses a ninth value to represent unknown signal values. By this extension, the method can be used for circuits containing flip-flops but no feedback (other than that within the flip-flops).

Example 6.13   For the circuit of Figure 6.33 we reconsider the three transitions $I_1 \rightarrow I_2$, $I_3 \rightarrow I_4$, and $I_5 \rightarrow I_6$ as defined in Example 6.10. The circuits of

AND	1	0	+	−	S1	S0	D+	D−
1	1	0	+	−	S1	S0	D+	D−
0	0	0	0	0	0	0	0	0
+	+	0	+	S0	D+	S0	D+	S0
−	−	0	S0	−	D−	S0	S0	D−
S1	S1	0	D+	D−	S1	S0	D+	D−
S0	S0	0	S0	S0	S0	S0	S0	S0
D+	D+	0	D+	S0	D+	S0	D+	S0
D−	D−	0	S0	D−	D−	S0	S0	D−

(a)

OR	1	0	+	−	S1	S0	D+	D−
1	1	1	1	1	1	1	1	1
0	1	0	+	−	S1	S0	D+	D−
+	1	+	+	S1	S1	D+	D+	S1
−	1	−	S1	−	S1	D−	S1	D−
S1	1	S1	S1	S1	S1	S1	S1	S1
S0	1	S0	D+	D−	S1	S0	D+	D−
D+	1	D+	D+	S1	S1	D+	D+	S1
D−	1	D−	S1	D−	S1	D−	S1	D−

(b)

x	$\bar{x}$
0	1
1	0
+	−
−	+
S0	S1
S1	S0
D+	D−
D−	D+

(c)

Figure 6.34   Tables for 8-valued algebra

Figure 6.35(a), (b), (c) show the signal values in the 8-valued algebra for these three cases. It is clear that the 8-valued algebra correctly computes the output in all three cases. ∎

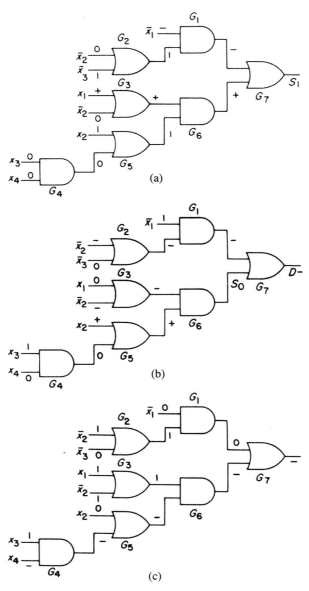

Figure 6.35 (a) Circuit transition $I_1 \rightarrow I_2$ (b) Circuit transition $I_3 \rightarrow I_4$ (c) Circuit transition $I_5 \rightarrow I_6$

6.8.2   Sequential Hazards

The model of asynchronous sequential circuits which we have been considering has a delay element in each feedback loop. The presence of these inserted delays ensures that the combinational excitation logic will have completed its response to an input change before it sees any state variable changes produced by that input change. This along with the other precautions we have taken regarding the state assignment, design of hazard-free combinational logic, and the single input variable change assumption are sufficient to ensure proper operation. In analyzing such circuits, it is usually assumed that there are no restrictions on the relative magnitudes of stray delays in the circuit, but that these delays are non-negative and the upper bound D' is known. The lower bound on the magnitudes of the inserted delays D is assumed to be known and it is usually assumed that $D > > D'$. The minimum time between successive input changes for fundamental mode operation is determined by the state assignment and the bounds on the magnitude of stray and inserted delays. In some cases the circuit may function properly without some or all of these inserted delay elements. However, in general their removal may cause the circuit to malfunction in which case the circuit is said to have a *sequential hazard*. We shall restrict our attention to normal mode flow tables. Similar techniques are applicable to non-normal tables.

There are two types of hazards that may be present in asynchronous sequential circuits. A circuit is said to contain a *steady state hazard* if there exists some distribution of stray delays such that the circuit may reach an incorrect state for some input transition. An *output hazard* (sometimes called a *transient hazard*) is said to be present if a spurious output pulse may be produced during some transition for some distribution of stray delays.

It may seem incongruous to give potential speed as a reason for asynchronous design and then to intentionally insert delays in feedback loops to slow up the circuit. However as we shall see these delays are actually being used to "fix" potential "critical races" between an x-variable and a y-variable. If no such potential races actually exist then the delay can be removed.

Consider the flow table segment of Figure 6.36(a) and the transition from $1 \rightarrow 2$. The actual sequence of events corresponding to this transition is as follows:

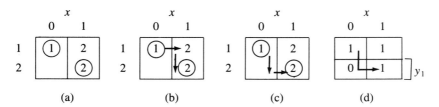

Figure 6.36   Possible transition paths in a state transition

1. x changes from $0 \rightarrow 1$
2. The x change causes y_1 to change from $0 \rightarrow 1$.

However due to the presence of stray delays of varying magnitudes in the logic circuit, to ensure that this sequence of changes is seen in the correct order a delay element is inserted in the feedback loop generating y_1. This ensures that the transition is made along the path shown in Figure 6.36(b). If this delay element were not inserted the transition could conceivably occur along the path shown in Figure 6.36(c). If some state excitation logic were as shown in Figure 6.36(d), this could result in a critical race between x and y_1.

Figure 6.37(b) shows a realization of the flow table of Figure 6.37(a) using the state assignment shown to its right. Let us consider the transition from 3 to 4. When x changes from 0 to 1, the output of AND gate a changes from 0 to 1 and the output of gate b changes from 1 to 0. As a result, Y_1 may undergo a $1 \rightarrow 0 \rightarrow 1$ transient. If the $0 \rightarrow 1$ change on a is delayed sufficiently with respect to the $1 \rightarrow 0$ change on b, the circuit may pass through state 2 represented

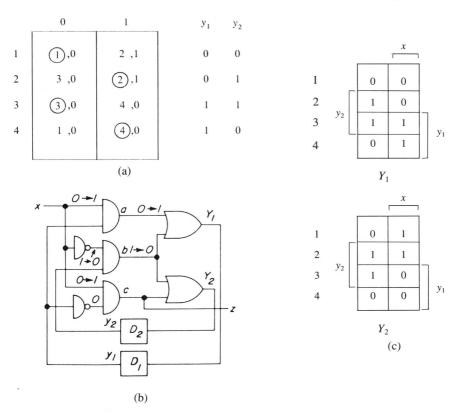

(a)

(b)

(c)

Figure 6.37   (a) A flow table and state assignment (b) Its realization (c) Karnaugh maps of Y_1 and Y_2

by $y_1 = 0$, $y_2 = 1$. Since this is a stable state in the $x = 1$ column, the circuit may stabilize in state 2 instead of reaching state 4 as specified in the flow table. This is a steady state hazard caused by the static hazard in the realization of Y_1. Similarly, a steady state hazard exists during the transition from state 2 to state 3. The circuit may reach state 1 instead of state 3. From the Karnaugh maps of Figure 6.36(c), we see that the static hazards and consequently the steady state hazard can be removed by adding the term $y_1 y_2$ and $\bar{y}_1 y_2$ to the realizations of Y_1 and Y_2 respectively.

The above circuit also contains an output hazard for the transition from state 3 to state 4. The $1 \rightarrow 0 \rightarrow 1$ transient resulting from the static hazard in Y_1 may produce a $0 \rightarrow 1 \rightarrow 0$ transient in the output z or an incorrect $0 \rightarrow 1$ change in the output. In this circuit, removal of the steady state hazard will also eliminate the output hazard.

The delays used in the feedback loops and/or as memory elements should be such that the effects of input changes reach all parts of the circuit before any change produced by state variable changes. If the delay element in some feedback path is eliminated or does not satisfy this constraint malfunctioning may occur even if all prime implicants of the next state functions are used in the realization.

Consider the circuit realizing the flow table of Figure 6.37(a) and assume that it is initially stable in state 1, with input $x = 0$. Now let us analyze the circuit behavior when the input changes to 1, if the delay memory elements do not satisfy the aforementioned constraints. The circuit first changes to state 2 (y_2 changes to 1). Due to large stray delays in the circuit, the effects of the y_2 change may reach some part of the circuit before the $0 \rightarrow 1$ input change. The next state for state 2, input 0 is 3 and therefore the circuit undergoes the $2 \rightarrow 3$ state transition (y_1 changes to 1). Finally, when the effects of the $0 \rightarrow 1$ change in x reaches all parts of the circuit, the circuit may reach the stable state 4 (y_2 changes back to 0), instead of state 2.

This type of hazard is a property of the flow table. Let I_1 and I_2 be two adjacent input states and q_i an internal state of a flow table, such that $N(q_i, I_1) = q_i$ and $N(q_i, I_2) = q_j$. The flow table contains an *essential hazard* for the $I_1 \rightarrow I_2$ transition from state q_i if the input sequence $I_2 I_1 I_2$ applied to the total state (q_i, I_1) results in a final state $q_k \neq q_j$.

Let the circuit realizing the flow table of Figure 6.37(a) be initially stable in state 1, with input $x = 0$. If the input changes to 1, the correct next state is 2, but the state reached by applying the input sequence 101 is 4. Thus the flow table has an essential hazard. In the flow table of Figure 6.37(a), all transitions involve essential hazards, although this is not generally true for arbitrary tables.

A realization of a flow table which contains an essential hazard may malfunction without inserted delay elements in some state variables due to possible critical races between the changing input variable and state variable(s) caused by stray delays. The problem can be solved by inserting delay elements in the feedback paths thus ensuring that the circuit completes its response to the input change before any changes in the state variable occur. The necessity of inserted delay elements in realizations of flow table containing essential hazards is stated in the following theorem due to Unger and proven in [8,10].

Lemma 6.6   Inserted delay elements are required for eliminating steady state hazards in a sequential circuit if and only if its flow table contains at least one essential hazard.   ∎

It is only necessary to delay those variables which change during the hazardous transitions. Unger has also shown constructively that one inserted delay element is sufficient for realizing any normal flow table, assuming that only one input variable changes during any transition. (See Problem 6.12.) Later in this chapter, we shall present a method of realization requiring only one delay element, but also permitting multiple-input changes, provided that all input changes associated with any input transition are completed within a fixed interval of time.

Flow tables without essential hazards can be realized without inserted delays, but special state assignments may be necessary in some cases. Consider the flow table segment shown in Figure 6.38 (referred to as a d-trio).

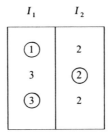

Figure 6.38   A d-trio

The transition from the total state $(1, I_1)$ to $(2, I_2)$ does not involve any essential hazard. If an STT assignment is used, the circuit may reach any point in the transition subcube $T(1,2)$ during the transition from state 1 to state 2, before the input change reaches some gate in the circuit. Since $N(2, I_1) = 3$, the circuit may then begin the transition from state 2 to state 3. Let the set of state variables which change in the transitions from 1 to 2 and 2 to 3 be denoted by A and B respectively. If no inserted delay elements are used, the set of variables $C = A \cup B$ must be assumed to change in any order and the circuit may pass through any coding which can be reached from state 2 in this manner. To ensure proper operation the state assignment must be such that for all such codings, the next state entry in column I_2 of the Y-matrix can be specified with the coding for state 2.

In the manner explained above flow tables without essential hazards can be realized without inserted delay elements. Such realizations will not contain steady state hazards but may contain output hazards (which cannot be removed).

It may not be necessary to insert delay elements in all feedback loops for flow tables with essential hazards. Delay elements will be necessary only for state variables that change during transitions involving essential hazards.

Example 6.14   The flow table of Figure 6.39(a) has no essential hazards and hence can be realized without any inserted delay elements. Using the state

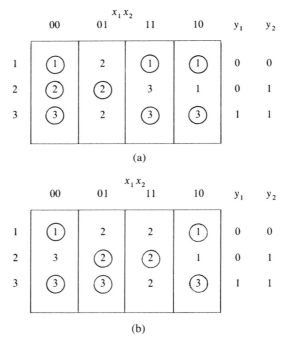

(a)

(b)

Figure 6.39   (a) Flow table without essential hazards, (b) Flow table containing an essential hazard

assignment shown to the right of the table, to prevent malfunctioning in the transition $(1,11) \rightarrow (2,01)$, associated with the only d-trio, we must specify the entry in column 01 and row 10 of the Y-matrix with the coding 01 associated with state 2. This results in the excitation functions

$$Y_1 = \bar{x}_2 \, y_1 + x_1 \, y_1 + x_1 \, x_2 \, y_2$$
$$Y_2 = y_1 + \bar{x}_1 \, y_2 + x_2 \, y_2 + \bar{x}_1 \, x_2$$

The flow table of Figure 6.39(b) has an essential hazard associated with the transition from the total state $(1, 00)$ to the total state $(2, 01)$. Since this is the only essential hazard and the only state variable that changes during this transition is y_2 (using the state assignment shown), a delay element is reqired only for this variable. The only d-trio is associated with the transition $(3, 10) \rightarrow (2, 11)$. By specifying the entry in row 10 and column 11 with the coding for state 2, the resulting circuit will operate properly.   ∎

The three-valued algebra previously introduced for detecting hazards in combinational logic circuits may also be used for detecting steady state hazards in sequential circuits with or without inserted delay elements, and for single-input or multiple-input variable changes. If the circuit contains delay elements (pure or inertial), their magnitudes are assumed to be greater than the time taken by the circuit to respond to the x-input changes.

Procedure 6.3   (Hazard detection in sequential circuits.)

1. Consider a transition from a stable total state (q_i, I_j) resulting from the input change $I_j \to I_k$. For every input variable x_i that changes during the transition, set $x_i = 1/2$. Leave the other input variables and all state variables at previous known values.
2. Compute the values of all the gates in the circuit as specified previously, assuming that the outputs of inserted delay elements do not change yet. Repeat until all gate outputs stabilize.
3. Change all the input variables which were assigned the value $1/2$ in step 1, to their new values corresponding to the input state I_k and recompute gate outputs as in step 2 until they stabilize, still not permitting delay element outputs to change.
4. Change the outputs of pure delay elements to values of their respective inputs at the end of step 2. For inertial delays, change their outputs to the values of their respective inputs at the end of step 3. Recompute all gate outputs, until they stabilize.
5. Change the outputs of pure delay elements to values of their respective inputs at end of step 3. Recompute all gate outputs until they stabilize.
6. If any delay element inputs computed in steps 4 or 5 are different from the delay outputs change those outputs to the respective input values and recompute gate outputs. Repeat until no further changes occur. If some state variables remain at $1/2$, the circuit contains a steady state hazard for the transition under consideration.   ∎

Example 6.15   Consider the circuit of Figure 6.40(a), which is intended to realize the flow table of Figure 6.40(b). Let us first consider the case when there are no inserted delay elements in the feedback paths. With the circuit initially stable with $x = y_1 = y_2 = 0$, the effect of changing x to 1 can be determined by setting x to $1/2$. If $x = 1/2$, Y_2 becomes $1/2$. With no delay elements, y_2 becomes $1/2$, which in turn causes Y_1 and then y_1 to become $1/2$. Since no further change is possible, we now change x to 1. Y_1 and Y_2 remain at $1/2$, indicating the presence of a steady state hazard for this transition. This flow table contains an essential hazard for this transition as shown previously.

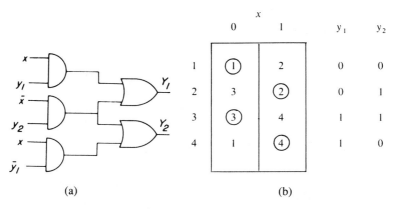

Figure 6.40 (a) An asynchronous circuit, (b) Flow table of the corresponding machine—Example 6.13

Now, let us consider the same circuit with a pure delay element of suitable magnitude inserted in each of the feedback paths. Analyzing the same transition, we note that Y_2 changes to 1/2 when x is changed to 1/2. However, the delay element prevents this change from reaching y_2 immediately. Changing x from 1/2 to 1 results in $Y_1 = 0$, $Y_2 = 1$. If we now change y_2 to 1/2, Y_1 and Y_2 remain at 0 and 1 respectively, indicating that the transition is hazard-free.

If the circuit is initially stable with $x = 1$, $y_1 = 0$, $y_2 = 1$, and x changes to 0, we change x to 1/2. This results in $Y_1 = Y_2 = 1/2$. Changing x to 0, assuming that the delays are pure, produces $Y_1 = Y_2 = 1$, the correct state. However, when we set $y_1 = y_2 = 1/2$, as specified in step 4 of Procedure 6.3, Y_1 and Y_2 both become 1/2, indicating a steady state hazard. This hazard is the result of the static hazard present in the combinational excitation logic. If the inserted delays in the circuit are assumed to be inertial, then it is not necessary to set $y_1 = y_2 = 1/2$ because the inertial delay will mask the transients in Y_1 and Y_2 and the transition is hazard-free.

Now, let us consider the case where a pure delay is inserted in the feedback path of y_2, but none in the other feedback path. Let the circuit be initially in the state $y_1 = 0$, $y_2 = 1$ and let the input change from 1 to 0. Letting $x = 1/2$ as before, we obtain $Y_1 = Y_2 = 1/2$. Since there is no delay in the y_1 path, we change y_1 to 1/2 and recompute Y_1 and Y_2, which are both still 1/2. Changing x to 0, Y_1 and Y_2 are both still 1/2 indicating a steady state hazard. ∎

6.9 MULTIPLE-INPUT CHANGES

The single-input change restriction which we have been using in our discussion so far can be relaxed. We allow any number of input variables to change simultaneously. Since it may be impossible to ensure that all the variables that change during a transition do so in synchronism, we shall treat all changes that occur within some time interval δ_m as having occurred simultaneously. We also assume that successive input changes occur at intervals greater than some $\delta_M > \delta_m$, thereby permitting fundamental mode operation as defined earlier. We shall refer to multiple-input changes satisfying these assumptions as *simultaneous input changes*. If the restriction that input changes associated with an input transition occur within a specified interval is removed, the changes are called *unrestricted input changes* [12]. This case will not be considered here.

The main problem associated with the design of sequential circuits under these assumptions is that of distinguishing the final input state of an input transition from the transient input states that may be passed through during the transition. Although different techniques may be used for this, only one method, applicable to normal mode flow tables will be presented here [13]. The method also serves as a proof of the sufficiency of a single delay element in realizing any normal mode flow table, even when simultaneous input changes are permitted.

The realization consists of two subcircuits as shown in Figure 6.41. The circuit C_1 produces a "1-hot" output for each input state; i.e., for each input state,

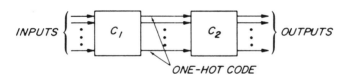

Figure 6.41 Circuit realization for simultaneous input changes

exactly one output variable of C_1 is 1. A transition from any input state I_j, represented by $x_j = 1$, $x_i = 0$, $i \neq j$, to any other input state I_k, represented in the 1-hot code by $x_k = 1$, $x_i = 0$, $i \neq k$, is always made in such a manner that the only intermediate state is the all-zeros state, which we shall call a *spacer*. This implies that x_j is first changed to 0, and then x_k is changed to 1. Furthermore, we shall require that the spacer input persists long enough for the circuit C_2 to complete its response to it and reach a stable state.

Assuming that a circuit C_1 of the type specified above can be designed, any normal mode flow table M can be realized permitting simultaneous input changes, by augmenting the given flow table to a flow table M' and designing the circuit C_2 to realize M'. The flow table M' is obtained by adding a column corresponding to the spacer input to the flow table M. The spacer column contains only stable states, and the outputs are specified to be unchanged from their previous values and denoted by S in the flow table. An example of a flow table M and its augmented flow table M' are shown in Figure 6.42. A transition in M corresponds to two transitions in M', one from a 1-hot code word to the all-zero spacer followed by a transition from the spacer to a different 1-hot code word. Thus, M' effectively operates in pulse mode.

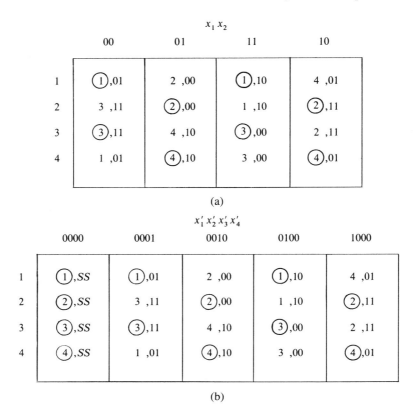

$$x_1 x_2$$

	00	01	11	10
1	①,01	2 ,00	①,10	4 ,01
2	3 ,11	②,00	1 ,10	②,11
3	③,11	4 ,10	③,00	2 ,11
4	1 ,01	④,10	3 ,00	④,01

(a)

$$x_1' x_2' x_3' x_4'$$

	0000	0001	0010	0100	1000
1	①,SS	①,01	2 ,00	①,10	4 ,01
2	②,SS	3 ,11	②,00	1 ,10	②,11
3	③,SS	③,11	4 ,10	③,00	2 ,11
4	④,SS	1 ,01	④,10	3 ,00	④,01

(b)

Figure 6.42   Flow table transformation

With input transitions occuring only between the all-zero spacer and 1-hot code points, the flow table M' is subjected to single-input changes only. Furthermore since all transitions are to or from the spacer column, M' does not contain any essential hazards or d-trios even if M contains essential hazards. Thus M' can be realized without delay elements. Since all transitions are to or from the spacer column which contains only stable states, it can also be shown that any STT assignment can be used for such a realization.

The outputs in the spacer column are specified to be unchanged from their previous values. For example, if M' of Figure 6.42 is stable in state 1 under input 0001 and the spacer input is received, the outputs are required to remain at 01. However, if the circuit is stable in state 1 under input 0100, the outputs are required to remain at 10. The outputs can be maintained at their previous values by using set-reset flip-flops, which will be unexcited during the spacer input.

A realization of the circuit C_1 is shown in Figure 6.43. The circuit labeled decoder is combinational and produces 1-hot outputs (in the steady state) on the

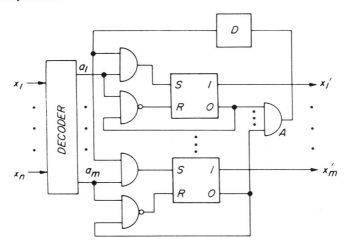

Figure 6.43   Realization of subcircuit C_1

leads, a_1, a_2, . . . , a_m. However, when the inputs to the decoder change, transients may be present on the leads a_i. Let the circuit C_1 initially be stable with a 1-hot output. The output of the AND gate A will be 0 and the AND gates connected to the set side of the flip-flops will thus be disabled. Now, let the inputs to the decoder change. This may result in changes in several a_i's (including transients). If an input a_i changes to 1 it is prevented from setting the corresponding flip-flop by the 0 output to the AND gate. If the jth flip-flop was initially set and a_j changes to 0, the flip-flop is reset through the NOR gates. The output of the AND gate A changes to 1 after all the flip-flops have been reset. After delay time D, the outputs of the decoder are allowed to set the flip-flops. By this time, the decoder outputs should have become stable and only one output should be 1. Thus, the spacer output has a duration of approximately D, after which the outputs change to the new 1-hot code word.

In this realization of C_1, all input changes associated with an input transition are required to occur within a fixed interval determined by the magnitude of D and the stray delays. The realization also proves the sufficiency of a single delay element for realizing any flow table, even when multiple-input changes are allowed, provided that the input changes are suitably constrained.

6.10   OTHER DELAY MODELS

We have assumed that there are no restrictions on the relative magnitudes of stray delays in gates and connecting lines. In some practical circuits it may be reasonable to assume that line delays are less than gate delays. Under this assumption the result of Lemma 6.6 is no longer valid and any normal mode flow table can be realized without inserted delays, provided only a single input variable is allowed to change during any input transition [14].

The results derived in this chapter depend on the assumptions that we have made about delays. Other models have been presented in the literature and we now summarize some of the important results for their cases. For more detailed presentations the reader is referred to the original references.

A different model of asynchronous circuits has been proposed by Muller and Bartky [15]. The lines in the circuit are assumed to have no stray delay, whereas bounds on the magnitudes of stray delays associated with gates are assumed to be unknown, except that they are positive and finite. These assumptions are useful in studying the behavior of circuits in which gate delays may vary over a wide range. Circuits whose behavior is independent of the magnitudes of stray delays are called *speed independent circuits*.

Under the unbounded gate delay assumption it is impossible to determine the required interval between successive input changes for fundamental mode operation. Therefore, it is necessary for the circuit itself to generate a signal to indicate its readiness for receiving the next input. Several techniques have been proposed for designing circuits that generate such *ready (completion) signals* to operate under the unbounded gate delay assumption [7,16,17].

In designing large circuits, it is convenient to be able to interconnect modules realizing simpler functions. Such interconnections are possible between modules generating completion signals. If the outputs of a module A are connected to a module B, the completion signals generated by B are fed back to A. The modules themselves should be designed so that the outputs of A do not change until B has completed its response to the previous output of A. This can be accomplished by connecting memory devices (such as flip-flops) to the outputs. The basic approach for designing combinational and sequential circuits discussed above can be modified to provide output storage within each module. Larger circuits can be realized by interconnecting both combinational and sequential circuit models designed in this manner.

REFERENCES

1. McCluskey, E.J., "Fundamental Mode and Pulse Mode Sequential Circuits," *Proc. IFIP Congress*, Munich, Germany, North Amsterdam Publishing Company, Amsterdam, pp. 725–730, 1962.
2. Huffman, D.A., "The Synthesis of Sequential Switching Circuits," *J. Franklin Inst.*, vol. 257, pp. 161–190, March 1954 and pp. 275–303, April 1954.
3. Huffman, D.A., "A Study of Memory Requirements of Sequential Switching Circuits," Technical Report No. 293, Research Laboratory of Electronics, Massachusetts Institute of Technology, Cambridge, Mass., 1955.

4. Saucier, G., "Ecodings for Asynchronous Sequential Networks," *IEEE Trans. Elec. Computers*, vol. EC-16, pp. 365–369, June 1967.

5. Liu, C.N., "A State Variable Assignment Procedure for Asynchronous Sequential Switching Circuits," *J. ACM* vol. 10, pp. 209–215, April 1963.

6. Tracey, J.H., "Internal State Assignments for Asynchronous Sequential Machines," *IEEE Trans. Elec. Computers*, vol. EC-15, pp. 551–560, August 1966.

7. Armstrong, D.B., Friedman, A.D. and P.R. Menon, "Design of Asynchronous Circuits Assuming Unbounded Gate Delays," *IEEE Trans. Computers*, vol. C-18, pp. 1110–1120, December 1969.

8. Unger, S.H., *Asynchronous Sequential Circuits*, Wiley Interscience, New York, 1969.

9. Eichelberger, E.B., "Hazard Detection in Combinational and Sequential Switching Circuits," *Proc. Fifth Annual Symposium on Switching Circuit Theory and Logical Design*, pp. 111–120, 1964. Also *IBM J. of Res. & Dev.*, pp. 90–99, 1965.

10. Unger, S.H., "Hazards and Delays in Asynchronous Sequential Switching Circuits, *IRE Trans. Circuit Theory*, vol. CT-6, pp. 12–25, March 1959.

11. Fantauzzi, G., "An Algebraic Model for the Analysis of Circuits," *IEEE Trans. Computers*, vol. C-23, pp. 576–581, June 1974.

12. Unger, S.H., "Asynchronous Sequential Switching Circuits with Unrestricted Input Changes," *IEEE Trans. Computers*, vol. C-20, pp. 1437–1444, December 1971.

13. Friedman, A.D. and P.R. Menon, "Synthesis of Asynchronous Sequential Circuits with Multiple-Input Changes," *IEEE Trans. Computers*, vol. C-17, pp. 559–566, June 1968.

14. Armstrong, D.B., Friedman, A.D. and P.R. Menon, "Realization of Asynchronous Sequential Circuits Without Inserted Delay Elements," *IEE Trans. Computers*, vol. C-17, pp. 129–134, February 1968.

15. Muller, D.E. and W.S. Bartky, "A Theory of Asynchronous Circuits," *Proc. of an International Symp. on the Theory of Switching*, vol. 29, Annals of the Computation Laboratory of Harvard Univ., Harvard Univ. Press, pp. 204–243, 1959.

16. Hammel, D., "Ideas on Asynchronous Feedback Networks," *Proc. Fifth Annual Symposium on Switching Circuit Theory and Logical Design*, pp. 4–11, 1964.

17. Miller, R.E., *Switching Theory*, vol. 2. Wiley, New York, 1965.

PROBLEMS

6.1 Consider the flow table of Figure 6.44. The entry N (2,01) has been denoted as A. Characterize the table as SOC, MOC, normal mode, fundamental mode, etc.

 a) if $A = 1$
 b) if $A = 2$
 c) if $A = 3$
 d) if $A = 4$

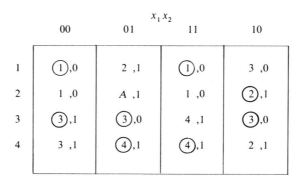

Figure 6.44   Problem 6.1

6.2 Construct a primitive flow table for an asynchronous circuit which operates as follows:

a) The circuit has two binary inputs, x_1 and x_2 and one binary output z, and only one input can change for any transition;

b) starting in stable initial state 1, with $x_1 = x_2 = 0$, and $z = 0$, the output changes value if and only if x_1 changes value 3 successive times or x_2 changes value 2 successive times.

Then reduce the primitive table so as to minimize the number of states.

6.3 Consider the Boolean expression

$$f = (x_1 \, x_2 + \bar{x}_1 \, x_3) \, (x_1 \, (x_4 + x_5) + \bar{x}_1 \, \bar{x}_3 \, \bar{x}_4 \, x_5)$$

and the corresponding combinational circuit.

a) Does the circuit have any static hazards for single variable changes?

b) Does the circuit have any dynamic hazards for single variable changes?

c) Find a hazard-free sum-of-products realization for the function of Figure 6.45.

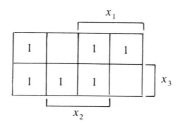

Figure 6.45   Problem 6.3

6.4 For each of the state tables of Figure 6.46 determine if possible a unicode state assignment in which each transition requires only a single state variable change, under the single input variable change assumption.

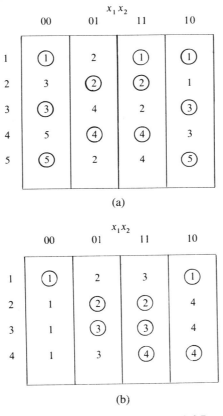

(a)

(b)

Figure 6.46 Problems 6.4 and 6.7

6.5 Using the state variable assignment specified in Figure 6.13 for the flow table of Figure 6.12 specify the Y-matrix.

6.6 For the flow tables of Figure 6.47:

a) find minimal variable connected row set state assignments;

b) find minimal variable shared row set state assignments.

6.7 Find a unicode STT assignment for each of the flow tables of Figure 6.46.

6.8 For each of the following combinational functions derive hazard-free sum-of-products and product-of-sums realizations.

$$x_1 x_2$$

	00	01	11	10
1	(1)	2	3	(1)
2	5	(2)	4	(2)
3	(3)	5	(3)	1
4	1	(4)	(4)	1
5	(5)	(5)	6	2
6	5	4	(6)	(6)

(a)

$$x_1 x_2$$

	00	01	11	10
1	(1)	2	—	3
2	(2)	(2)	4	(2)
3	4	—	5	(3)
4	(4)	6	(4)	2
5	1	(5)	(5)	6
6	7	(6)	7	(6)
7	(7)	5	(7)	2

(b)

Figure 6.47   Problem 6.6

a) $f(x_1, x_2, x_3, x_4) = \Sigma m_0, m_1, m_7, m_{15}$
b) $f(x_1, x_2, x_3) = \Sigma m_0, m_1, m_3, m_4, m_7$

6.9 For the combinational function

$$f(x_1, x_2, x_3, x_4) = \Sigma m_0, m_2, m_3, m_4, m_5, m_6, m_7, m_{12}, m_{13}, m_{15}$$

does the sum-of-products realization

$$f = \bar{x}_1 \bar{x}_4 + \bar{x}_1 x_3 + x_2 x_4 + x_2 \bar{x}_3$$

have any hazards for single input changes? What does this imply about the necessity of a hazard-free realization containing *all* prime implicants?

6.10 For each of the tables of Figure 6.48, find all essential hazards, and *d*-trios, and indicate which state variables in the proposed state assignments must have inserted delay elements to insure proper operation, assuming single input variable changes.

$x_1 x_2$

	00	01	11	10	y_1	y_2
1	①,0	2 ,0	4 ,0	①,0	0	0
2	1 ,0	②,0	②,1	1 ,0	0	1
3	③,1	4 ,1	2 ,1	③,1	1	1
4	1 ,0	④,1	④,0	3 ,1	1	0

(a)

$x_1 x_2$

	00	01	11	10	y_1	y_2
1	①,0	2 ,0	①,0	①,0	0	0
2	1 ,0	②,0	3 ,1	②,0	0	1
3	③,1	③,1	③,1	2 ,0	1	1

(b)

Figure 6.48   Problem 6.10

6.11 The circuits of Figure 6.49 have been proposed as models of inertial delays where M is a majority gate. Discuss the classes of inputs for which they will work.

6.12 a) The circuit of Figure 6.50(a) has been proposed as a three state variable *delay box* which can be used to realize circuits with a single delay element for certain types of state assignments where M is a majority gate. For what types of state assignments can this delay box be utilized?

b) Repeat for Figure 6.50(b) where $B_i = CY_i + \overline{C}y_i + y_i Y_i$.

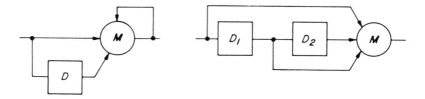

Figure 6.49   Inertial delay models

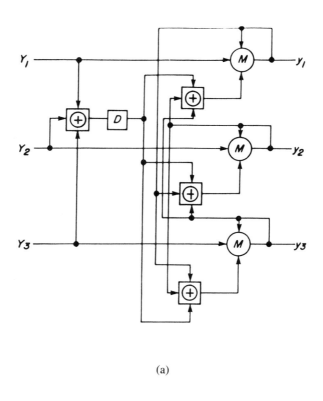

(a)

Figure 6.50   Realizations of three variable delay boxes—Problem 6.12

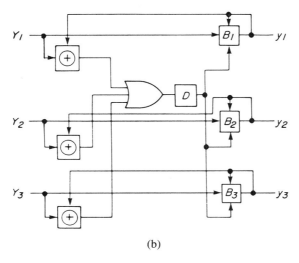

(b)

Figure 6.50   (continued)

6.13 The circuit of Figure 6.51(b) represents an attempt to realize the flow
table of Figure 6.51(a). Determine whether there are circumstances under
which the terminal behavior of the circuit *may not* conform to the flow
table. If so, describe them and indicate remedies. Assume that only one
input at a time may change, and that ample time is allowed between
consecutive input changes. Will the circuit work correctly if the inertial
delay element is replaced by a pure delay element? Explain. (Line delays
are not restricted in relation to gate delays.)

6.14 Consider 2-level realizations corresponding to the Boolean expressions

a) $x_1 (\overline{x}_1 + x_2)$

b) $x_1 \overline{x}_1 + x_1 x_2$

In each case determine if there are any dynamic hazards. What can you
infer about the hazard preserving capabilities of the distributive law?

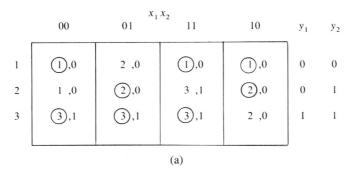

(a)

Figure 6.51   Problem 6.13

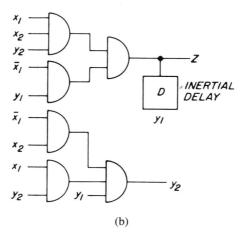

(b)

Figure 6.51   (continued)

6.15 The assignment of Figure 6.52 is a universal 8-state assignment using $2S_0$ = 6 state variables. Show that no transition requires more than two transition times. Show how this can be generalized to a $2S_0$ state variable, two transition time universal state assignment for all S_0.

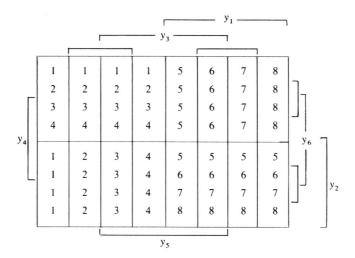

Figure 6.52   Problem 6.15

Chapter 7

FUNDAMENTALS OF
SYSTEM LEVEL DESIGN

Up to now we have considered the design of *circuits* in which the basic elements, gates, and memory elements were interconnected in such a manner as to realize functions which were specified by a state table (or truth table). In this chapter we will consider the design of digital systems in which the basic elements are related sets of memory elements called *registers*. Combinational and sequential circuits are used to perform computations on the contents of these registers under the control of other circuits. In system level design we are primarily interested in how these subsystems may be defined and interconnected so as to properly execute a sequence of information processing tasks rather than the detailed synthesis of the particular subsystems. Frequently the design of systems to perform relatively complex computations is simplified considerably if such design is done on the system level rather than the circuit level (as considered in the previous chapters). This is especially true for complex computations such as binary multiplication which can be done by a sequence of relatively simple information processing operations, register shifting and register addition. We will assume that operation is synchronous, all operations being controlled by a master clock so as to occur only at fixed clock times.

7.1   DESIGN LANGUAGE

In circuit level design, truth tables or state tables are used to specify the function to be designed. Languages which can be used to represent the flow of information on a system level are helpful in system level design. Such languages are frequently referred to as *Register Transfer Languages* (RTL's) [1]. In this chapter we will use a language which may be considered to be a prototype of many similar languages.

Register Transfer Languages greatly facilitate the conceptualized design of complex digital circuits with hundreds of flip-flops which would be virtually impossible using a state table approach. Many researchers have also attempted to use RTL's as an approach to automated logic design. Since our goal here is strictly limited to the educational, we will avoid the pitfall of complicated syntactic rules and propose a very simple and intuitive language. Our choice of this specific language is based solely on the relative ease of representing and interpreting the specificiation of the system designs we will be considering herein. The essential features of this language are as follows.

Representation of Systems Inputs, Outputs, and Registers

1. The inputs of a system will be denoted by X (or Y, V, W) and a particular input bit by x_i (or y_i, v_i, w_i). A constant input will be represented by a number n.
2. The outputs of a system will be denoted by Z, and a particular output bit by z_i.
3. The registers of a system will be denoted by capital letters (excluding those letters used to represent inputs or outputs) or by a sequence of capital letters such as A, MBR, etc. A particular flip-flop (bit) of register R will be denoted by R_i. We assume that the bits of an n-bit register are numbered from right to left as shown in Figure 7.1, or from left to right depending on the type of register. For example the bits of a shift register are frequently numbered from left to right whereas counter registers are normally numbered from right to left. A set of consecutive bits R_i, R_{i+1}, . . . , R_j will be denoted by $R_{i,j}$.

Figure 7.1   A register

Basic System Operations

The basic system operations result in a modification of some register or registers. Usually a control signal S_i is used to control the execution of a specific operation so that it is performed if and only if $S_i = 1$. It is assumed that system behavior is synchronous, all operations being controlled by a master clock so as to occur only at fixed clock times, and that master-slave flip-flops are used to prevent malfunctions as previously explained. Each operation is executed by a set of circuits, which perform the operation in response to a single control signal (rather than a sequence of control signals). Thus the use of a particular instruction in the description of an algorithm implies the existence of the corresponding hardware circuits to execute the instruction (within one clock period). The basic instructions and the associated implied circuits to perform these instructions are as follows.

Data Movement Instructions

1. Transferring the contents of register B to register A:

$$S_j: \quad A \leftarrow B.$$

It is assumed that A and B have the same number of bits and B_i is transferred to A_i for all i, when $S_j = 1$. The corresponding circuit (for a single bit) is shown in Figure 7.2(a). The circuit will also be represented as shown in the block diagram of Figure 7.2(b).

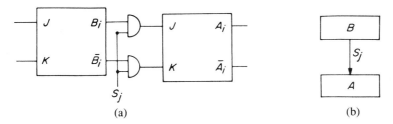

(a)   (b)

Figure 7.2   (a) A circuit implementation of S_j: $A \leftarrow B$ (b)The corresponding block
diagram

2. Setting register R to the value of an input X:

$$R \leftarrow X$$

It is assumed that if R has bits $R_0, \ldots, R_{n-1}$ then X consists of $x_0, \ldots, x_{n-1}$ and bit R_i of R is set to x_i.

3. Setting register R to the value of a constant number k:

$$R \leftarrow k$$

If R is an n-bit register then $0 \leq k \leq 2^n - 1$. For a 3-bit register the circuit of Figure 7.3(a) would implement the instruction,

$$S_i: \quad A \leftarrow 4$$

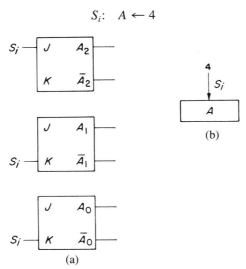

Figure 7.3   (a) A circuit implementation of S_i: $A \leftarrow 4$ (b)The corresponding block
diagram

since when $S_i = 1$, A_2 is set and A_1 and A_0 are reset. It may be necessary to modify the contents of a register A in different ways for different control signals. This is readily implemented by having the excitations of the individual memory elements correspond to the logical OR of the excitation signals corresponding to the individual operations. Thus the circuit of Figure 7.4 implements the two instructions

$$S_i: \quad A \leftarrow 4$$
$$S_j: \quad A \leftarrow B$$

It may also be desirable to have the same control signal cause the execution of several independent operations (i.e., operations not affecting the contents of the

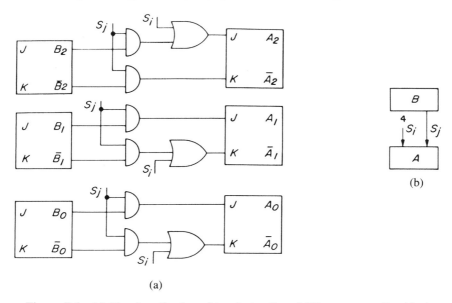

(a)

Figure 7.4 (a) Circuit realization of two instructions (b)The corresponding block diagram

same register). This is represented by listing the operations separated by semi-colons corresponding to the same control signal as follows:

$$S_i: \quad \text{Operation } \Theta_1; \quad \text{Operation } \Theta_2; \quad \ldots, \text{etc.}$$

For example the instruction

$$S_i: \quad A \leftarrow B; \quad C \leftarrow D; \quad D \leftarrow 4$$

causes the contents of registers B and D to be transferred to A and C, respectively, and the constant 4 to be stored in D. Note that the previous value of D is transferred to C. The same destination register cannot be used for two simul-taneous operations.

Data Manipulation Instructions

In addition to moving data between registers it is also frequently necessary to be able to perform arithmetic and logical operations on the data. Some of the most common arithmetic and logical operations are shown in the table of Figure 7.5. The use of any operation implies the existence of a hardware circuit to perform that operation. Frequently there is more than one way of representing a given computation. For instance the operations of Figures 7.6(a) and (b) both add one to the contents of Register B. The instructions of Figure 7.6(a) make use of addition and hence imply the schematic circuit represented by the block diagram of Figure 7.6(c). The instructions of Figure 7.6(b) imply that register C is a counter and hence require the schematic circuit of Figure 7.6(d).

Name	Notation	Description
Arithmetic Operations		
Addition	$C \leftarrow A + B$	A and B are added and the result is stored in C
Subtraction	$C \leftarrow A - B$	B is subtracted from A and the result is stored in C
Multiplication	$C \leftarrow A * B$	The producer of A and B is stored in C
Division	$C \leftarrow A/B$	A is divided by B and the result is stored in C
Bit by Bit Logical Operations		
OR	$C \leftarrow A \vee B$	The logical OR of bits A_i and B_i is stored in C_i for all i
AND	$C \leftarrow A \wedge B$	The logical AND of bits A_i and B_i is stored in C_i for all i
NOT (Complement)	$B \leftarrow \overline{A}$	The complement of bit A_i is stored in B_i for all i
Register Operations		
Shift Right	$A \leftarrow \mathrm{SR}(A)$	Shift the contents of A one bit right $(0 \rightarrow A_0, A_i \rightarrow A_{i+1}$ for all $i = 0, \ldots, n-2)$
Shift Left	$A \leftarrow \mathrm{SL}(A)$	Shift the contents of A one bit left $(0 \rightarrow A_{n-1}, A_{i+1} \rightarrow A_i$ for all $i = 0, \ldots, n)$
Increment	$A \leftarrow \mathrm{INC}(A)$	Increment (add 1 to) A
Decrement	$A \leftarrow \mathrm{DEC}(A)$	Decrement (subtract 1 from) A

Figure 7.5 Common arithmetic and logical operations

S_1: $A \leftarrow B$ S_1: $C \leftarrow B$
S_1: $A \leftarrow A + 1$ S_2: $C \leftarrow \text{INC}(C)$ (increment
                                                                        the contents of register C)
S_3: $B \leftarrow A$ S_3: $B \leftarrow C$
          (a)   (b)

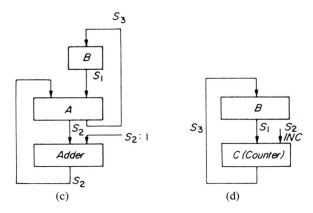

Figure 7.6   Two systems for the same data processing task

7.2   SIMPLE ALGORITHMS

Our language has now been specified to a sufficient extent so that it can be used to represent many algorithms as a sequence of fundamental register operations. Thus an algorithm to compute the 2's complement of input X may be specified as follows:

$$S_1: \quad A \leftarrow X$$
$$S_2: \quad A \leftarrow \overline{A}$$
$$S_3: \quad A \leftarrow A + 1$$

The system is assumed to operate in an essentially synchronous manner, controlled by clock pulses occurring at times T_i, $i = 1, 2, \ldots, $ p. Associated with each operation is a specific control signal. In general the order in which the instructions are executed is essential. Thus in order to execute the 2's complement algorithm the control signals must be generated in the order S_1, S_2, S_3. In general each operation (or set of operations) is associated with a specific clock pulse T_i, the ith clock pulse being associated with the ith set of instructions in the sequence. Figure 7.7 shows a sequence of instructions which computes the function $9*x$ using addition and shifting. In this instruction sequence operations and the corresponding control signals are repeated. The corresponding clock pulse for execution is also shown. Corresponding to each clock pulse T_i is a unique signal but the same control signal may be generated at different clock pulses.

$$T_0 \quad S_1: \quad A \leftarrow X$$

$$T_1 \quad S_2: \quad B \leftarrow A \qquad\qquad B = A$$

$$T_2 \quad S_3: \quad A \leftarrow A + A \qquad \text{Computes } 2 \cdot A$$

$$T_3 \quad S_3: \quad A \leftarrow A + A \qquad \text{Computes } 4 \cdot A$$

$$T_4 \quad S_3: \quad A \leftarrow A + A \qquad \text{Computes } 8 \cdot A$$

$$T_5 \quad S_4: \quad A \leftarrow A + B \qquad \text{Computes } 9 \cdot A$$

$$T_6 \quad S_5: \quad Z \leftarrow A$$

Figure 7.7   A program to compute $9*x$

In order to have a system perform a sequence of operations in the correct order it is necessary to generate the corresponding control signals in the correct order. A special circuit, called a *sequencer* or *control unit*, is used to perform this task [2]. This unit is a sequential circuit, which controls the order in which a sequence of operations are executed. After completing this task the control unit returns to its initial state and can then control the same operation sequence on different data. A control circuit which always transmits the same sequence of control signals in this manner is called a *simple* control circuit. A block diagram of a digital system which functions in this manner is shown in Figure 7.8.

A simple control circuit is in effect a one column sequential machine, whose only input is the master clock. The machine in effect counts clock pulses modulo n and outputs the corresponding signal for each clock pulse. Such a circuit is a

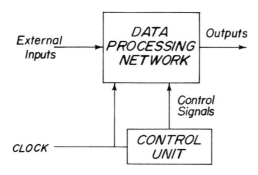

Figure 7.8   System with simple control circuit

modulo n counter whose state table is as shown in Figure 7.9(a). Here S_i is used to denote the control signal corresponding to clockpulse T_i. Hence different S_i are not necessarily distinct (i.e., S_i may be the same as S_j). For the instruction sequence of Figure 7.7 the corresponding control unit is defined by the state table of Figure 7.9(b). Note that the control unit has a state corresponding to each line in the sequence of instructions of Figure 7.7.

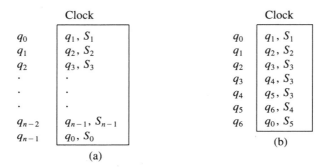

Figure 7.9   (a) State table for simple control unit (b) State table for control unit corresponding to instruction sequence of Figure 7.7.

The simple control circuit maps an individual clock pulse T_i into a corresponding control signal S_j. This correspondence may be represented as follows:

$$T_i : S_j : \quad \text{Operation } \#1$$

which is interpreted "at clock T_i the control unit generates control signal S_j in response to which the data processing network performs Operation #1."

Thus it is implicitly assumed that each operation can be completed in a single clock period. This in turn implies a correlation between the logic circuitry required in the data processing network and the basic operations which it can perform within a clock period.

The outputs of the control unit, the control signals, must be generated as a set of binary signals, $\lceil \log_2 n \rceil$, such signals being required to generate n distinct control signals. If these binary signals are input to a decoder, a single output signal S_i is generated for each distinct control signal (Figure 7.10). Once the control unit for an algorithm has been specified, the data processing network can be designed. This network uses the appropriate control signals as gating or enabling signals to control the execution of the individual data processing operations.

Thus a digital system to perform an algorithm may be designed as outlined in the following procedure.

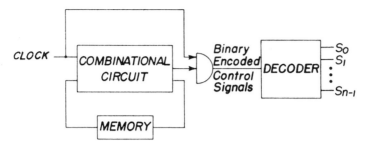

Figure 7.10   Representation of simple control circuit

Procedure 7.1

1. Specify the algorithm as a sequence of basic operations in a Register Transfer Language. (The use of a basic operation implies the existence of a subsystem which can perform that operation.)*
2. Specify the (simple) control unit to generate the correct control signal sequence to enable correct execution of the algorithm.
3. Design the data processing network using the appropriate control signals as enabling signals to control the execution of the individual data processing operations. ∎

Example 7.1   We will design an input-output buffer (IOB) to operate as follows. Data is transmitted to the IOB in 8-bit groups called *bytes*. The IOB accumulates four successive bytes and then transmits them as a 32-bit word to the computer. The general system for the IOB is shown in Figure 7.11. Note that each register R has associated with it a circuit N_i which generates the excitation inputs to R.

The 8-bit bytes occur on inputs $x_0, x_1, \ldots, x_7$, and are accumulated and stored in A, a 32-bit register of JK flip-flops, under the control of the control unit. Then a control signal is generated which gates the 32-bit word to the B register of the computer. The circuit N_1 is a combinational circuit which uses the control signals to gate the inputs into the appropriate bit of A, and N_2 is a similar circuit which gates the 32-bit word to B. The following sequence of basic operations must be executed.

---

*We have assumed that the control unit generates control signals each clock period, thus implicitly assuming that the logic circuits performing the implied computation can do so in a single clock period. In practice different computations may require different periods of time thus complicating somewhat the design of the control unit.

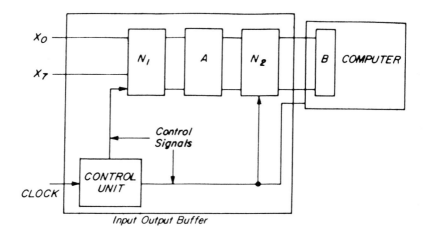

Figure 7.11   Input-output buffer

$$T_1: \quad A_{1,7} \leftarrow X$$
$$T_2: \quad A_{8,15} \leftarrow X$$
$$T_3: \quad A_{16,23} \leftarrow X$$
$$T_4: \quad A_{24,31} \leftarrow X$$
$$T_5: \quad B \leftarrow A$$

The control unit must generate a sequence of five control signals to control the execution of these operations. Such a control unit is defined by the state table of Figure 7.12.

	Clock
q_0	q_1, S_1
q_1	q_2, S_2
q_2	q_3, S_3
q_3	q_4, S_4
q_4	q_0, S_0

Figure 7.12   IOB control unit state table

The network N_1 is a combinational circuit which generates the excitations for the memory elements of register A. Assuming JK flip-flops, these excitation functions are of the form

$$\left. \begin{array}{l} J_i = S_1 \cdot x_i \\ K_i = S_1 \cdot \bar{x}_i \end{array} \right\} \quad 0 \le i \le 7$$

$$J_i = S_2 \cdot x_{(i-8)}$$
$$K_i = S_2 \cdot \overline{x}_{(i-8)} \qquad 8 \le i \le 15$$

$$J_i = S_3 \cdot x_{(i-16)}$$
$$K_i = S_3 \cdot \overline{x}_{(i-16)} \qquad 16 \le i \le 23$$

$$J_i = S_4 \cdot x_{(i-24)}$$
$$K_i = S_4 \cdot \overline{x}_{(i-24)} \qquad 24 \le i \le 31$$

The network N_2 is a combinational circuit which generates the excitations for the B register. These are of the form

$$J_i = S_0 \cdot y_i$$
$$K_i = S_0 \cdot \overline{y}_i \qquad 0 \le i \le 31$$

where y_i is the state of B_i. ∎

Example 7.2 Another computation which can be performed under the control of a simple control circuit is the 2's complement. We shall now design a digital system which computes the 2's complement of input X as previously defined

$$T_1: \quad A \leftarrow X$$
$$T_2: \quad A \leftarrow \overline{A}$$
$$T_3: \quad A \leftarrow A + 1$$

The execution of this algorithm requires a control unit to generate a sequence of three control signals repetitively. Such a control unit is described by the state table of Figure 7.13.

Clock

q_0	q_1, S_1
q_1	q_2, S_2
q_2	q_0, S_0

Figure 7.13 Control unit state table for 2's complement addition

The system can be represented schematically as shown in Figure 7.14.

The excitation inputs to the A register are generated by N_1 and are such as to generate the state behavior specified by:

$$Y_{Ai} = S_1 \cdot x_i + S_2 \overline{y}_{Ai} + S_0 \cdot z_i, \quad 1 \le i \le n$$

where z_i are the outputs of the addition logic. Similarly, N_2 generates the excitation inputs to the adder in accordance with the following

$$X_i = S_0 \cdot A_i$$
$$Y_0 = S_0 \cdot 1$$ ∎

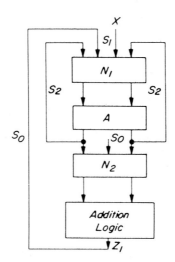

Figure 7.14 System for 2's complement addition

7.3 STATUS DEPENDENT CONTROL UNITS [2]

A simple control unit generates a repetitive sequence of control signals and hence can be used for repetitive execution of certain types of operations. However, some types of computations may require a sequence of control signals which may depend upon and vary with the specific data upon which the computation is performed. The description of such an algorithm requires a new type of instruction called a conditional branch. Such an instruction is of the form

IF (STATUS CONDITION) THEN CONTROL SIGNAL 1:
OPERATION 1, ELSE CONTROL SIGNAL 2:
OPERATION 2

which causes operation 1 to be executed if the status condition is satisfied while operation 2 is executed if the status condition is not satisfied.

The instruction sequence of Figure 7.15 illustrates the use of a conditional branch statement to compute the difference between two positive numbers which appear on inputs X and Y. The use of a status condition implies the existence of a circuit to perform the implied computation. For the program of Figure 7.15 a comparison circuit must be used to compare A and B upon receiving the control signal S_2. The comparison circuit should generate an output $Z = 1$ if $A \geq B$ and $Z = 0$ if $A < B$. The control unit would then generate a next control signal of S_3 if $Z = 1$ which would cause the operation $D \leftarrow A - B$ to be performed or S_4 if $Z = 0$ which would cause the operation $D \leftarrow B - A$ to be performed.

S_1: $A \leftarrow X; B \leftarrow Y$
S_2:   COMPARE (A, B)
       IF $(Z = 1)$ THEN S_3: $D \leftarrow A - B$: ELSE S_4: $D \leftarrow B - A$

Figure 7.15   Instruction sequence to compute difference between two numbers

The generation of control signals corresponding to conditional branch operations necessitates that the control unit must receive input information from the data processing network to generate the control sequences. Such a controller is said to be *status dependent*. A general system with a status dependent controller is as shown in Figure 7.16.

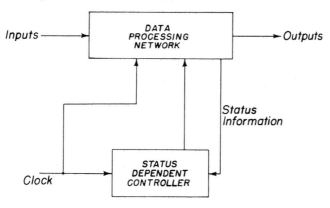

Figure 7.16   System with status dependent control unit

Some algorithms require a given sequence of instructions to be repeated several times. By adding another type of operation it is possible to express such an algorithm while only explicitly writing the repeated sequence of instructions once. The instruction

GO TO T_i

where T_i is the clock pulse associated with the first instruction in the repeated sequence, enables the complete sequence of instructions to be repeated an indefinite number of times. When used in conjunction with the conditional branch statement (e.g., IF (STATUS CONDITION) THEN GO TO T_i), the sequence to be repeated can be restricted to a specific number of iterations. This type of statement also permits a sequence of instructions to be either executed or skipped depending on the status condition. The GO TO statement causes the control unit to change state but does not cause any computation to be performed and thus does not necessitate the generation of a corresponding control signal.

An example of an algorithm requiring the use of a conditional branch—GO TO statement is the following procedure which computes the square root of a number through a process of convergence. This algorithm uses the arithmetic operations of addition, division, and comparison. The algorithm, which computes the square root to within an accuracy specified by a constant, k, is as follows.

1. Approximate the square root of N as $N/2 = X_0$ as a first approximation.
2. Take a next approximation as $X_1 = 1/2(X_0 + N/X_0)$.
3. Continue calculating the $(i + 1)$th approximation as

$$X_{i+1} = \frac{1}{2}\left(X_i + \frac{N}{X_i}\right)$$

where X_i is the ith approximation. The algorithm terminates when two successive approximations differ by $<k$, a constant.

If $N = 6$ and $k = .2$, the computation of the square root of N requires two iterations of this procedure and is as follows:

Iteration	Result
0	$X_0 = 3$
1	$X_1 = \frac{1}{2}\left(3 + \frac{6}{3}\right) = 2.5$
2	$X_2 = \frac{1}{2}\left(2.5 + \frac{6}{2.5}\right) = \frac{1}{2}(4.9) = 2.45$

However, if $N = 20$ and $k = .2$, three iterations are required.

Iteration	Result
0	$X_0 = 10$
1	$X_1 = \frac{1}{2}\left(10 + \frac{20}{10}\right) = 6$
2	$X_2 = \frac{1}{2}\left(6 + \frac{20}{6}\right) = \frac{1}{2}(9.33) = 4.67$
3	$X_3 = \frac{1}{2}\left(4.67 + \frac{20}{4.67}\right) = \frac{1}{2}(8.96) = 4.48$

We can specify the procedure to compute the square root of X in our register transfer language as follows:

Explanation

S_1: $A \leftarrow X$, $C \leftarrow k$ Store input in Register A and constant k in Register C.

S_2: $AP \leftarrow SR\ [A]$ $X/2$ is input to AP as (as initial approximation) (Note that division by 2 is equivalent to a right shift).

S_3: $B \leftarrow A/AP$ $\left.\begin{array}{}\\ \\ \\ \end{array}\right\}$
S_4: $B \leftarrow AP + B$ Generate next iteration result.
S_5: $B \leftarrow SR(B)$

S_6:   COMPARE (B, AP) $\left.\begin{array}{}\\ \\ \\ \\ \end{array}\right\}$
      IF $(Z = 1)$ THEN S_7:   Compute difference with previous approximation and store in D.
      $D \leftarrow B - AP$ ELSE S_8:
      $D \leftarrow AP - B$

S_9:   COMPARE (D, C) $\left.\begin{array}{}\\ \\ \\ \\ \end{array}\right\}$
      IF $(Z = 0)$ THEN S_0:   If $D < k$, output result, and prepare for
      OUTPUT $\leftarrow B$; GO TO T_1,   next computation. If $D \geq k$, begin computation of next approximation.
      ELSE S_{10}: $AP \leftarrow B$;
      GO TO T_3

This procedure must be executed under the control of a status dependent control unit. Such a control unit can be specified as a finite state sequential machine whose input columns correspond to the possible values of the status inputs which affect the generation of control signals. In the square root algorithm there are two status dependent operations both of which are the result of the comparison of the contents of two registers. The use of these instructions requires the existence of a comparison subcircuit. We assume that this circuit generates an output $Z = 1$ if $B \geq AP$ and $Z = 0$ if $B < AP$ and similarly $Z = 1$ if $D \geq C$ and $Z = 0$ if $D < C$. This output Z is then the status input of the control unit. The sequential machine of Figure 7.17 will generate the appropriate sequence of control signals (assuming initial state q_0) for the execution of the square root

	z	
	0	1
q_0	q_1, S_1	q_1, S_1
q_1	q_2, S_2	q_2, S_2
q_2	q_3, S_3	q_3, S_3
q_3	q_4, S_4	q_4, S_4
q_4	q_5, S_5	q_5, S_5
q_5	q_6, S_6	q_6, S_6
q_6	q_7, S_8	q_7, S_7
q_7	q_8, S_9	q_8, S_9
q_8	q_0, S_0	q_2, S_{10}

Figure 7.17   Control unit for square root system

algorithm previously specified in register transfer language form. Note that the
next state and output for states q_0 through q_4, which correspond to the first five
instructions in the algorithm, are the same for $Z = 0$ and $Z = 1$ and hence are
independent of the status signal Z. In state q_5 the control signal S_6 is generated
and this causes B and AP to be compared. Depending on the result of this
comparison, if $B \geq AP$, $Z = 1$, and control signal S_7 is generated in state q_6,
or if $B < AP$, $Z = 0$ and S_8 is generated. Then in state q_7, control signal S_9 is
generated which causes D and C to be compared. If $D \geq C, Z = 1$, and control
signal S_{10} is generated and the next iteration started by the transition N (q_8, 1)
$= q_2$. If $D < C, Z = 0$ and control signal S_0 is generated and the next computation
initiated by the transition N (q_8, 0) $= q_0$. The general structure of the system
is shown in Figure 7.18.   ∎

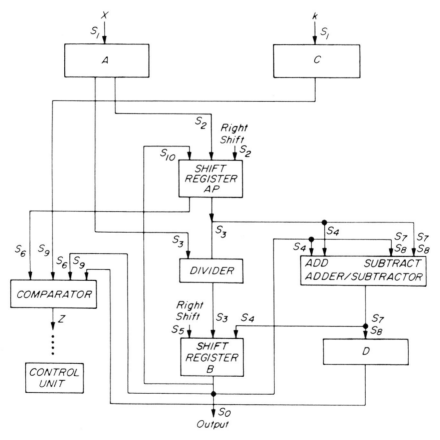

Figure 7.18   Square root system

In the previous example the desired computation could not have been performed without reference to a status signal. However in other cases such as the

Input-Output Buffer previously considered, a status signal can be used to permit counting to be done within the data processing network rather than within the control unit. This enables the control unit to be simplified and also enables the derivation of a control unit which can direct a "family" of circuits with different sizes of registers, thus providing a canonical system design for some classes of problems as illustrated in the following two examples.

The following two examples illustrate the derivation of switching systems corresponding to other algorithms.

Example 7.3 In this example we describe a system level design of a generalized I/O Buffer which can be used to create a k-byte word from a serial collection of k single bytes, where k is an input parameter. The parameter k is stored in an Up/Down Counter C which is decremented after each byte is input until all k bytes have been input. All bytes are input to the rightmost 8 bits of a register A and the contents of A are shifted left 8 bits ($A \leftarrow SL8(A)$) before each succeeding byte is input. When $C = 0$ indicating that all k bytes have been read, A is output into B and the next word formation begins.

The RTL level description of this system is shown in Figure 7.19(a). The control signal S_4 causes the contents of C to be input to the All-Zero Detector (AZD). Then depending on the status of Z either another byte is input or the completed word is transferred to B. ∎

T_1: S_1: $C \leftarrow k$
T_2: S_2: $A_{[n-7, n]} \leftarrow X$
T_3: S_3: $C \leftarrow DEC(C)$
T_4: S_4: $AZD(C)$
T_5:   IF $Z = 0$ THEN S_5: $B \leftarrow A$; GO TO T_1
                    ELSE S_6: $A \leftarrow SL8(A)$; GO TO T_2

(a)

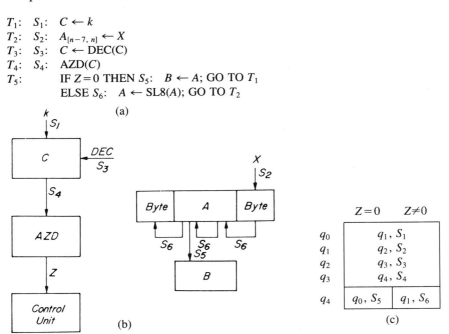

(b)   (c)

Figure 7.19 (a) RTL Program, (b) System block diagram, (c) Control Unit State diagram

In the previous example the design description was greatly simplified by loading all bytes into the same bits of the A register and then shifting the bytes into the correct position in the A register, rather than loading each byte directly into the correct bits. In conjunction with the use of a decrementable counter this eliminated the necessity for the control unit to be concerned about how many of the k bytes had already been loaded. The following example illustrates a similar approach to the design of a generalized r digit BCD to Binary Converter.

Example 7.4 Procedure 2.3 of Chapter 2 can be used to convert a BCD number to binary. We shall now derive a system which can implement that procedure. The basic system is as shown in Figure 7.20. The original BCD number is stored

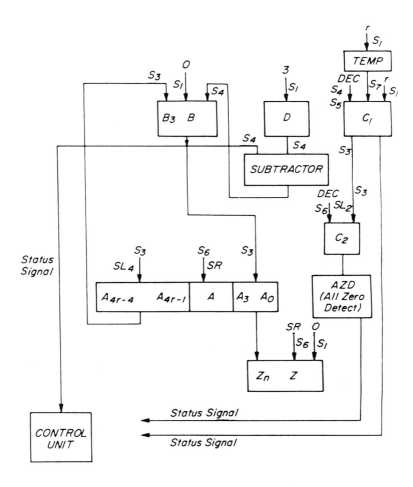

Figure 7.20 BCD to binary system

in a register A. This register is combined with a 4-bit register B into a circulating shift register. This is done so that the constant 3 can always be subtracted from the same digit rather than from different digits of A. Two counters C_1 and C_2 are used to count the r possible subtractions in each iteration and the $4r$ iterations respectively. An RTL level system description and the corresponding control unit is shown in Figure 7.21. ∎

q_0	q_1, S_1	
q_1	q_6, S_2	
q_2	q_3, S_3	
	$B_3 = 0$	$B_3 = 1$
q_3	q_4, S_5	q_4, S_4
	$C_1 = 0$	$C_1 \neq 0$
q_4	q_5, S_3	q_3, S_3
q_5	q_6, S_6	
	$C_2 = 0$	$C_2 \neq 0$
q_6	q_0, S_8	q_2, S_7

Figure 7.21   Control unit state table for BCD to binary conversion

T_1: S_1: $A \leftarrow X; B \leftarrow 0; D \leftarrow 3, C_1 \leftarrow r; \text{TEMP} \leftarrow r; Z \leftarrow 0$

T_2: S_2: $C_2 \leftarrow \text{SL2}(C_1); \text{GO TO } T_6$

T_3: S_3: $A \leftarrow \text{SL4}(A); A_{0,3} \leftarrow B; B \leftarrow A_{[4r-4,\, 4r-1]}$

T_4:   IF $(B_3 = 1)$ THEN S_4: $B \leftarrow B - D$: $C_1 \leftarrow \text{DEC}(C_1)$ ELSE S_5: $C_1 \leftarrow \text{DEC}(C_1)$

T_5:   IF $(C_1 \neq 0)$ THEN S_3: $A \leftarrow \text{SL4}(A); A_{[0,3]} \leftarrow B$: $B \leftarrow A_{[4r-4,4r-1]}; \text{GO TO } T_4$ ELSE S_3: $A \leftarrow \text{SL4}(A)$: $A_{[0,3]} \leftarrow B$: $B \leftarrow A_{[4r-4,4r-1]}$: GO TO T_6

T_6: S_6: $A \leftarrow \text{SR}(A); Z_n \leftarrow A_0; Z \leftarrow \text{SR}(Z); C_2 \leftarrow \text{DEC}(C_2)$

T_7:   If $(C_2 \neq 0)$ THEN S_7: $C_1 \leftarrow \text{TEMP}; \text{GO TO } T_3$ ELSE S_8: GO TO T_1

In the first step X is input to A, the counter C_1 is initialized to r, the number of digits, and registers Z, B, D, and TEMP are initialized. Then counter C_2 is initialized to the number of bits (i.e., $4*r$) and the first output bit is input to Z. In the third step, the most significant digit of A is shifted into B. It is then tested to see if $B_3 = 1$, in which case 3 is subtracted from B, and then C_1 is decremented. The contents of B is then restored to the least significant digit of the A register and this subtracting operation is repeated on each digit of A (step 5). Then the least significant bit of A is stored as the least significant bit of the output, and counter C_2 is decremented. This process is repeated $4r$ times (step 7), at which time Z contains the correct binary output.

7.4 INSTRUCTION DEPENDENT CONTROL UNITS

So far we have considered the design of control networks which can carry out a single data processing task repetitively. For each data processing task requiring a different control signal sequence generation a new control unit must be designed. However, it is possible to design a single control network which can generate control signal sequences for several different information processing operations. Such a controller is referred to as an *instruction-dependent* unit. This controller must have inputs that specify which instruction is currently being executed. In response to the inputs specifying the instruction, and the status inputs (if any), the controller generates the appropriate control signal sequence. A general system with an instruction dependent control unit is shown in Figure 7.22. The control signals may be input to the instruction source to ensure that the

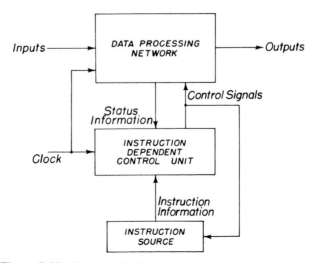

Figure 7.22   System with instruction dependent control unit

instruction information changes at the appropriate time. Specifying the control unit is essentially the same as deriving the state table for individual instruction control units. However, minimizing the number of outputs in the control unit is an added problem, as illustrated in the following example.

Example 7.5   We will design a control unit to generate the appropriate control sequence to execute either of two instructions as specified by the value of an input I. If $I = 0$ the 2's complement of X is computed. If $I = 1$, the complement of $Z + 1$ will be computed. We can express an algorithm for both of these instructions in our RTL as follows:

$$I = 0$$

$$S_1: \quad A \leftarrow X; B \leftarrow 1$$
$$S_2: \quad A \leftarrow \overline{A}$$
$$S_0: \quad C \leftarrow A + B$$

$$I = 1$$

$$S_3: \quad A \leftarrow X; B \leftarrow 1$$
$$S_4: \quad C \leftarrow A + B$$
$$S_5: \quad C \leftarrow \overline{C}$$

The state table for this controller is shown in Figure 7.23(a), where we have assumed that I can only change value when the control unit is in state q_0.

	$I=0$	$I=1$
q_0	q_1, S_1	q_3, S_3
q_1	q_2, S_2	-
q_2	q_0, S_0	-
q_3	-	q_4, S_4
q_4	-	q_0, S_5

(a)

	$I=0$	$I=1$
q_0	q_1, S_1	q_1, S_1
q_1	q_2, S_2	q_2, S_0
q_2	q_0, S_0	q_0, S_2

(b)

$$S_3 = S_1$$
$$S_4 = S_0$$

Figure 7.23   Control unit for Example 7.5

If $I = 0$, the control unit passes through states q_1 and q_2 before returning to initial state q_0 and generates the control signal sequence $S_1 S_2 S_0$. If $I = 1$, the control unit passes through states q_3 and q_4 before returning to q_0 and generates the control signal sequence $S_3 S_4 S_5$. We assume that the input I only changes value when the control unit is in state q_0 so the entries in states q_1 and q_2 in column 1 and q_3, q_4 in column 0 are left unspecified. In effect, in state q_0 the only input sequences are 000 or 111. This table can be reduced by combining states q_1, q_4 and q_2, q_3 to that of Figure 7.23(b). It is also possible to reduce the number of distinct control signals which must be generated. Note that S_1 and S_3 produce the same logic operations $A \leftarrow X$ and $B \leftarrow 1$. Therefore, S_3 can be replaced by S_1.

Similarly, S_0 and S_4 produce the operation $C \leftarrow A + B$, so S_4 can be replaced by S_0. The signals S_2 and S_5 produce the operations $A \leftarrow \overline{A}$ and $C \leftarrow \overline{C}$ respectively. These operations affect different registers and hence may be considered to be independent. If we replace S_5 by S_2 the control signal S_2 will cause both $A \leftarrow \overline{A}$ and $C \leftarrow \overline{C}$ and the effective computation will not be changed. Applying these control signal reductions to the table of Figure 7.23(a) results in the reduced table of Figure 7.23(b).   ∎

We have assumed that the inputs which specify the instruction to be executed are controlled by a source external to the control unit. However, this source must be synchronized with the control unit since these inputs are assumed to remain constant until the complete control signal sequence for the current instruction has been generated. Let us now consider an extension of this model in which the control unit generates a control signal that also controls the inputs which specify the instruction. This extended capability of the instruction dependent control unit enables it to automatically sequence through a series of operations (called a program). These operations are assumed to be contained in a list that indicates the order in which these instructions must be executed. Such a system might be referred to as a programmed computer. In most computers the program is stored in a subunit of the computer called the memory unit, thus the term *stored program computer*.

7.5 DIGITAL COMPUTER MODEL

The basic organization of the stored program computer system is as shown in Figure 7.24 [3]. The *Memory Unit* is used to store the program to be executed and the data upon which the program operates. The *Central Processing Unit (CPU)* consists of the registers and logic required to perform the basic logical and arithmetic operations which constitute a program. The *Control Unit* controls

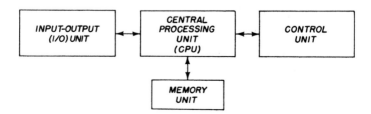

Figure 7.24   Block diagram of stored program computer

the sequence in which instructions are executed and also controls the CPU and other system units during the execution of each instruction. The *I/O Unit* serves as an interface between the stored program processor and the outside world. We shall now consider the manner in which a program that is stored in the memory unit is executed.

Assume that each instruction is stored in one word of memory. To execute the program the control unit must read an instruction from memory, determine the operation specified by the instruction, generate the sequence of control signals required to perform this operation, and then determine the location of the next instruction in memory, read that instruction, etc. We shall first consider the process by which information in memory is located and read.

The memory unit is made of 2^k r-bit registers. The content of each register is called a *word*, and each register has a unique *address* associated with it to distinguish it from all the other registers.

To access the memory systematically, two specially designated registers called the *Memory Buffer Register (MBR)* and the *Memory Address Register (MAR)* are utilized. The *MAR* is used whenever memory is accessed (read or written into) to store the address (name) of the specific register in memory which is being accessed. The contents of this register, in the case of a read, or the contents to be written in this register, in the case of a write, are stored in the *MBR* which serves in effect as an interface between the *CPU* and the memory. In order to read a memory register M_L located at address L, the following 3-step process is executed:

	Operation	*Explanation*
1.	$MAR \leftarrow L$	The address of the word to be accessed is stored in *MAR*
2.	$MBR \leftarrow M_{[MAR]}$; $M_{[MAR]} \leftarrow 0$	The contents of the memory register at the address specified by *MAR* (which is denoted by $M_{[MAR]}$) are transferred to *MBR* and that location is set to 0.
3.	$M_{[MAR]} \leftarrow MBR*$	The contents of the *MBR* are written into the memory register at address L.

After completion of this process the desired word has been restored in its original memory location and is also available in the *MBR*. The process by which data in a register D is written into the memory unit at location L is similar to the reading process and consists of the following steps.

---

*This is required to restore the information read from memory assuming "destructive readout."

Operation	*Explanation*
1. $MAR \leftarrow L$; $MBR \leftarrow D$	The location to be written into is stored in the MAR and the data to be written is stored in the MBR.
2. $M_{[MAR]} \leftarrow 0$	The memory unit at address M_L is cleared.
3. $M_{[MAR]} \leftarrow MBR$	The contents of the MBR are written in the memory unit at address M_L.

After this process the specified address L of the memory unit contains the data D.

The control unit has two basic phases of operation, the *fetch phase*, in which instructions are fetched from memory in the proper sequence, and the *execute phase*, in which the instructions are executed by the control unit's generation of the proper sequence of control signals.

Each instruction word in memory is partitioned into disjoint groups of bits (called *fields*), which contain specific types of information. One such field, the operation code field, identifies the type of operation being performed. Assuming that the number of bits in the operation code field is constant (fixed field length) then c bits in this field are adequate if the system has at most 2^c types of instructions. The remaining fields of an instruction word supply additional information required to execute the instruction. In the most general case this information includes the addresses of the two operands, the address where the result is to be stored, and the address where the next instruction to be executed is stored. Thus four address fields may be required. However, several possible simplifications can be used to reduce this requirement.

The result address field can be eliminated if the result of a particular type of operation is always stored in a special register (the particular register may depend on the operation). Similarly, one of the operand fields can be eliminated if for each type of operation one of the operands is always stored in a special register (which again may vary with the operation). Thus a single address field is adequate if all of these simplifying assumptions are used. The address field must consist of k bits in order to specify 2^k possible memory locations. Alternatively, we can partition the memory unit into $2^{k'}$ segments of $2^{k-k'}$ words and specify a memory location by using a k' bit register (frequently called an *index register*) to specify the segment in which the specific location is, and a $k-k'$ bit address field to specify the particular location within that segment. This reduces the number of bits required for the address field. However, additional instructions are required to transfer data to the index registers.

During the fetch phase, the control unit must keep track of the next instruction address. However, this address need not be specified in the instruction being executed, if the instructions of a program are stored in sequential address positions of the memory unit. In this case if the address of the current instruction is I, the address of the next instruction is $I + 1$, unless the current instruction is a *transfer* instruction, which specifies some other next instruction address. A special register, the *instruction address register (IAR)*, is used to store the address of the next instruction to be executed. After each instruction is executed, the contents of the *IAR* are incremented by one unless the instruction executed is a transfer operation. In this case the operand address fields can be used to specify the contents of the address of the next instruction, which is then stored in the *IAR*.

Thus the fetch phase consists of the following status dependent control sequence.

Control Sequence	*Explanation*
S_1: $MAR \leftarrow IAR$	The next instruction to be executed,
S_2: $MBR \leftarrow M_{[MAR]}$	the location of which is specified in
S_3: $M_{[MAR]} \leftarrow MBR$	the *IAR*, is fetched and the operation
S_4: $IR \leftarrow MBR_{i,j}$	code bits $(MBR_{i,j})$ are stored in *IR*, the *Instruction Register*.
S_5: IF (*IR* indicates Transfer Operation) THEN	The address of the next instruction to be executed is stored in the *IAR*. This address is determined by increment-
S_6: $IAR \leftarrow MBR_{ADD\ FIELD}$ ELSE	ing the contents of *IAR* by 1 unless the present instruction is a transfer
S_7: $IAR \leftarrow IAR + 1$	operation in which case the next instruction is in the memory location whose address is specified in the current instruction address field in *MBR*.

Thus the state table of the control unit for the fetch phase is as shown in Figure 7.25, where the output of a decoder is $T = 0$ if the present operation is not a transfer operation and $T = 1$ if it is a transfer operation.

During the execution phase the contents of the *IR* and the values associated with related status signals determine the control signal sequence.

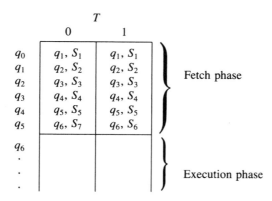

Figure 7.25 State table describing control unit fetch phase

7.6 MACROINSTRUCTIONS AND MICROINSTRUCTIONS

Once the basic RTL instructions that must be performed and the control signals that enable these operations have been specified, the CPU logic can be implemented using standard logic design techniques. The execution of a single computer instruction may require a complex sequence of RTL instructions as illustrated previously for the square root function. Such an instruction, whose execution may require a sequence of control signals, is called a *macroinstruction*.

The basic RTL instructions that are assumed to be executable in one clock period and require one control signal are called *microinstructions* [3,4]. The following sequence of steps defines the fundamental design process of a programmed computer.

1. Define basic macroinstructions.
2. Define the sequence of logical and arithmetic microinstructions and the corresponding control signal sequence for each macroinstruction.
3. Design control unit to generate the appropriate control signal sequence for each macroinstruction including access of next instruction.
4. Design CPU to perform logical and arithmetic microinstructions using appropriate control signals as enabling signals.

An important aspect of this procedure is the selection of an algorithm of microinstructions for each macroinstruction. The following example illustrates the specification of a sequence of RTL microinstructions for the arithmetic macroinstruction of multiplication.

Example 7.6   Consider the design of a binary multiplier. Assume that we wish to form the product $X \cdot Y$ where $Y = y_n \, y_{n-1} \ldots y_0$, $y_i = 0, 1$. Then

$$X \cdot Y = X \cdot (y_n \, 2^n + y_{n-1} \, 2^{n-1} + \ldots + y_1 \, 2^1 + y_0 \, 2^0)$$
$$= (X \cdot y_0) + 2(X \cdot y_1) + 2^2(X \cdot y_2) + \ldots + 2^n(X \cdot y_n)$$
$$= \sum_{i=0}^{n} 2^i(X \cdot y_i).$$

However, since $y_i = 0, 1$, $X \cdot y_i = X$ if $y_i = 1$, and $X \cdot y_i = 0$ if $y_i = 0$. Thus $2^i(X \cdot y_i) = 2^i X$ or 0. Furthermore, $2^i X$ is simply X shifted to the left i positions. Thus multiplication of two n-bit numbers can be performed by a sequence of n shift and add operations. Such an algorithm can be specified as follows.

Multiplication Algorithm	Explanation
T_1: S_1: $A \leftarrow 0; M \leftarrow X; Q \leftarrow Y;$ $D \leftarrow n$	The two operands X and Y are stored in Registers M and Q respectively. The result register A (which has $2n$ bits) is initialized to 0. The number of bits, n, is stored in D.

T_2: IF ($Q_o = 1$) THEN S_2:   If the least significant bit of Q,
$A_{[n,2n-1]} \leftarrow A_{[n,2n-1]} + M$; Q_o, is 1, add M to the n most
ELSE GO TO T_3 significant bits of A. Shift A to
the right one bit,* shift Q to the
right one bit and decrement D
T_3: S_3; $Q \leftarrow SR(Q)$; $A \leftarrow SR(A)$;   (independent of Q_o).
$D \leftarrow D - 1$

T_4: IF ($D = 0$) THEN S_o: read   This is iterated n times until D
next instruction; ELSE GO $= 0$.
TO T_2.

The control unit state table for this algorithm is shown in Figure 7.26. In this algorithm we have used a microinstruction that decrements the contents of the D register by one. Hence the counting part of the procedure is carried out by CPU logic. Alternatively the control unit could count up to n and the D register would not be needed. For instance, for $n = 3$ the state table of Figure 7.27

q_{M0}	q_{M1}, S_1	
q_{M1}	$Q_0 = 0$ q_{M2},	$Q_0 = 1$ q_{M2}, S_2
q_{M2}	q_{M3}, S_3	
q_{M3}	$D = 0$ q_{M0}, S_0	$D \neq 0$ q_{M1},

Figure 7.26 Control unit for binary multiplication

q_{M0}	q_{M1}, S_1	
q_{M1}	$Q_0 = 0$ q_{M2},	$Q_0 = 1$ q_{M2}, S_2
q_{M2}	q_{M3}, S_3	
q_{M3}	$Q_0 = 0$ q_{M4},	$Q_0 = 1$ q_{M4}, S_2
q_{M4}	q_{M5}, S_3	
q_{M5}	$Q_0 = 0$ q_{M6}	$Q_0 = 1$ q_{M6}, S_2
q_{M6}	q_{M0}, S_3	

Figure 7.27 Alternative multiplication control unit

---

*Alternatively, instead of shifting A to the right after each iteration we could shift M to the left. In this case M must have $2n$ bits, and if $Q_i = 1$, $A \leftarrow A + M$.

defines a control unit that generates the necessary signal sequence for a 3-bit multiplication.

The control unit in effect counts up to 3 by the state sequence q_{M_2}, q_{M_4}, q_{M_6} and then generates the completion signal S_0 and returns to the initial state of the fetch phase q_0. ∎

For each macroinstruction an algorithm of microinstructions must be selected to be implemented. The choice of this algorithm will affect the logical complexity of both the control unit and the CPU as well as the speed of operation of the system. Thus in choosing an algorithm the designer must consider what microinstructions are required by other macroinstructions (to select a basic set of microinstructions) and the tradeoff between speed and complexity involved in implementing other microinstructions. A choice may also have to be made between implementing a given instruction as a macro- or microinstruction. For instance if addition is a microinstruction, the CPU must contain a parallel adder. Alternatively, addition can be implemented as a macroinstruction in which case the CPU only needs a 1-bit adder. This tradeoff is between increased speed and reduced control unit complexity (if implemented as a macroinstruction) and reduced CPU complexity (if implemented as a microinstruction). The considerations and ramifications of these tradeoffs may be quite complex. Consequently, digital system design is very much a heuristic rather than an algorithmic process, and is highly dependent on the experience of the designer.

REFERENCES

1. Bartee, T.C., Lebow, I.L. and I.S. Reed, *Theory and Design of Digital Machines*, McGraw-Hill, New York, N.Y., 1962.
2. Booth, T.L., *Digital Networks and Computer Systems*, John Wiley and Sons, New York, N.Y., 1971.
3. Chu, Y., *Commputer Organization and Microprogramming*, Prentice-Hall, Englewood Cliffs, N.J., 1972.
4. Husson, S.S., *Microprogramming: Principles and Practices*, Prentice-Hall, Englewood Cliffs, N.J., 1970.

PROBLEMS

7.1 Design a subsystem including the control unit to increment (if $I = 1$) or decrement (if $I = 0$) a 3-bit number by 1; assuming that logic exists to complement an individual bit.

7.2 A machine is to be designed to add two floating point numbers X and Y. Bits 1–3 of each number are the 2's complement representation of the exponent and bits 4–10 are the 2's complement representation of the mantissa. The system works as follows. A pulse on S initiates the addition of X and Y and the normalized sum $X + Y$ appears on outputs Z. A pulse on D is to be generated at completion. If the result is too small or too large to be normalized with these bit fields a pulse is generated on output U or O respectively. Specify a detailed design at the register transfer level assuming the operators, shift, increment by one, binary addition, and less than or equal to.

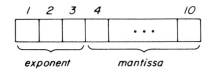

Figure 7.28 Problem 7.2 number representation

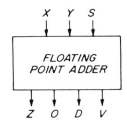

Figure 7.29 Problem 7.2 floating point adder

7.3 Consider the following RTL description of a digital system.

$T_1 : S_1 : A \leftarrow X; C \leftarrow 1$
$T_2 : S_2 : \text{COMPARE } (A,0)$
$T_3 : \text{IF } (Z_c = 1) \text{ THEN } S_3 : C \leftarrow C \cdot A; A \leftarrow \text{DEC}(A); \text{GO TO } T_2$
  $\text{ELSE } S_4 : Z \leftarrow C; \text{GO TO } T_1$
  where $Z_c = 1$ indicates $A > 0$.

a) Derive a state table for the system control unit and a system level block diagram.

b) Assume that X is a positive (binary) integer, A is an up-down counter and $A \leftarrow \text{DEC}(A)$ results in decrementing the number in A by 1; and Z is the output. What mathematical function is this system computing?

7.4 Consider the following RTL description of a digital system.

$T_1 : S_1 : A \leftarrow X; B \leftarrow Y; C \leftarrow 0$
$T_2 : S_2 : \text{IF } (A > 0) \text{ THEN}$
    $S_3 : C \leftarrow C + B; A \leftarrow \text{DEC}(A); \text{GO TO } T_2$
    $\text{ELSE } S_4 : Z \leftarrow C; \text{GO TO } T_1$

a) Derive a state table for the system control unit.

b) Assume that X and Y are non-negative integers, A is an up-down counter and $A \leftarrow DEC(A)$ results in decrementing the number in A by 1 and Z is the output. Describe what mathematical function this system is performing.

7.5 The following control unit and block diagram describe a digital system. The status signal Z_c is the output of a comparison unit as shown below. The circuit also has a counter A with an input and a decrement signal (DEC A), registers B and C and a multiplier.

q_0	q_1, S_1	
q_1	q_2, S_2	
q_2	$Z_c = 1$ q_1, S_3	$Z_c = 0$ q_0, S_4

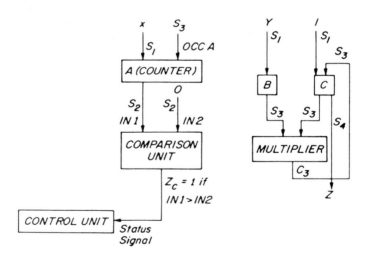

Figure 7.30   Problem 7.5

a. Derive an RTL program description of the computation being performed by this system, where q_0 is the initial state.

b) What function is being computed by the system?

7.6 Consider the following RTL description of a digital system.

$T_1 : S_1 : A \leftarrow X; C \leftarrow 1; B \leftarrow Y; E \leftarrow 1$

$T_2 : S_2 : \text{COMPARE } (A,0)$

$T_3 : \text{IF } (Z_c = 1) \text{ THEN } S_3 : C \leftarrow C \cdot A; A \leftarrow \text{DEC}(A); \text{GO TO } T_2$

    $\text{ELSE } S_4 : A \leftarrow C; Z_1 \leftarrow C$

    where $Z_c = 1$ indicates $A > 0$

$T_4 : S_2 : \text{COMPARE } (A,0)$

$T_5 : \text{IF } (Z_c = 1) \text{ THEN } S_6 : E \leftarrow E \cdot B; A \leftarrow \text{DEC}(A); \text{GO TO } T_4$

    $\text{ELSE } S_5 : Z \leftarrow E; \text{GO TO } T_1$

    where $Z_c = 1$ indicates $A > 0$

a) Derive a state table for the system control unit.

b) Assume that X and Y are positive integers, A is an up-down counter and $A \leftarrow \text{DEC}(A)$ results in decrementing the number in A by 1 and Z and Z_1 are the outputs. Determine the mathematical functions computed by this system.

7.7 Derive a generalized RTL description of a system to convert a binary number to BCD, including a system block diagram and the state table for the status dependent control unit.

7.8 Derive a generalized RTL description of a system to add two BCD numbers, including a system block diagram and the state table for the status dependent control unit.

7.9 Derive a generalized RTL description of a system to subtract a BCD number B from another BCD number A, including a system block diagram and the state table for the status dependent control unit.

INDEX

A

Acyclic circuits, 41
Arithmetic logic unit (ALU), 14
Asynchronous sequential circuits,
    161– 218

B

Binary arithmetic, 19, 25–35
    addition, 26
    division, 34
    multiplication, 33
    subtraction, 27
Binary coded decimal (BCD), 23
Binary number representation, 19
Bipolar logic, 7
Boolean Algebra, 8
Boolean Algebra laws, 11
    absorption, 11
    associativity, 11
    idempotence, 11
Branching, 61
Buses, 148

C

Carry lookahead adder, 91
Central processing unit (CPU), 14
Checkerboard function, 83
Circuit level design, 14
Closed cover, 131
Column dominance, 63
Combinational circuits, 41
Combinational functions, 41
    minimization, 47

Comparator, 87
Compatible set, 125
Complementary metal-oxide
    semiconductor (CMOS), 7
Complete product term, 48
Control unit, 233
Control unit, instruction dependent, 246
    simple, 234
    status dependent, 238
Counters, 146
Cube, 49
Cyclic tables, 61

D

D-trio, 211
Data manipulation instructions, 231
Data movement instructions, 228
DeMorgan's Law, 10
Decoders, 91
Delay box, 223
Delay element, 116
Delay, inertial, 198
    pure, 198
    stray, 198
Demultiplexer, 93
Dichotomy, 192
Digital circuits, 1
Digital computers, 1, 248–251
Diodes, 3
Double rail inputs, 46

E

Emitter-coupled logic (ECL), 7
Essential hazard, 210

Essential prime implicant, 60
Execute phase, 250

F

Fan-in, 7
Fanout, 7
Fetch phase, 250
Field effect transistors (FET), 7
Fields, 250
Finite state machine, 105
Fixed point representation, 35
Flip-flops, 109
  characteristic equation, 110
  D, 115
  edge-triggered, 113
  JK, 113
  master-slave, 112
  SR, 110
  T, 114
Floating point representation, 35
  exponent, 35
  mantissa, 35
  normalized, 35
Flow table reduction, 167–170
Flow tables, 163
Flow tables, multiple output change
    (MOC), 165
  non-fundamental mode, 164
  non-normal fundamental mode, 164
  normal mode, 164
  single output change (SOC), 165
Fundamental mode, 164

G

Gate level design, 14
Gates, 2
  AND, 4
  NAND, 5
  NOR, 5
  OR, 4
Good prime implicant, 64
Gray code, 37

H

Hazards, 171, 198–201
Hazards, combinational, 203
  dynamic, 199
  output, 208
  sequential, 208–214

static, 199
steady state, 208
Hexadecimal code, 23
Huntington's Postulates, 9
  closure, 9
  commutativity, 9
  complementation, 9
  distributivity, 9
  identity elements, 9

I

Implicant, 49
Implication graph, 131
Index register, 250
Input output (I/O) unit, 249
Input/output devices, 14
Instruction Address Register (IAR), 251
Integrated circuits, 2
Integrated injection logic (I^2L), 7
Iterative arrays, 91, 104

K

Karnaugh map, 53

L

Large scale integration (LSI), 2
Levels, 46
Light emitting diodes (LED's), 43
Literals, 48
Logic design, 1

M

Macroinstructions, 252
Maximal compatible, 126
Maxterm, 45
Mealy machine, 107
Medium scale integration (MSI), 2
Memory Address Register (MAR), 249
Memory Buffer Register (MBR), 249
Memory elements, 109
Memory unit, 14, 248
Metal oxide semiconductor (MOS), 7
Microinstructions, 252
Minimal two level realization, 68
  NAND, 69
  NOR, 69
Minterm, 44
Modulo number representation, 28

Moore machine, 107
Multiple input changes, 214–217
Multiple level combinational functions, 83–101
Multiple output combinational circuits, 71
Multiple output prime implicant, 73
Multiplexers, 97

N

N-channel metal-oxide semiconductor (NMOS), 7
Negative logic, 4
Noise margin, 7

O

One's complement addition, 32
One's complement representation, 32
Output compatible, 125
Overflow, 32

P

Packing density, 7
Pair chart, 126
Parallel adder, 89
Parity check circuit, 94
Parity check code, 37
Parity check function, 83
Planar Logic Arrays (PLA's), 98
Positive logic, 4
Power dissipation, 7
Prime implicant, 49
   covering problem, 59
   covering table, 59
   cost, 51
Prime implicate, 67
Principle of duality, 11
Principle of substitution, 12
Product of maxterms, 45
Propagation delay, 7

Q

Quine-McCluskey procedure, 52

R

Race, 173

Race, critical, 173
   non-critical, 173
Read-Only Memory arrays (ROM's), 98
Reed-Muller representation, 82
Register Transfer Language (RTL), 227
Register level design, 14, 227–254
Registers, 144, 228
Ripple counter, 146
Row dominance, 60

S

Sequential circuits, 41
   functions, 41, 105
   machine, 105
Shift registers, 145
Simultaneous input changes, 215
Single rail inputs, 46
Small scale integration (SSI), 2
Speed independent circuits, 218
State assignment, 135, 142–144, 174–194
   Liu type, 189
   Tracey type, 192
   connected row set, 176–183
   one-shot, 188
   shared row, 185–188
   single transition time (STT), 188–194
   universal, 183
State diagram, 106
State table, 105
State table reduction, 120–135
State variable, 135
Structured design, 15
Sum of minterms, 44
Switching circuits, 1
Switching theory, 1

T

Transistor-transistor logic (TTL), 7
Transition table, 110
Transition time, 177
Trigger time, 112
Truth table, 2
Turing machines, 150
Two's complement addition, 30
Two's complement representation, 29

U

Underflow, 32

Unicode state assignments, 175
Unrestricted input changes, 215

V

Very large scale integration (VLSI), 2

Y

Y-map, 137, 194
Y-Z map, 137